D1519869

Clear-Cutting Eden

Clear-Cutting Eden

Ecology and the Pastoral in Southern Literature

Christopher Rieger

The University of Alabama Press
Tuscaloosa

Copyright © 2009
The University of Alabama Press
Tuscaloosa, Alabama 35487-0380
All rights reserved
Manufactured in the United States of America

Typeface: Minion and Goudy Sans

∞

The paper on which this book is printed meets the minimum requirements of American National Standard for Information Sciences-Permanence of Paper for Printed Library Materials, ANSI Z39.48-1984.

Library of Congress Cataloging-in-Publication Data

Rieger, Christopher.
    Clear-cutting Eden : ecology and the pastoral in Southern literature / Christopher Rieger.
        p.   cm.
    Includes bibliographical references and index.
    ISBN 978-0-8173-1641-9 (cloth : alk. paper) — ISBN 978-0-8173-8124-0 (electronic)
1. American fiction—Southern States—History and criticism. 2. American fiction—20th century—History and criticism. 3. Literature and society—Southern States—History—20th century. 4. Human ecology in literature. 5. Nature in literature. 6. Pastoral fiction, American—History and criticism. 7. Caldwell, Erskine, 1903–1987—Criticism and interpretation. 8. Rawlings, Marjorie Kinnan, 1896–1953—Criticism and interpretation. 9. Hurston, Zora Neale—Criticism and interpretation. 10. Faulkner, William, 1897–1962—Criticism and interpretation. I. Title.
    PS261.R45 2009
    810.9′35875—dc22

                                                                        2008024438

For Wendy

Contents

Acknowledgments

I would like to thank several people for their help in the early stages of this project: John Lowe, Peggy Prenshaw, Richard Moreland, and Carolyn Jones-Medine. John Lowe was invaluable as a teacher, reader, mentor, and friend. His encouragement and suggestions made this project possible. Equally important were the support, advice, and friendship I received from Bob Beuka, Dan Gonzalez, and Brian Arundel.

I also want to thank Westminster College for its support of my work, particularly my friends and former colleagues in the English department, Carolyn Perry, Dave Collins, Wayne Zade, and Theresa Adams. I am grateful to the University of Alabama Press and copyeditor Robin DuBlanc for their help and hard work.

Portions of this work appeared elsewhere in somewhat different forms, and I would like to acknowledge and thank the journals and presses for their permission to use this material. Portions of chapter 1 appeared as the essay "Silent Spring on Tobacco Road: The Degradation of the Environment in Erskine Caldwell's Fiction" in *Reading Erskine Caldwell: New Essays* (2006), edited by Robert L. McDonald, published by permission of McFarland & Company, Inc. Part of chapter 2 was first published in the Spring 2004 (57, no. 2) issue of *Mississippi Quarterly*. Portions of chapter 3 were originally published in different form in the Winter 2002–3 (56, no. 1) issue of *Mississippi Quarterly* and in the 2004 (vol. 13) issue of the *Marjorie Kinnan Rawlings Journal of Florida Literature*.

I want to thank my grandparents, whose bravery and perseverance have made all that I do possible: William and Karla Rieger and Kenneth and Inez Partridge. My father, Branimir Rieger, has been a model as a teacher and scholar and was also a huge help as an editor of this project. I also want to thank my mother, Marilyn Rieger, for all of her support and encouragement in helping me explore my interests in the South, literature, and nature, and my brother, Andrew, especially for his musical support. I must also mention Jackson and Griffin Rieger for giving me reasons to work and to come home.

Most of all, I want to thank my wife, Wendy, whose love, generosity, humor, and patience have made this book possible.

Clear-Cutting Eden

Introduction

Changes in the Air and on the Ground:
Nature, the Great Depression, and Southern Pastoral

The American South has always been a region closely aligned and identified with nature and the land, both in the popular imagination and in the realities of its agrarian past. From the lush, Edenic descriptions of the landscape in the reports of early explorers like John Smith to the reactionary essays of the Nashville Agrarians in *I'll Take My Stand* (1930), writers have consistently sought for their own purposes to construct versions of a South defined by its relationship to nature. Whether seeking to lure new settlers and investors to the New World or trying to make a case for Southern exceptionalism in the twentieth century, authors writing about the South have relied on specific conceptions of nature in creating a definition of the region, and these conceptions vary widely from author to author. That is, the *idea* of nature is an important tool in the construction of the idea of the South and in the construction of the actual, physical conditions of Southern society. Notions of the South as an abundant paradise, as a pastoral haven of order and simplicity, as a feudal, aristocratic anachronism, or as a place cursed and ruined by its legacy of chattel slavery all depend on particular versions of the relationship between the South and the natural world for their force. The region and its inhabitants may be portrayed as either in harmony with or in opposition to a specific view of the natural world in order to justify certain social systems as natural or to deride them as unnatural.

Although there is no clear linear development of the way the idea of nature is used in Southern literature, the period often termed the Southern Renaissance is fueled by a new wave of authors who reconfigure the use of nature in their fiction in conjunction with modernist analyses of the self and the South. The relatively belated arrival of modernism in the South—generally dated to around the end of World War I—means that its effects were arguably more pronounced and intense compared to other regions. Daniel Singal, for instance, claims that "the South offers a special opportunity for studying the shift from nineteenth- to twentieth-century culture" because change proceeded "in far more concentrated fashion [and] with greater tension and drama," and the culture clash was "fiercest in the South," as well as "comparatively self-contained."[1] Issues of race, class, and gender figure prominently in modernist reappraisals of the contemporary and historical South, and representations of the natural world are inextricably tied to such analyses. At the same time these intellectual changes were sweeping the South between the two World Wars, significant social, political, and economic revolutions were creating another "New South." This period of profound upheaval includes the great migration of blacks out of the South, increased industrialization and urbanization, a decreasing number of Southern farmers, as well as the myriad effects of the Great Depression. This book examines how Southern literary representations of the natural world were influenced by, and influenced, the historical, social, and ecological changes of the 1930s and 1940s, focusing on the work of four representative authors: Erskine Caldwell, Marjorie Kinnan Rawlings, Zora Neale Hurston, and William Faulkner. It is in reaction to the Great Depression, I argue, that these Southern authors reinvent and reinterpret the pastoral literary mode as a way of reconceiving Southerners' relationship with the natural world.

In Southern literature, the pastoral mode plays a vital and central role in the creation of popular images of the "Old South." Because the pastoral relies on the juxtaposition of city and country, culture and nature, for its force, it has helped both to characterize and define Southerners and their connections with the natural environment. A concise definition of pastoral is not possible. As I will argue, the variety and mutability of this literary mode account for its durability and continued relevance. Paul Alpers uses the entirety of *What Is Pastoral?* (1996) to work toward a better critical understanding of this mode, to restrict the "ungoverned inclusiveness" of the modern use of the term, and to dissuade readers from the view that "pastoral is motivated by naïve idyllicism." Alpers admits that there is no consensus on the meaning of the term and that "it sometimes seems as if there are as many versions of pastoral as there are critics and scholars who write about it." Despite the limitations Alpers seeks to impose, his book covers pastoral texts from the poetry of Virgil and Theocritus to the novels of Thomas Hardy and Sarah Orne Jewett. Pastoral novels comprise works "in which theme or subject matter, usually but not necessarily rural, is given literary form that derives from or is made intelligible by the usages of traditional pastoral," Alpers says, adding that "some of the most interesting fictional pastoral is in books that do not, as wholes, count as pastoral novels."[2]

Other critics have applied decidedly more liberal standards to what may be called pastoral. Lawrence Buell offers a specifically American understanding of the term: "'Pastoral' is used in an extended sense, familiar to Americanists, to refer not to the specific set of obsolescent conventions of the eclogue tradition, but to all literature—poetry, prose, fiction or nonfiction—that celebrates the ethos of nature/rurality over against the ethos of the town or city . . . [including] all degrees of rusticity from farm to wilderness." British critic Terry Gifford, in *Pastoral* (1999), echoes Buell's point, saying that pastoral may refer to "any literature that describes the country with an implicit or explicit contrast to the urban." Both Gifford and Buell concede that there exist many pastoral texts that uncritically idealize country life, following Leo Marx's differentiation between "sentimental" and "complex" pastorals in his landmark study of American pastoral, *The Machine in the Garden*.[3] Briefly put, while the former escapes the complexities of the city, the latter critically investigates them. Although Gifford identifies a pattern of retreat and return as fundamental to all pastoral and Buell stresses its double-edged character, both critics canonize new versions of the pastoral that are quite distinct from those traditionally associated with the term. More specifically, they agree that the pastoral has gained new importance and significance because of increased environmental awareness over the course of the twentieth century. I apply this theory to literature of the Southern Renaissance and find that new versions of human/nature relationships emerge in response to the Great Depression, giving rise to what I call ecopastorals.

These new versions of pastoral break away from an older Southern pastoral tradition, which I want to delineate briefly. Jan Bakker, in *Pastoral in Antebellum Southern Romance,* examines the roots of Southern pastoral, which have typically been dismissed as superficial and escapist.[4] The works of John Pendleton Kennedy, William Gilmore Simms, and John Esten Cooke initiate a Southern tradition of using the pastoral to critique industrialization and modernization through scenes of idyllic, bucolic country life. Bakker argues that pastoral's inherent dualism may lull readers into "accepting its picturesque bucolic nostalgia on face value alone," but that there exist many serious (or complex) works of antebellum pastoral that possess a "dialectic force whose contrasts of dream and reality work to compromise or question the pastoral's recurring images of a Southern *locus amoenus*."[5] While not everyone would agree that these antebellum works are complex rather than sentimental pastorals, it is clear that the pastoral mode is centrally important to Southern literary expression from its early roots. Even at that time, there is the typical pastoral mood of nostalgia for a bygone, simpler era, a tendency only exacerbated in postbellum Southern pastoral works.

The Southern pastoral tradition is most closely identified with the Reconstruction era and the late nineteenth century, notably the poetry of Sidney Lanier and the "plantation school" fiction of Thomas Nelson Page and Joel Chandler Harris. Lucinda MacKethan examines these influential writers in *The Dream of Arcady*, finding that Page and Harris in particular use nostalgic versions of the Old South in order to offer "the plantation regime . . . and its pleasant rural peace . . . as an alternative to the confusion of the materialistic New South." The antebellum plantation is portrayed in these works as a refuge of order and stability, a harmonious blend of city and country. Although this aspect is quite similar to the earlier pastorals of Simms, Kennedy, and others, the postbellum versions differ significantly in their emphasis on difference and racial hierarchy. Ex-slave narrators, like Harris's Uncle Remus and Page's Sam from what is perhaps his best-known story, "Marse Chan," are employed to sing the praises of the prewar system and decry the disarray of the present era. The sense of a lost golden age pervades the stories as the ideal of pastoral balance is located in an irrecoverable past—like the Garden of Eden—rather than an actual place of the present or future. The feeling that a particular way of life was ending and another beginning is fertile ground for the blossoming of the pastoral, and MacKethan explains that the specific variety of plantation school, sentimental pastoral arises in response to the upheaval of Reconstruction: "A seemingly simple kind of rural society finds itself being irrevocably set upon a more complex, urban course; it can be seen that in the process much that has always been held to be of spiritual value is being discarded or has already been lost, and in the resulting confusion the cultural aims of the society in question become divided between the pull towards progress and the grip of the past."[6] While Page and Harris succumb to the lure of an idealized past in response to their own "New South," it is my contention that writers of the Southern Renaissance create new versions of the pastoral that look in the other direction, taking, for instance, a form used to extol slavery and racial subjugation and using it for contrary purposes.

The 1930s and 1940s find the South at a similar moment to that described by MacKethan above, a time of palpable and jarring transition from an agrarian society to a more industrialized, modern one. The ecopastorals that emerge become more complex than their predecessors even in their retention of the basic pastoral strategy of criticizing present society by a set of purer standards. Whereas traditional Southern pastoral looked to the past to provide these standards, the Southern Renaissance is a time of critically interrogating and demythologizing the past. Thus, these ecopastorals tend to be highly ironic and self-questioning. When the past no longer represents a stable center of meaning, the pastoral impulse itself is subject to greater scrutiny. In the works I examine in this project, there is also a tendency to turn toward the nature side of the pastoral equation. That is, natural landscapes, and more specifically wilderness, assume many of the qualities of purity and legitimacy associated with the past in the Southern pastoral tradition. Although older versions of Southern pastoral contain a theoretical model for relating to the natural world, this aspect is often buried under the more overt romanticizing of the past and propagandizing for racial hierarchy. Ecopastorals bring the natural world from the background to the foreground, making nature a presence in its own right, a force that influences humans rather than simply a passive entity to be acted upon.

The Great Depression creates the conditions for new versions of the pastoral in a number of ways, especially through a greater emphasis on work and through the evident failings of humans' work in nature. The same sets of socioeconomic and environmental conditions give rise to both the ecopastorals of Caldwell, Rawlings, Hurston, and Faulkner and the more traditional pastoral philosophy of *I'll Take My Stand*. The Agrarians openly advocate turning away from industrialization back toward an agricultural society, using the past to rebuke the present. The ecopastorals tend to accept that modern industrial society will be a part of the South, and, accordingly, they seek a middle ground that can accommodate rural, agrarian ways along with modern, industrial ones. The various nostalgias of antebellum pastoral, the plantation school, and *I'll Take My Stand* may indeed critique the ills of the present, but they also tend to whitewash the ills of the past. As I will show, the ecological destruction wrought by the South's historical abuse of the land reaches a point where it can no longer be masked by moonlight and magnolias.

The wildly popular *Gone with the Wind* (1933) also tackles themes of land, race, gender, and class, but with significant differences from the novels I examine in the following chapters, which makes it a useful counterexample of traditional pastoral in the Depression era. Margaret Mitchell's work casts the Old South as an anachronistic society, but does so with a certain nostalgia. There is little of the dogged interrogation of the past that characterizes so much of the work of the Southern Renaissance. While Scarlett does challenge gender norms as a strong, independent businesswoman, she also pays a heavy price for her flaunting of conventions. She becomes despised by her friends and family for her actions, and she is even blamed for the death of her second husband, Frank Kennedy, because her riding alone in a carriage to her sawmill provokes an attack that he dies trying to avenge: "She had killed Frank. She had killed him just as surely as if it had been her finger that pulled the trigger. . . . God would punish her for that."[7] The novel sends a mixed message to its Depression-era audience. Scarlett's resolve, hard work, and business acumen save her extended family from ruin in the aftermath of the Civil War, but the cost seems to be her honor, her morals, and her social standing.

The natural world of *Gone with the Wind* is decidedly in the background, and Mitchell's novel falls somewhere between the late nineteenth-century plantation school pastorals and even earlier Southern varieties, as described in Bakker's study of the genre: "The formula of pastoral imagery in pre-nineteenth century writing about the South depicts a fallen garden, and muses upon humankind's lost estate. . . . What evolves in early tracts, histories, and later fictions about the nascent South is an apposite and subtle commentary upon the fallacy of humanity's age-old and hopeless dream of re-acquiring somehow, somewhere, someday an idyllic, tranquil earthly Eden."[8] Mitchell's representation of nature, women, and blacks contrasts strikingly with those of the authors examined in the following chapters. She represents the land of Tara in traditional, sentimental pastoral terms, a passive landscape of the improved garden fringed by an unknown and unruly wilderness: "The plantation clearings and miles of cotton fields smiled up to a warm sun, placid, complacent. At their edges rose the virgin forests, dark and cool even in the hottest noons, mysterious, a little sinister" (8). The free blacks of the Reconstruction are aligned by Mitchell with the threatening, unruly side of nature, while the slaves of Tara remain devoted to their masters even when the war is over: "Negroes were provoking sometimes and stupid and lazy, but there was loyalty in them that money couldn't buy, a feeling of oneness with their white folks which made them risk their lives to keep food on the table" (472). The overall implication of Mitchell on race is one similar to Page, that blacks are childlike and were better off as slaves.

Mitchell is more critical of traditional gender roles, but the intersections of nature and gender reveal a more circumscribed conception in comparison to Rawlings and Hurston. Scarlett and the other Southern belles must forgo eating in public, hide their true intelligence, and dress in layers of restricting, shape-altering clothes, all of which disguise women as something they are not, just as the pastoral version of nature on the plantation is false, "nature improved" but actually less natural. Scarlett complains that Yankee girls don't "have to act like such fools," but the mothers of the South "impressed on their daughters the necessity of being helpless, clinging, doe-eyed creatures" (79–80). Mitchell does, in fact, criticize this aspect of the culture, suggesting that Southern women have been brainwashed and would be better off if they were free to express themselves openly: "There was no one to tell Scarlett that her own personality, frighteningly vital though it was, was more attractive than any masquerade she might adopt. Had she been told, she would have been pleased but unbelieving. And the civilization of which she was a part would have been unbelieving too, for at no time, before or since, had so low a premium been placed on feminine naturalness" (80). These dissonant notes are few and far between in the novel, though, and Scarlett's later public displays of her intelligence and true personality are tied by Mitchell to her supposed ethical and moral shortcomings.

Scarlett is virtually the only character with a strong attachment to the natural world, and in some ways the strength she draws from the land links her with strong women like Hurston's Janie Starks or Rawlings's Piety Jacklin. However, there are also differences among these characters that make Scarlett's association with nature more troubling. Mitchell at one point makes explicit the woman-as-Southern-garden metaphor when she openly associates Scarlett's body with the land of Tara. Ashley Wilkes puts the dirt of Tara into Scarlett's hand in order to remind her of her connection to her family estate at a moment when the pair are considering giving into their carnal desires: "Had Ashley yielded, she could have gone away with him and left family and friends without a backwards look but, even in her emptiness, she knew it would have torn her heart to leave these dear red hills and long washed gullies and gaunt black pines" (536). Having an affair with Ashley would mean giving up Tara, and rejecting him means keeping her body to herself and keeping Tara. Scarlett later even wears the curtains from Tara as a dress, and this equation of the female body with the land is reinforced in the novel as Southern women repeatedly assume that the invading Yankee soldiers who are destroying their crops and homes also want to rape them. The rather traditional pastoral elements of *Gone with the Wind* help to underscore how radically new and different the ecopastorals of Caldwell, Rawlings, Hurston, and Faulkner are with respect to their representations of the natural world and people's interdependence with it.

Caldwell, Rawlings, Hurston, and Faulkner each reject the static, passive conception of nature implied in the traditional pastoral garden, where humans are above nature, controlling and shaping it at will. Employing an ecocritical approach to their works, I suggest that these writers posit a network model of the natural world that includes humans, placing people and their environments in a reciprocal relationship. Moreover, these authors more consciously intertwine representations of nature with issues of class, race, and gender, connections that the field of ecocriticism now finds axiomatic. My approach will illuminate relationships among seemingly disparate authors who are usually not linked but who are actually all inventing similar versions of the pastoral for a New South and, in the process, critiquing older versions of both. I also ground my ecocritical approach in the material and economic history of the time and the region. The fundamental changes that occur in the Depression-era South provide the impetus for a literary renaissance, and by emphasizing this historical context I want to elucidate the connections between nature and culture with which the pastoral mode is explicitly concerned. In spite of its prior uses, the pastoral mode remains viable in this period because it seeks to present a social model that achieves an appropriate balance of culture and nature, city and country, at a time when this relationship seems particularly unstable.

The domination of agriculture in the economy and culture of the South was already on the decline prior to 1930, but the Great Depression sped the pace of change, compelling Southern authors to examine more closely the causes and effects of industrialization and urbanization on a historically rural farming region.[9] Since the very identity of the South as an entity distinct from the rest of the country had been inextricably tied to its agricultural economy, these changes destabilized and threatened to destroy traditional ways of life, and, indeed, challenged the assumption that a clearly definable South exists at all. According to Jack Temple Kirby, the South lost over 1.5 million farms from 1920 to 1960, creating a particularly intense and traumatic sense of change in the region.[10] The resulting sense of dislocation made the land itself a logical starting place both for attempts to sustain the institutions of the past in the chaotic present (e.g., the Nashville Agrarians' *I'll Take My Stand*) and for modernist critiques of the validity and usefulness of inherited knowledge (e.g., W. J. Cash's *The Mind of the South*).

An underlying assumption of this study is that the natural world is more than just the passive physical background against which the substance of life (or fiction) is played out. Nature is at once a cultural construct and an external reality not fully contained by human constructions. Taking my cue from the insights offered in the fields of humanistic and cultural geography in recent decades, I emphasize the dynamic element of natural places. As geographer E. V. Walter suggests, there is a reciprocal influence between human beings and their environments: "People and things in a place participate in one another's natures. Place is a location of mutual immanence, a unity of effective presences abiding together." Similarly, J. Nicholas Entrikin reminds us that lived places resonate with the energies of their inhabitants: "We live our lives in place and have a sense of being part of place, but we also view place as something separate, something external. . . . Thus place is both a center of meaning and the external context of our actions."[11] Of course, not all natural environments can properly be called lived places, especially those commonly classified as wilderness. Nonetheless, the tenet of cultural geography that a profound interdependency exists between people and places is readily adaptable to a wide variety of lived and uninhabited natural places, and the mutually constitutive nature of place and social reality informs the ecopastorals of the Depression.

In the field of sociology, Rupert Vance's classic 1932 study *Human Geography of the South* shows that the interaction and reciprocal influences of humans and nature is a topical matter for Southern academics as well as novelists.[12] Vance's study coincides with a growing environmental awareness, both nationally and in the South, and with the compositions and publications of the works examined in this study. Judith Bryant Wittenberg rightly notes that "although the environmental crisis in the United States was deep-rooted and increasing with each decade, the public perception that it was fast assuming disastrous proportions grew during the 1930s and 1940s."[13] These factors help explain the increased prominence of nature in Southern fiction between 1930 and 1950. While mass deforestation, soil erosion, and depleted fertility were hardly new phenomena in the twentieth century, they were not major themes for Southern writers until the Southern Renaissance period. Part of my argument is that the traditional Southern pastoral views of nature did not adequately recognize the symbiotic relationship of humans and their natural environment, so exploitation of natural resources and consequent environmental damage were not areas of concern. The new versions of ecopastoral that emerge in the Depression posit nature as a network that includes humans, taking cues from ecology.[14]

One reason that environmental concerns began to affect the popular psyche more significantly is that the results of nineteenth-century policies and practices were being felt decades later. Albert Cowdrey has called the South of 1900–1930 "a theater of environmental disasters," featuring a boll weevil infestation, a tularemia outbreak among rabbits, a yellow fever epidemic, a great flood, widespread droughts, drastic erosion, and the clear-cutting of millions of acres of forests.[15] As I will discuss in more detail in subsequent chapters, the most damaging of these disasters to people trying to live off the land were deforestation and the loss of soil fertility, both direct consequences of human activities in nature. The monocrop planting in the South, first of tobacco and then of cotton, wore out the soil and increased its susceptibility to erosion, while the commercial fertilizers used to compensate for lost fertility eventually exacerbated both problems.[16] Don H. Doyle, in *Faulkner's County: The Historical Roots of Yoknapatawpha*, grimly concludes that by the time Faulkner began writing about his native Mississippi in the 1920s, the "evidence of destruction" was vivid and abundant: "He grew up in a land torn apart by gullies that ran down the hillsides, with creeks and rivers clogged by quicksand sludge, a landscape also of denuded fields pocked with stumps left by the lumbermen who had cut their way through the woods like locusts."[17]

The landscapes were much the same throughout the South following more than a century of intensive agriculture and widespread, mechanized logging of Southern forests from 1880 to 1920. Nor were these two chief sources of environmental problems unrelated, as Cowdrey explains in the language of the network model: "The relationship between forests and soil, rivers, and wildlife amplified the losses, implying disruption of the linked systems which constituted the natural regimen of the landscape." Hugh Bennett, the first head of the Soil Conservation Service, estimated in 1930 that 97 million acres were completely decimated by erosion in the South alone and that the amount of farmland denuded of topsoil ranged from 1.5 million acres in Virginia to over 5 million in Georgia. The Dust Bowl phenomenon of the 1930s, a consequence of the earlier agricultural practices of the so-called sodbusters, displaced thousands of farming families and helped fuel the public perception that a crisis of disastrous proportions was already under way by casting environmental problems in visible and tragic human terms. Donald Worster refers to the Dust Bowl as "one of the three greatest ecological blunders in history" and argues that it must be understood as closely connected to the Great Depression: "Both events revealed fundamental weaknesses in the traditional culture of America, the one in ecological terms, the other in economic. Both offered a reason, and an opportunity, for substantial reform of that culture." Historian Richard Pells additionally notes the connection between environmental problems and the sense of total collapse engendered by the Depression: "Men became preoccupied with floods, dust storms, and soil erosion not only because these constituted real problems but also because they were perfect metaphors for a breakdown that appeared more physical than social or economic."[18] The apparent collapse of nature itself provided Southern writers not only a metaphor for chaotic, fragmented modern society, but also fertile ground (so to speak) for a changed pastoral vision, a reimagining of humans' relations with the natural environment.

Events like the Dust Bowl, along with the publication of a number of influential environmental texts, contribute to a wider acceptance of the idea that human communities—and individuals' livelihoods—are not separate from the natural world but part of the same larger system. Paul Sears's *Deserts on the March* (1935), for instance, was an influential study condemning the land-use practices that led to both erosion and the Dust Bowl. Other works that had a significant impact on the public environmental discourse in the 1930s and 1940s were Albert Schweitzer's autobiography, the journals of John Muir, Aldo Leopold's landmark environmental work *Sand County Al-*

manac, Charles Elton's *Animal Ecology*, and a reissued edition of George Perkins Marsh's *Man and Nature*, which had originally warned readers in 1864
of the "hostile influence of man." As Wittenberg puts it, such works continue
the "gradual tipping of the conceptual scales from nature-as-commodity to
nature-as-community."[19] The shift was not purely conceptual, however, as
the Soil Conservation Act was passed by Congress in 1935, six Southern states
passed legislation in 1937 authorizing local districts to work with the Soil
Conservation Service, the Civilian Conservation Corps planted millions of
trees throughout the cut-over South, and the Southern Pulpwood Conservation Association promoted more responsible forestry.[20]

Southern literature reflects these developments not only in novels that
deal directly with land-use issues, like Caldwell's *Tobacco Road* (1932), Rawlings's *South Moon Under* (1933), and Faulkner's *Go Down, Moses* (1942), but
also in works that posit something of a sociological corollary to what is often
called the First Law of Ecology: everything is connected to everything else.[21]
SueEllen Campbell has identified an intriguing similarity between the idea
of intertextuality and this concept of ecological interdependence, and she
demonstrates that post-structuralism and ecology both critique "the traditional sense of a separate, independent, authoritative *center* of value or
meaning; both substitute the idea of *networks*."[22] In essence, both literary
and ecological theory challenge the notion of autonomous individuality.
For example, the existence of billions of microscopic creatures on our bodies problematizes any rigid distinction between self and other. In this way,
the ideas of someone like Foucault, who says that an individual is a "node
within a network," can be compared to the principle of contemporary biology and ecology that "the individuality of an organism is not definable
except through its interaction with its environment, through its interdependencies."[23]

The philosophical underpinnings of such notions of interdependence are
elucidated by Alfred North Whitehead, best known for his influential *Science
and the Modern World* (1925), who says that no unit can exist independently
of others and that "an actual entity by its very nature requires other actual entities as ingredients." Whitehead extends this challenge to Cartesian subject/
object duality into the realm of temporality as well, claiming that "the whole
past world of actualities is in some way present in a present actual occasion. . . . Whatever is in a certain occasion's past . . . is objectively present in
it."[24] Faulkner articulates a strikingly similar principle in his famous formulation that "the past is not dead; it's not even past." He also demonstrates this
idea in *Go Down, Moses*, where we see the rippling effects of L. Q. C. McCaslin's actions on his descendents mirrored by the juxtaposition of past and

present in the book's jumbled chronology. It is perhaps not coincidental, then, that this novel about the long-term, unintentional effects of the past and the interrelations of black and white Southern families also tackles issues of land ownership, hunting ethics, logging practices, and the destruction of wilderness.

While the other authors examined in this study do not use the same sort of chronological and structural experimentation as Faulkner, each suggests in his or her fiction an interdependency among people as well as between humans and nature. A new tradition of communal values that replaces hierarchies is implicit in the ideas of nature as conceived by the formerly marginal voices of African Americans and women. When nature is perceived as an interdependent network that affirms multiplicity, diversity, and equality (as in the novels of Rawlings and Hurston), then the claim can be made that similar values in the human community are, in fact, more "natural" than the hierarchical structures attributed to a previously dominant and oppressive system. Whether this system is identified as pastoralism, Victorianism, the patriarchy, slavery, or Jim Crowism depends on the particular author and text in question (and on the critic discussing them). However, the validity of each of these hierarchies, like the network model, also rests on the assumption that they are merely replicating the natural order—only the idea of nature is much different.[25]

This concept of a system of communal values based on an environmental model is very close to what prominent ecocritic Lawrence Buell calls "ecocentrism," an attitude that exhibits a "shift from representation of nature as a theater for human events to representation in the sense of advocacy of nature as a presence for its own sake."[26] Although ecocriticism remains a loosely defined theoretical and critical movement that derives from ecological, biological, platial, and sociological bases, this flexible interdisciplinary approach is perhaps its greatest asset. A basic premise of my approach to this study is the inherent usefulness of an open, interdisciplinary method for creating fresh readings of even the most analyzed literary classics. Moreover, a combination of theoretical strategies seems only appropriate for a study that posits—and examines how authors represent—a fundamental interdependency among individuals, specific environments, cultural and historical trends, socioeconomic systems, and the biotic community of nature. Thus, the following chapters use a combination of historical, psychological, genre-based, feminist, and ecocritical hermeneutics in order to demonstrate the degree to which human relationships with nature affect nearly every aspect of culture.

The ecopastorals counter the prevailing assumption that humans are inherently separate from, over and above, the natural world. For the antebellum and Reconstruction-era pastorals, the improved garden of the plantation was primarily window dressing, a convenient backdrop that symbolized the gentility and stability of a romanticized past: a passive nature amid a chaotic world. Bakker refers to the *locus amoenus* (pleasant place) in his study of antebellum Southern pastoral, while MacKethan expounds on "the dream of arcady" in the postbellum era. Both are idealized versions of nature imagined as orderly and easily controlled, unlike so much else in the South in periods of tumultuous change. Rarely in any pre-twentieth-century Southern pastoral work are there people actually working the land. One of the primary differences, then, in the ecopastorals is their emphasis on work and on knowing nature through labor. Before discussing the four principal authors on whom I will focus, I want to further address the differences and similarities of the ecopastorals and earlier Southern versions. Why should the pastorals of the Depression era be considered different from their predecessors? And why, if they are so different, should they be called pastorals at all?

As I have touched on already, much recent scholarship on the pastoral warns against attempting any strict definition of this contentious category. Critic Annabel Patterson calls the attempt to define the nature of the pastoral "a cause lost as early as the sixteenth century, when the genre began to manifest the tendency of most strong literary forms to propagate by miscegenation," and Alpers cites her in encouraging us to think not about what pastoral is, but about what pastoral can do and how it is used.[27] Nonetheless, I want to offer some central tenets of pastoral in order to better explain where ecopastoral differs and how it is still essentially pastoral, not only in terms of literary conventions but, more importantly, I think, in attitude, intention, and philosophical outlook.[28]

There is always to be found in the pastoral a comparison of two ways of life, rural and urban (which often also correspond with past and present). A simple, rustic spokesperson represents the country or rural, while the author is usually identified with the city or urban. Sometimes there is an actual character who leaves the city to make the typical pastoral journey of retreat and return; sometimes the reader stands in for this character as he or she is transported to the rural setting. The pastoral middle ground idealizes a blending of the poles of urban and rural, culture and nature, which Leo Marx cleverly links to the human psyche: "The contrast between city and country in the pastoral design . . . implies that we can remain human, which is to say, fully integrated beings, only when we follow some such course, back and forth, between our social and natural (animal) selves."[29] Besides this personal reformation that often occurs in nature, the simplicities of the more natural rural setting serve to highlight the problems with a contemporary social situation. For instance, in several of Page's stories an ex-slave narrator laments the current lack of work to be found and the uncertainties of the Reconstruction South while illustrating the "natural" affinities blacks and whites shared before the war, when at least there was enough food and everyone knew his or her place in the order of the world.

The pastoral is about finding a middle ground between the extremes of culture and nature, but the locale itself can vary from shepherd's pasture to family farm and even to slave plantation. For instance, the most common ending to the "plantation romance," as MacKethan points out, is the marriage of an ex-Union soldier and a Southern belle, which saves the old plantation home from ruin and also restores belief in the old order.[30] A key difference in the ecopastorals is the way they approach the idea of a middle ground. The Southern authors of the Depression tend to view social divisions of class, race, and gender as more fluid and less rigid (based on the network model of nature), and thus the middle ground for them is more of a combination of opposites. Traditional pastoral tends to maintain strict poles of opposing states, perhaps modifying one slightly by imitating the other without any real attempt at radically combining the two and thereby changing both.

The marriage of Yankee soldier and Southern belle restoring the old order is a good example of this, and *I'll Take My Stand* illustrates the same principle as the older versions of pastoral through its insistence on strict binary terms. In the first paragraph of "Introduction: A Statement of Principles," the authors proclaim that "the best terms in which to represent the distinction are contained in the phrase, Agrarian *versus* Industrial." The whole tenor of the introduction (and, indeed, most of the book) is of setting up oppositions, not to reconcile them but to stake out competing grounds. The third paragraph almost wistfully recalls the idea of an independent South still taking on the role of defiant combatant: "Nobody now proposes for the South . . . an independent political destiny. That idea is thought to have been finished in 1865. But how far shall the South surrender its moral, social, and economic autonomy to the victorious principle of Union?" Likewise, John Crowe Ransom suggests in his opening essay "Reconstructed but Unregenerate" that although the "American progressivist doctrine" is on top now, it is possible that this will be reversed and the "Southern idea" will be on top.[31] This typifies the thinking of polarized oppositions; one must be dominant over the other. The new ecopastorals are much more about combining oppositions, an almost dialectical process of synthesizing something new.

While the improved garden (or its modern equivalent of farm and plantation) is ostensibly the pastoral middle ground combining the best of nature and culture, the ecopastorals acknowledge that humans have so ravaged, polluted, and manipulated the garden that there is scarcely anything "natural" about it. The texts of Caldwell, Rawlings, Hurston, and Faulkner together represent a shift toward wilderness as the new pastoral locale. For as the way we think about nature changes, our versions of the pastoral naturally change as well. Wilderness has traditionally represented the primitive extreme of the pastoral equation, "the opposite pole from the cacophonous, machine-driven city," in the words of ecocritic Glen A. Love. Writing in the early 1990s, Love argues that nature writing and environmentalism "in the last two decades or so" have helped stimulate a profound pastoral shift: "Wild nature has replaced the traditional middle state of the garden and the rural landscape as the locus of stability and value, the seat of instruction. . . . Under the influence of ecological thought, wilderness has radicalized the pastoral experience."[32]

In this book, I show how this shift is occurring in Southern literature of the early twentieth century. Lewis Simpson, in *The Dispossessed Garden*, describes it as a time when Southern authors began to counter the "culture of alienation" that had stultified Southern letters: "[I]n its experience of alienation as a pastoral reaction to modernity, in its devotion to the plantation image, the Southern literary mind had engaged in a withdrawal from memory and history."[33] The radicalization that Love speaks of can be seen in the Depression-era texts that shift the pastoral from a rather conservative mode for writers like Simms, Cooke, Page, Harris, and the Nashville Agrarians to a more progressive vehicle for Caldwell, Rawlings, Hurston, and Faulkner. These authors are at the leading edge of the types of changes Love is describing in both the way Americans conceive of nature and the way American writers portray it: "If the key terms for relatively untrammeled nature in the past were *simplicity* and *permanence*, those terms have shifted in an ecologically-concerned present to *complexity* and *change*. [Wilderness is] the model of a complex diversity and a new pattern for survival."[34] This idea of wilderness as naturally complex, diverse, and dynamic is used to counter a historically negative association of Native Americans, African Americans, and women with nature: "When nature is viewed . . . as the 'terra nullius,' or empty background for culture, as a passive resource for human domination, those persons equated with nature may analogously be treated as natural inferiors, and ensuing inequitable and divisive social interrelations may be cast as natural rather than humanly created, as inevitable rather than open to question and reform."[35] Novelists like Rawlings and Hurston, rather than deny a bond between women and nature, reconstitute the relationship as active and potentially empowering. Specifically, they represent wilderness as more than merely a passive field for the exercise of masculine power, and they identify their female characters with a vital, active nature rather than with virginal or despoiled Southern gardens.

While all four of the authors on whom I focus may not address gender and/or race in this way, one feature that links all of their ecopastorals (and differentiates them from earlier pastorals) is a pronounced emphasis on labor in nature. Work of any kind is extolled during the Depression, and the idea of knowing nature through labor runs throughout the texts of these authors. Working with the land provides a more intimate connection with the natural world than viewing it as an aesthetic object or as an arena for recreation or as an exotic "other" that needs protection. Any sort of return to the Garden of Eden is precluded in the ecopastorals because it has already been clear-cut, plowed under, and worn out. Rather, learning to live and work in nature responsibly, combining the social and the natural, is the only hope for a future that benefits all of nature, including its human inhabitants.

Rather than survey a wide range of authors from this time period, I have selected four distinct and important writers for more detailed examination. The four principal authors selected for this study were chosen because they all make Southern relationships to the natural world central concerns of their work and because each creates distinct new versions of the pastoral in the process. In many ways these writers are representative figures in that their specific renderings of human relationships with the natural environment attest to a variety of more general cultural anxieties about the destabilizing effects of the Great Depression and the creation of the modern New South. I also wanted to select diverse yet well-known authors who exemplify wider trends or strains in Southern literature. I see each of them contributing to a new category of what I am calling ecopastoral, though each creates a different version within that broad category.

I examine the fiction of Caldwell, Rawlings, Hurston, and Faulkner as much for their different approaches to writing about the natural world as for any similar awareness of the importance of natural environments in "purely" human affairs. Caldwell's focus is on poor white farmers and Southern agricultural use and abuse of the soil. He creates antipastoral works, depicting the opposite of a romanticized notion of the bucolic American family farm. Rawlings, as a transplanted "Yankee," brings an outsider's perspective to the "crackers" who become both her neighbors and her fictional characters. Her best work is set in the backwoods of north Florida, and she produces a wilderness pastoral that critiques society, even as it questions and revises the pastoral mode itself. Hurston examines both black and white folk culture, focusing on the concept of knowing nature through labor and contemplating how attitudes toward the natural world intersect with issues of race, class, and gender. She crafts what I call a personal pastoral in both the novels I examine here, altering the mode to fit her female protagonists' quests for identity. Faulkner, as we might expect, confronts virtually all of these issues in a single "postpastoral" novel, *Go Down, Moses,* exploring the connections of a degraded environment to a degraded culture and specifically probing the idea of wilderness in relation to the McCaslin family plantation.[36]

Rawlings and Caldwell may not be well known to many readers (or at least not as well known as Hurston and Faulkner), and therefore they are perhaps the least obvious choices for this project. A major reason for their selection is perhaps best explained considering the two together. Rawlings's work falls closest to the loose category of "nature writing" of any of these four authors. An apt moniker for her major works, all set in the backwoods of Florida, might be "environmental fiction" in that they directly focus on the struggles of people in rural and wilderness settings where the specter of ever-encroaching modern civilization always looms. Caldwell, on the other hand, is identified with the milieu of social criticism or social protest fiction much more than any of the other three authors in this study. Sometimes classified as a proletarian writer, Caldwell, at first glance, appears least concerned with natural environments per se, as opposed to the human activities occurring within them. Thus, my approach is to show, on the one hand, how Rawlings's environmental fiction incorporates significant subtexts regarding social issues (particularly gender) and, on the other, to reveal how Caldwell's social criticism expands from, and largely depends on, his conceptions and representations of the natural world.

In the last thirty years, Hurston has become an indispensable part of the Southern and American canons. Much of the current scholarship, however, tends to examine her work primarily in relation to African American literary traditions or considers her a protean writer who defies inclusion in any literary movements or traditions. By discussing her work in the contexts of Southern and environmental studies, I offer readings that suggest her continuity with seemingly disparate authors, while also juxtaposing her portraits of nature, women, and African Americans with those of white authors from the same era and region. Hurston appropriates key aspects of the white-dominated pastoral mode and creates personal pastorals of women who often must navigate between untenable extremes. Her creation of what I call a working-class pastoral in *Seraph on the Suwanee* (1948), her "white novel," uses pastoral to engage issues of race, class, and gender simultaneously.

In *Go Down, Moses,* nature is similarly entangled with these categories, and Faulkner constructs a postpastoral novel that examines the complex connections in fascinating ways. What makes the work postpastoral is Faulkner's metapastoral approach of using pastoral elements while questioning the efficacy of the mode, as well as the novel's ecocentric sensibility, which anticipates some core principles of the modern environmental movement. Faulkner's emphasis on nature's destruction establishes the novel as a precursor to, or early example of, a postpastoral that overtly responds to environmental issues.

Despite the wide variety of ways these authors choose to represent nature and investigate the mutually constitutive relationship of humans to their natural environments, each of the four responds to, contests, and revises, in some manner, the pastoral traditions of American and Southern literature. The mutability of pastoral is a key factor in its enduring relevance, and part of my argument (building on those of others) is that a variety of texts can be called pastoral though they may have obvious differences from the classical varieties. The ecopastorals that emerge from the Southern Depression are forerunners of their type, creating new versions that can still be found in the twenty-first century.

Leo Marx predicts that the "wholly new conception of the precariousness of our relations with nature is bound to bring forth new versions of the pastoral." Buell cites this same passage in his argument that pastoral has continuing or even increasing relevance in an age of environmentalism: "[P]astoralism is sure to remain a luminous ideal and to retain the capacity to assume oppositional forms for some time to come. . . . Pastoral's likely future as an ideological force makes it all the more important to grasp its double-edged character."[37] This double edge of pastoral, its ability to be both regressive and progressive, is prominent in traditional and modern variants, and it permits a single text to appear both sentimental and complex. Thus, while the ecopastorals I analyze are largely complex and progressive in their representations of the natural world, they can be at times more sentimental and regressive on social issues.

Although my textual analyses in the chapters that follow are characterized by their attention to race, class, and gender dynamics, I also strive to remain focused on the natural environment itself as "expressive space," in E. V. Walter's terms, which fosters these dynamics. For as Barbara Ching and Gerald Creed shrewdly note, quite often in contemporary literary and cultural theory, the representation of "social distinctions primarily in terms of race, class and gender . . . masks the extent to which these categories are influenced by place identification." Buell, too, makes a similar complaint of current criticism (even including much ecocriticism) that "marginalizes the literal environment too much when it portrays the green world as little more than projective fantasy or social allegory."[38] Accordingly, in this study I am mindful of natural environments as places inextricably linked with social processes and the lives of their inhabitants, in addition to their symbolic or metaphorical functions.

Chapter 1 analyzes Caldwell's two best and most popular novels, *Tobacco Road* and *God's Little Acre* (1933), as antipastorals forged in reaction to the Great Depression. Critiquing a spirit of "acquisitive individualism," Caldwell identifies the social factors that have depleted the soil and dispossessed independent farmers of their place in the Jeffersonian yeoman tradition. In both novels, I argue, Caldwell emphasizes the impotence and frustration of male characters who can no longer work to grow cotton in the fields nor transform the cotton to textiles in mills. Farmers who cannot farm and weavers who cannot weave lose touch with a feminine natural world and find their manhood threatened. Caldwell links women and nature through the physically deformed women of *Tobacco Road* who reflect the scarred landscape and through the sexual vitality of the women in *God's Little Acre* who embody a natural energy that Will Thompson, Caldwell's mill worker *übermensch,* cannot find in the earth or in the idle machinery of the closed mill. Economic and social factors are the root causes of Caldwell's degraded natural environments, which, in turn, exert a debilitating influence on their human inhabitants, demonstrating E. V. Walter's notion of place as a "location of mutual immanence" where people and their environment "participate in one another's nature."[39] Ultimately, however, Caldwell's works fall short of envisioning a new model for relating to nature as he replicates many traditional pastoral attitudes even as he discredits the traditional pastoral model.

In chapter 2, I examine three works by Marjorie Kinnan Rawlings—*South Moon Under, Cross Creek* (1942), and *The Yearling* (1938)—and argue that she relocates the pastoral garden to the heart of the wilderness in order to free her characters from traditionally confining and artificial gender identities. Rawlings finds many of the positive attributes of the middle ground in an environment typically considered an untenable extreme in traditional pastoral modes. The elemental qualities of life in the isolated Florida "scrub" country necessitate more "natural" conceptions of gender, in Rawlings's formulation, by virtue of its proximity to pristine wilderness. The distance of the scrub from modern civilization reveals that gender inequities are justified by positing social constructions of gender as natural and therefore immutable. Rawlings essentially suggests that an interdependent, fluid model of nature that she finds in the wilderness is more accurate than traditional pastoral versions of an ordered and static garden. Therefore, dynamic and changeable gender roles are more natural, and thus more correct, than the fixed hierarchy of a purely cultural construction that subordinates women to men. Rawlings's version of nature is not necessarily more accurate than others and, in fact, her conception of wilderness as a corrective to the ills of society threatens to replicate the problematic pastoral ideal in the new setting of the wilderness.

Chapter 3 expands this investigation of the relationship of nature to gender by considering two novels by Zora Neale Hurston—*Their Eyes Were Watching God* (1937) and *Seraph on the Suwanee*—that reconstruct the passive association of women and nature as active and empowering. Hurston uses the controlling symbol of a pear tree for the story of Janie in *Their Eyes* and a mulberry tree for Arvay Henson's tale in *Seraph*. Both women undertake journeys of self-discovery, and the trees they identify with as young women serve as paradigms of their future relationships: Janie's pear tree as a positive symbol of egalitarian love and Arvay's mulberry tree as a poisoning reminder of poor "cracker" roots she would like to forget. Moreover, both novels use what I call a personal pastoral as a method of framing these women's quest for internal harmony and balance. I also argue that, in *Their Eyes*, Hurston's burgeoning knowledge of Afro-Caribbean Vodou informs her representation of nature as a vital, active force that counters attempts of white- and male-dominated culture to objectify nature, women, and African Americans. In both works Hurston considers practical land-use issues in conjunction with pastoral ideals. In *Seraph*, I read Hurston's choice to focus on white characters as a method of emphasizing class and gender dynamics, while matters of race hover on the periphery. Hurston combines the personal pastoral with a working-class pastoral to produce a complex text that celebrates the diverse environments of Florida as well as the economic rise of the Meserve family, which is facilitated by Jim's labor in his natural environments.

In chapter 4, I propose that Faulkner's *Go Down, Moses* is an early example of what Terry Gifford calls the postpastoral. Using Gifford's definition of the term as a guide, I analyze the novel's treatment of Mississippi's ecological history, the ownership of land and people, the consequences of environmental and human exploitation, the veneration of wilderness, and hunting both as personal communion with nature and as cultural ritual. *Go Down, Moses* exemplifies Gifford's characterization of postpastoral as literature that goes "beyond the closed circuit of pastoral and anti-pastoral to achieve a vision of an integrated natural world that includes the human."[40] I then use this discussion of the novel as a springboard to wider issues, including the role of pastoral in contemporary Southern literature and the relevance of ecocriticism to Southern studies.

The notion of society as composed of separate, independent persons seems no longer tenable in the depths of the Great Depression. The past, thoroughly dismantled and discredited by modernist analyses, is useless as a guide for the future. Through reappraisals of nature, Southern writers find a model for social collectivism (as well as a justification for it as natural) in the conception of ecosystems as networks of interdependent, inseparable relations. The natural world also can provide a physical place for connecting with the "Other" of nature and with other people: through the communal labor of the muck in the Everglades, the dangerous work in Florida shrimping communities, the joint efforts to save orange groves from frost or livestock from bears, and transcendent experiences that one's existence is, in Rawlings's words, "a torn fragment of the larger cloth." My title reference to clear-cutting Eden, then, works in more ways than one: there is the literal environmental destruction that these authors portray and respond to, and there is the demythologizing of an idealized view of the past as a lost golden age. This study suggests how these four authors answer the question that remains: What is the nature of the future?

1
Depleted Land, Depleted Lives

Erskine Caldwell's Antipastoral

Erskine Caldwell is the single greatest influence on the popular conception of the white Southern farmer. By the time of his death in 1987, Caldwell had sold over 80 million copies of his books worldwide in over forty languages. While his best-known novels, *Tobacco Road* (1932) and *God's Little Acre* (1933), sold modestly but steadily upon their initial releases, they were stunningly successful as paperback reissues in 1946. *Tobacco Road* sold over 1 million copies in the first year alone, and *God's Little Acre* sold a staggering 6 million copies within five years of its paperback release, making it the most successful book Penguin had ever published. Additionally, the stage version of *Tobacco Road* was a sensation almost immediately after its December 1933 Broadway debut. In an era when going to the theater had become a luxury, *Tobacco Road* was the longest-running show in Broadway history, finally closing in 1941 after 3,180 shows, over 900 more than any other play in American history at the time. On top of that, several traveling shows operated at once, playing in all but seven states and breaking attendance records everywhere. Estimates suggest over 7 million people saw the play nationwide from 1934 to 1940.[1] Caldwell's works helped make the sharecropper into a national symbol of the Great Depression, and they called the attention of the nation to the plight of poor Southern farmers.

In *Tobacco Road* and *God's Little Acre,* Caldwell exposes the conditions of poor farmers and workers in the South and advocates the need for social change. The natural environment of these novels mirrors the depressing, barren, and stagnant lives of his characters, suggesting the betrayal of the pastoral ideal in the American South of the Great Depression. While the traditional pastoral landscape implies a harmonic blend of culture and nature, city and country, Caldwell shows that, in this place and time, anyway, culture and nature both work against the people caught between them. The ideal of balance is replaced by a nightmarish cycle of reciprocal causes and effects in which socioeconomic forces hasten the depletion of the land, and diminishing agricultural returns further subject families like the fictional Lesters and Waldens to the capriciousness of the Depression-era marketplace.

Over the course of these two novels, Caldwell develops an antipastoral representation of the Southern farmer and gropes unsuccessfully for a new and viable alternative. *Tobacco Road* thoroughly dismantles the pastoral convention of an independent yeoman farmer working in harmony with the land, and Caldwell's portrayal of the Southern landscape as a ruined garden is directly linked to the crushing poverty of the Depression. Jeeter Lester, for instance, clings to a romantic cultural myth of unity with the land, further exacerbating his family's dire straits by equating a mill job with an "unnatural" violation of God's plan. In *God's Little Acre,* Caldwell openly mocks pastoral idealization of the farmer by having Ty Ty Walden dig for gold rather than plant cotton on his land, a folly that, by comparison, actually seems no more foolish than Jeeter's attempts to make a living on worn-out land with no credit, tools, or seed.

Tobacco Road is about stasis and a reciprocity of stagnation between humans and nature. Similarly, the novel's narration is full of repetition and a lack of movement. I read *God's Little Acre* almost as a sequel in which Caldwell adds a mill town to the setting of the depleted family farm in order to investigate whether the textile mills might offer more hope for rural Southerners than do the now unproductive cotton farms. Stylistically, this novel is also shifting. Just as Ty Ty Walden ceaselessly moves the location of God's little acre, Caldwell continually shifts the novel's setting and its narrative style, which reflects his hesitancy about the potential of the mill town as a replacement for the pastoral ideal of the farm.

The idea of knowing nature through work is important in all of the eco-pastorals. Caldwell, however, is different from the authors treated in subsequent chapters because of his characters' inability to work, their lack of labor. Jeeter Lester, for instance, is prevented from working his land by numerous factors, and his idleness signals—and helps create—an alienation from nature. In *God's Little Acre,* labor is certainly valorized, but the characters do not consistently work either in the mill or on the farm. This inability to work is especially devastating for men in Caldwell's work. For the most part, Caldwell genders land and nature in his work as strictly feminine, replicating traditional pastoral gendering patterns. Ecocritical and ecofeminist insights on the relationship of gender and nature can help to recognize the importance of a gendered landscape and to understand its implications. Ultimately, I argue, Caldwell's failure to challenge the gendered assumptions of the Southern pastoral tradition is part of a more general incapability on his part to reconceptualize human relationships with the natural world in the way the other ecopastoral authors do. His antipastoral inverts and dismisses traditional Southern pastoral but does not offer a new and workable substitute.

The depleted soil and barren landscapes in the two novels are the result of a set of values that have traditionally been coded as masculine, particularly a scientific, mechanistic worldview that encounters nature as a feminine site for the exercise of male power. Louise Westling, for example, describes in *The Green Breast of the New World* how a gendering of nature as feminine in the American pastoral tradition sentimentalizes the conquest and destruction of the wilderness. While Westling finds in Ernest Hemingway's work "an exclusively masculine code of values," the same may be said of Caldwell's images of death and decay in *Tobacco Road* and *God's Little Acre.* The marginalization of traditionally feminine natural symbols of life and growth signify the consequences of, in Westling's words, "a sentimental masculine gaze at a feminized landscape."[2] Even though this gendered construction of the landscape is part of a failed way of interacting with nature, Caldwell shows little willingness to challenge such fundamental assumptions in his presentations of these farmers' plight. Instead, his focus is more on how economic factors deny men their customary roles of masters of the soil. At times these two novels present a less hierarchical interdependency of humans and nature, the type of model that might be employed as a critique of traditional pastoral gender roles. Yet despite glimpses of a more active natural world endowed with agency of its own, Caldwell relies on a fairly conventional conception of a feminine, passive natural world.

In his nonfiction collaboration with the photographer (and his future wife) Margaret Bourke-White, *You Have Seen Their Faces* (1937), Caldwell clarifies the implicit material connection between humans and nature in his fiction. Not only is the soil depleted and eroded, he claims, but its tenants also are "worn out physically and spiritually" because "the institution of sharecropping does things to men as well as to land."[3] The paternalistic plantation owners and absentee landlords, whom he equates with the scions of industrial manufacturing, are castigated as representatives of "the agricultural system that acquires sharecroppers and mules for their economic usefulness, and disposes of them when no more profit can be extracted from their bodies" (113). The body of the earth has been a similarly disposable commodity in the history of Southern agriculture, as Caldwell asserts in a later interview: "Nobody thought of saving the land. . . . If the soil was depleted, you moved on to somewhere else. Land was so cheap they could afford to abandon it."[4] By portraying human beings as little more than raw materials and economic resources, like mules and land, Caldwell moves beyond a purely symbolic construction of nature. In this way, he combats the notion of nature as *terra nullius*—a mere backdrop for more important human affairs—by positing an interdependent relationship between humans and their environment in which specific places play an active role in the formation of culture and material reality.

It is useful to turn briefly to the realm of cultural geography for its insights into the relationship of human agency, social process, and spatial location. Martyn Lee claims that spatial location is in danger of assuming subordinate status to the cultural points of this tripartite structure, but he argues that the influence of place should not be undervalued: "[S]pace, when taken culturally, represents a relatively coherent and autonomous social domain which exercises a certain determinacy upon both the population and the social processes located upon its terrain, and as such should be seen as far more than the mere aggregation of the actions and activities of those populations and processes." Lee extends Pierre Bourdieu's notion of "habitus" to the realm of place studies in order to explain how places exist fairly autonomously, as more than simply passive sites for the actions of humans and social processes. Lee defines the habitus of location as "a set of relatively consistent, enduring and generative cultural (pre)dispositions to respond to current circumstances, or 'the outside world,' in a particular way." In other words, habitus, as experienced by individuals, is a "conceptual lens through which particular understandings or interpretations of the social world are generated and as such invite particular forms of response or action to the social world."[5] While Lee is speaking specifically of the habitus of cities, his ideas are equally applicable to rural locations, and, indeed, all of the authors examined in this book demonstrate the mutually constitutive nature of place and social reality in rural settings.

The austere landscape, for example, of the Lester farm in *Tobacco Road* can be seen not only as metaphorically related to the debased lives of its inhabitants but also as a presence that simultaneously constitutes and is constituted by the Lester family and their actions. As overfertilization and monocrop farming have contributed to the impoverishment of the soil, so has the barren and unproductive land helped create a family that accepts hunger, greed, lust, idleness, and sickness as the normal conditions of existence. The Lesters have been conditioned by the realities of their place to formulate particular conceptions of "the outside world," including the belief that all commodities are scarce, necessitating constant and violent competition. Despite debates among Caldwell critics, the moral depravity of the clan need not be categorized as either comic exaggeration in the vein of southwestern humorists or an overly sentimental portrait designed to induce pity and charity from middle- and upper-class audiences, just as the novel itself is neither a work of comedy nor social realism exclusively. Instead, this degeneracy can be read as a result of the specific effects of spatial location and social processes, while remembering that these factors are, in turn, affected by the actions of the Lesters: each aspect of the three-part structure constantly modifies, and is modified by, the other two.

Caldwell's illustration of the interdependence of the human and natural worlds suggests that barriers between self and other may be overcome, but his interest in nature is chiefly in its capacity as "place," that is, in its relationship to people rather than its potential as an entity or system that exists independent of human consciousness or action. For Caldwell's male characters, nature is invariably identified with a feminine vitality that is missing from their own lives. While the association of women and land is part and parcel of the Southern pastoral tradition, Caldwell removes the usual qualities of fecundity, beauty, and abundance for an antipastoral reflection of the decimated farms of the Depression. Similarly, Caldwell's women characters are not the civilized, honorable belles of Page and Simms. In *Tobacco Road*, Jeeter's wife, Ada, and Mother Lester are wracked with disease and perpetually on the verge of death; one daughter, Ellie May, is physically disfigured and barely able to control her sexual urges; another, Pearl, is a mute who refuses to be touched by men, including her husband; and an unknown number of other daughters are apparently prostitutes in nearby Augusta. In *God's Little Acre*, Ty Ty Walden's wife has died before the action of the novel; his daughter-in-law Griselda is an earth goddess type, similar to Faulkner's Eula Varner, who inspires lust in all men and happily obeys the commands of the dominating Will Thompson, whom she says she would follow "like a dog." Darling Jill Walden is a vapid nymphomaniac who seduces and discards men in rapid succession; and her sister Rosamond is content with mothering her husband—she feeds him, puts him to bed, and spanks him with a hairbrush after catching him in bed with Darling Jill—and graciously accepting whatever time and attention he deigns to give her. Caldwell offers distorted, even grotesque, versions of the stock female roles of virgin, whore, mother, and love goddess: promiscuous, emaciated, and deformed women living in a denuded Southern garden. Similarly, Caldwell's men are denied the traditional pastoral roles of masters of nature and protectors of virtuous women. They are more often emasculated by the land's infertility than empowered by ritual conquest of it, and Caldwell's impetus for this revision lies in the historical and social climate wrought by the exigencies of the Great Depression.

Historian Robert S. McElvaine has shown how the pressures of the Depression reawakened the conflict between the simultaneously held American desires for both "the Abundant Life," represented by large-scale mass production, and the life of "former simplicities," associated with the needs of the average person as opposed to big business. He understands these conflicting ideals as opposite ends of a continuum between which the middle class fluctuates based on historical circumstances: "The categories are far from absolute, but workers have tended to move toward cooperative individualism and businessmen toward acquisitive individualism." McElvaine describes how, in periods of liberalism and in trying economic times, the American middle class tends to identify with the cooperative values of the working class. During conservative eras and times of relative prosperity, on the other hand, "many in the middle class have tried to emulate those above them on the social scale and so adopted their values."[6]

The 1930s is, of course, a period both of liberalism and of widespread economic collapse. The previous decade of relative prosperity had successfully convinced much of the working and middle classes to adopt an ethic of acquisitive consumerism and to accept the premise of a scientific, amoral marketplace. Historian Richard Pells corroborates McElvaine's assessment of the national mood and argues that American writers saw the breakdown of America's financial and industrial systems as symptomatic of a deeper spiritual malaise: "The depression confirmed their belief that American ideals were dangerously distorted and unreal, that competition and acquisitiveness were eroding the country's social foundations, that the quality of human life under capitalism offered men no sense of community or common experience."[7] As the Depression worsened and affected more and more people, disillusionment with the unfettered marketplace grew, as did the cries for a moral economy that would stress collectivism as the means of achieving independence and individuality. To put this in the terms of the Edenic metaphor, the ideal of the paradisiacal, pastoral garden becomes consigned to an irrecoverable past, even as the desire to create a new utopia persists.

Caldwell's notorious ambiguity and penchant for self-contradiction in both style and philosophy reflect the increasing polarity of class division in the period and the conflicting impulses of cooperative and acquisitive individualism. Malcolm Cowley argues that there are two Erskine Caldwells— "Caldwell One, the sociologist," and "Caldwell Two," the imaginative writer— who work at cross purposes in his novels, but who sometimes achieve "an almost perfect union" in certain short stories. Cowley's implicit judgment of the novels as flawed combinations of the two tendencies is a fairly common attitude in the relatively thin annals of Caldwell criticism. Writing in 1979 about *Tobacco Road,* Robert Brinkmeyer Jr. summarizes the consensus opinion at that time: "Social realism and comedy, two separate and apparently incompatible purposes, seem to be at work in the novel; and the prevailing critical trend finds the novel flawed as a result of this mix: too comical for social indictment, and too socially zealous for pure humor."[8] While later critics like Sylvia Jenkins Cook and Richard Gray have taken a more positive view of Caldwell's ambiguities and discrepancies, there has been practically no mention of the relationship of "the two Caldwells" to the divided sentiments of the American lower and middle classes during the Depression: the simultaneous desire for "the Abundant Life" and for the imagined simplicities of a previous era that seemed a golden age during the hard times of the Depression.

Caldwell's bifurcated portrait of Jeeter might be read more profitably as a reflection of the social divisions of the era rather than as evidence of two Caldwells working against one another. The notion that Caldwell's comedic and reformist purposes are simply incompatible too hastily dismisses the more complex and potentially rewarding possibility of an intentionally contradictory depiction of Jeeter. He is a sympathetic victim of socioeconomic forces in his desire for "the Abundant Life" through more equitable division of wealth, a characterization that seems the product of Cowley's "Caldwell One, the sociologist." He is also a tragicomic figure (via "Caldwell Two") whose dire straits are a result of his own foolishness and ignorance and whose memories of the abundant credit and plentiful crops of the past only increase his present despair and lethargy. Or, to use McElvaine's terms, from the standpoint of acquisitive individualism, the Lesters are to be mocked, and perhaps pitied, for their comical ignorance and poor choices. From the view of cooperative individualism, an increasingly popular philosophy throughout the 1930s, they are hapless prey of vast, impersonal forces who deserve the aid of society (and particularly the government).

In terms of the pastoral, when Jeeter speaks in the novel he is the simple rustic spokesman of the pastoral tradition, with whom readers would reflexively sympathize. When the voice of "Caldwell Two" takes over the narrative, it is the perspective of the urban traveler come to the country, which often casts Jeeter in the role of worthless reprobate. Rather than blending the two perspectives into something like a harmonious, traditional pastoral middle state, Caldwell has them intentionally clash in his discordant antipastoral.

At the center of these disparate views is Jeeter's tenacious and simultaneously heroic and irrational attachment to the land. To focus only on the roles of the tenancy system and Jeeter's inaction is to subordinate the role of place in just the manner Martyn Lee cautions against. In a novel with a rambling, episodic plot structure and minimal character development, the setting of the story is perhaps its most important element, as Wayne Mixon has also noted: "Caldwell's depiction of an environment that is so brutal it can crush all decency from its victims gives the novel its great power."[9] Caldwell's focus on place in the novel illustrates the complexity and depth of the problem of Southern rural poverty. It is not a situation that can be fixed by either a change in lazy people's work habits or a reformation of an overly exploitative tenancy system. Caldwell shows that these issues are inextricably tied to human beings' relationships to their physical environments, which, in turn, affect (and are affected by) cultural predispositions. Jeeter's refusal to leave the decaying garden of his family's worn-out land for a more secure job in one of the nearby cotton mills is, ironically, practically his only redeeming quality. He is otherwise a man who has fathered countless children by neighboring wives, who exhibits little or no feeling for his family (including his silent, starving mother, whom he beats for stealing food), and who readily sells his preteen daughter into marriage. Nonetheless, Caldwell allows Jeeter to remain sympathetic as a distorted descendant of the Jeffersonian yeoman farmer who has been unfairly dispossessed of his agricultural inheritance. Thus, even a licentious reprobate who would sell his daughter and steal food from his mother can seem endearing and justified when he complains, "It don't look like everybody ought to be poverty-ridden just because they live on the land instead of going to the mills."[10]

Tobacco Road demonstrates that the present exhaustion of the soil stems from its historical abuse. A shortsighted approach to land management, particularly the monocrop cotton culture and extensive fertilization practices, ensured rapid rates of soil depletion and erosion, a devastating combination for those who depended on the land for their livelihood. Rupert Vance, in his famous study *Human Geography of the South* (1932), notes that there was widespread concern over Southern soil exhaustion as far back as the 1840s and 1850s, resulting in a subsequent period of heavy fertilization: "It was finally commercial fertilization which came both to repair the ravages of soil exhaustion and to extend to further reaches its primary cause, the culture of cotton." Erosion, which was more pronounced in the South than in other regions, created further problems for farmers by leaching chemicals from the soil.[11] Irresponsible farming techniques thus helped to create poor land for farming which, along with the severe impact of the Depression on small-scale farmers, produced a particularly crippling habitus of place that conditioned the responses and actions of its residents.

While most sectors of the American economy experienced a period of recovery and prosperity following the brief depression of 1920–22, agriculture remained mired in a slump that only worsened with the onset of the Great

Depression. With over one quarter of American agricultural income in 1929 coming from exports, individual farmers were extremely susceptible to the vagaries of the world market. A useful comparison can be drawn between the relationship of the marketplace mavens to the farmers and of the farmers to the land itself. During World War I, the American government, and particularly Food Administrator Herbert Hoover, encouraged massive increases in farm production, leading to a severe glut in the postwar world market.[12] During the general prosperity of the 1920s, abundant credit was extended to farmers in order to shore up the lagging agricultural sector, worsening the plight of many farmers when exports dropped severely beginning in 1929. Similarly, Caldwell has the Lesters, as a representative type for the independent farming family, overwork their land to the point of exhaustion. Jeeter's father, for example, switches his crop from tobacco to cotton in response to the dictates of the marketplace, hastening the depletion of soil that was too sandy and loose to support extensive cotton farming. Overproduction of crops and massive extensions of credit were not policies that would ensure the healthy, long-term existence of individual farmers, but rather expedient maneuvers for maximizing short-term profits. Monocrop farming and intensive fertilization also may yield large returns at first, but it is a combination that guarantees a rapid and lasting decline in soil fertility.

The Lester land, which seventy-five years earlier "had been the most desirable soil in the entire west-central part of Georgia" (83), has been so exhausted that Jeeter is forced to relinquish the entire "Lester plantation" to creditors about twenty years before the action of *Tobacco Road*.[13] For Jeeter, the loss of his family land is akin to being dispossessed of Eden. Unlike Faulkner's Ike McCaslin, who marks the claim of land possession as the original sin, for Jeeter the loss of ownership begins the fall into a life of hunger and despair, but the remnant of the idea of working "his" land keeps him there. At the opening of the novel, the fields around the Lesters' shack resemble a nightmarish wasteland of broom sedge, "gnarled and sharp stubs of a new blackjack growth," and thickets of "briars and blackjack pricks" where Jeeter's feeble and forgotten mother collects dead twigs "morning, noon and night" looking like "an old scare-crow, in her black rags" (17–18). Caldwell's bleak portrait offers a compelling counterpoint to the romantic agrarianism espoused by Andrew Lytle in his essay "The Hind Tit" in *I'll Take My Stand*. Lytle's essay promotes a self-sufficient agrarianism in which the trappings of consumerism are avoided through a return to home manufacturing. As *Tobacco Road* makes clear, however, removing one's family from a market economy is not so simple. Years of overproduction have left the land unable to produce much more than wormy turnips, and any type of extensive labor seems beyond the scope of the listless, malnourished, and diseased family. On top of that, Southern farmers tended not to raise any food of their own in order to devote all of their land and labor to their cash crops.[14] In calling the nation's attention to the plight of the Southern farmer, Caldwell sounds the death knell of the pastoral dream.

Caldwell shows in several passages that Jeeter's economic burdens are just as onerous as the depleted land. Even if the soil had been fertile and productive, he has no recourse for obtaining the seed and guano needed to raise cotton. Jeeter's experience with a predatory loan company, after failing to secure credit from the merchants in Fuller or the banks in Augusta, allows Caldwell to display how the ideal of the independent, yeoman farmer has become the peon of moneylenders. After an initial $200 loan, Jeeter pays interest that "amounted to three per cent a month to start with, and at the end of ten months he had been charged thirty per cent, and on top of that another thirty per cent on the unpaid interest" (148). Added to that is a $50 fee "for making the loan," leaving the family with $7 for a year's work, not including a $10 debt for renting a mule. In the end, "He had done all the work, furnished the mule and the land, and yet the loan company had taken all the money the cotton brought, and made him lose three dollars" (149).[15] Caldwell's naturalist depiction of the tenant farming system makes it difficult to blame Jeeter for his woes. He seems as defenseless against the forces of economics and history as the land appears to be against irresponsible and destructive farming practices. In moments like these, the idea of a reciprocal relationship between humans and nature seems replaced by a one-sided, hierarchical dominion of humans over a passive landscape.

The novel reveals that when the ideal pastoral balance of nature and culture is thrown out of whack, then the entire ecological system—which includes humans—degenerates into a veritable wasteland. Southern farmers, rather than working cooperatively with the land, have tried to force crops to grow based on economic, not ecologic, factors. The emblematic Jeeter is repeatedly described as out of touch with nature's rhythms, and he unswervingly holds to the idea that he must plant cotton, and only cotton, in his arid soil. Despite the apparent lack of a mutually constitutive human/nature relationship, evidence of the land's agency does, in fact, remain in the novel, if only on the margins. Almost as an aside, Caldwell mentions that the Lester land is sprouting fields of young pine seedlings, in addition to the broom sedge and tough-as-nails blackjack trees. Since the reciprocal relationship has become so one-sided, Jeeter fails to read this fact as an indicator of what might successfully grow here. He is so out of touch with the natural world that he tries to sell the unburnable blackjack wood while he burns the potentially marketable pine seedlings in slavish obeisance to habit: "If the wood that was burned had been sawn into lumber or cut into firewood, instead of burning to ashes on the ground, there would have been something for them to sell. . . . Jeeter always burned over his land, even though there was no reason in the world why he should do it" (124). In failing to heed what the land is telling him, Jeeter exhibits an allegiance to past cultural practices and an alienation from nature even as he remains bound to the land.

The issue of whom or what is to blame for the dire straits of the Lesters and countless families in like situations again illustrates Caldwell's famous ambiguity and inconsistency toward his subjects. At least some of the responsibility for the depleted land falls on the individual farmers and their ignorance of effective land use, even amid the pervading atmosphere of naturalistic determinism in which the Lesters seem unable to effect meaningful change. Yet Caldwell presents their ignorance of responsible farming practices as a consequence of a tenancy system that makes the land the de facto province of cotton brokers and mill owners. Forcing farmers to plant only cotton in soil ill suited to that purpose in order to repay loans and meet obligations to landlords might even be termed unnatural, or at least antiecological, in the sense that "any system which covers too many fields with the same plant falls afoul of the ecological principle which states the simplest systems are apt to be the most unstable."[16]

The implication is that a market based on the acquisitive individualism that McElvaine describes favors a very small percentage of the population and makes self-sufficiency practically impossible for many. It commodifies people as well as nature, and this objectification alienates individuals from one another and from the natural world. In the same way that the land is denied agency by Jeeter's burning away of its natural growth of pine trees, Jeeter is denied an active role by the gaggle of middlemen, "the rich people in Augusta," who dictate what crops to plant and even "tell him how to cultivate the cotton" (149). Thus, even as the Lesters' health is bound to that of the land in a network model, their creditors impose a hierarchical model, exploiting and denying agency to both the land and the farmers, which only hastens the destruction of both. The lenders and brokers fulfill the role of the pastoral counterforce, which, according to Leo Marx, always threatens the idyllic middle ground. Like the Yankee troops, carpetbaggers, and emancipated blacks of earlier versions of Southern pastoral, these middlemen represent an outside threat. Caldwell also suggests that threats may come from inside the garden as well, if not from Jeeter then from the pastoral notion of permanence, that the garden can remain an oasis of stasis amid the teeming chaos of the "outside" world. Planting cotton on every inch of soil year after year seems to assume that nothing will change ecologically. Thus, the pastoral lo-cus amoenus is overwhelmed by social processes (credit and labor systems) and by human agency (farming practices). In turn, place itself contributes to the demise with the resulting poor soil quality, and the final product is a barren and fruitless garden.

The annual renewal of life that occurs each spring is also a time of re-newal for farmers, at least according to the idealized bond with nature typical of much traditional pastoral. In a vain effort to participate in this cycle of renewal, Jeeter burns his fields each spring, despite the fact that he has not planted anything in seven years. His attachment to nature goes beyond the symbolic; his mental and physical health are profoundly affected by his in-ability to participate in spring planting. Explaining his disdain for the mills, Jeeter romanticizes farming and ignores his family's serious health prob-lems while suggesting a metaphysical superiority of the land to the mills: "[W]hen it comes time to break the land for planting, you feel sick inside but don't know what's ailing you. People has told me about that spring sickness in the mills. . . . But when a man stays on the land, he don't get to feeling like that this time of year, because he's right here to smell the smoke of burning broom-sedge and to feel the wind fresh off the plowed fields going down in-side his body" (29). He goes on to assert the presence of God in nature, say-ing that the workers are ill because the mills are made by humans and the land by God. However, his malnourished and disease-wracked family belies this claim of a healthy spiritual connection to nature. He is not so much in tune with nature's rhythms as he is enslaved by them, unable to break the cultural habits he views as natural. Jeeter's reverie seems more an example of the longing for simpler times, which McElvaine describes as a common reac-tion to the Depression, than an accurate assessment of the relative health of farmers and mill workers. Put another way, Jeeter's idealized pastoral long-ings mask the antipastoral reality.[17]

With each passing year, Jeeter's prospects for ever farming cotton again grow bleaker, and he begins to feel that he cannot sustain his own life without the internal recuperation he attributes to working the soil: "In all the past six or seven years when he had wanted to raise a crop he had kept his disap-pointment from crushing his spirit by looking forward to the year when he could farm again. But this year he felt that if he did not get the seed-cotton and guano in the ground he would never be able to try again" (153). This in-sistence on planting cotton even as he and his family slowly starve to death reveals how fully indoctrinated in the culture of tenant farming Jeeter has become. That is, Jeeter might regain agency and autonomy by stepping out-side of the sharecropping system, inside of which his freedom of choice has been taken away. Rather than harvest timber, plant food, or work in a cotton mill, where he and Ada "together could make twenty or twenty-five dollars a week," Jeeter clings to the notion that cotton farming defines him as a person: "I know it ain't intended for me to work in the mills" (152). The power he derives from working the land is more fundamental to his survival than food: "The urge he felt to stir the ground and to plant cotton in it, and after that to sit in the shade during the hot months watching the plants sprout and grow, was even greater than the pains of hunger in his stomach. He could sit calmly and bear the feeling of hunger, but to be compelled to live and look each day at the unplowed fields was an agony he believed he could not stand many more days. His head dropped forward on his knees, and sleep soon overcame him and brought a peaceful rest to his tired heart and body" (154). Jeeter's laziness and inactivity begin to seem less like character flaws than outward signs of the complete exhaustion of his will to live. The creeping broom sedge of despair can be burned away by the fire of hope only so many times before Jeeter's spirit and body lie barren and broken, vainly awaiting the rejuvenation of spring.

While Jeeter may say that alienation from the land and its natural cycles causes a kind of spiritual sickness, Caldwell implies that the absence of a material connection with nature, chiefly from lack of food, is the root of the problem, a more literal alienation from nature that threatens the family in numerous ways. In a 1980 interview, Caldwell explains that his characters' laziness, which seems to some readers to be at odds with his deterministic portrayal of them as victims of economic oppression, is primarily a by-product of malnutrition: "When you're in poverty and your sustenance consists of only one or two items . . . your body is just not getting all that it needs to function. . . . Often [poor whites] contracted pellagra and hookworm . . . [which] would not be apparent to the naked eye. So what happened was that even though nothing appeared to be wrong with these people, they had serious diseases which resulted in habitual laziness."[18] Caldwell's use of humor throughout the novel often blurs these realities by playing on traditional stereotypes of poor white Southerners as immoral, stupid, and lazy, characterizations that can be traced back as far as William Byrd's *Histories of the Dividing Line betwixt Virginia and North Carolina* (1728).[19] In the same interview Caldwell attributes the "apparent moral depravity" of Jeeter to the same conditions of poverty: "When a person is subjected to a very severe beating in life, he might get the feeling that he has to protect himself first. Therefore, he's not going to give his wife or his mother anything to eat; he's going to keep it for himself."[20] Thus, the loss of connection with the land produces a family that conspires to keep food from the oldest and weakest member, buries dead children in the fields, and plows over the unmarked graves. It is little wonder that none of the numerous children who have left home have ever returned or sent any messages to their family. Yet Jeeter seems oblivious to his paternal shortcomings when Dude relays to him a message from his son Tom telling his father he should move to the county poorhouse: "That don't sound like Tom talking. . . . Me and him never had no difficulties like I was always having with my other children. They used to throw rocks at me and hit me over the head with sticks, but Tom never did" (204). Despite such evidence of his affection, Tom concludes his message to Jeeter with a simple "go to hell."

However, it is not only the poor who exhibit moral depravity in *Tobacco Road*. Tom is the only one of the seventeen Lester children who we know has escaped poverty. His successful cross-tie business marks him as a "winner" in the economy of consumerism, but his conservative view of his parents as "losers" who should move to the county poorhouse is a rejection of the values of collectivism and cooperation, suggesting that Caldwell sees immorality as inherent in the current socioeconomic system as a whole. Through Tom and other well-to-do characters like the Augusta car salesmen who mercilessly taunt and brazenly cheat Sister Bessie, as well as the usurious bankers, Caldwell shows that the moral depravity that is so pronounced in the Lesters' behavior imbues the character of the "winners" in the consumerist competition as well.

The breakdown of family relationships is directly related to the impoverishment of the land and, more important, to the material poverty that prevents Jeeter from planting a crop. Especially for men, it seems, the inability to work the land weakens interpersonal relationships, deadens emotions, and isolates them from everyone and everything around them. The man who cannot work, cannot love—a theme Caldwell returns to in greater detail in *God's Little Acre*. Jeeter's estrangement from the world is represented as a turning inward, and Caldwell's description of the tough and wiry blackjack tree that flourishes on the Lester land parallels his characterization of Jeeter: "The blackjack never grew much taller than a man's head; it was a stunted variety of oak that used its sap in toughening the fibres instead of growing new layers and expanding the old, as other trees did" (173). The inability to establish and maintain meaningful human relationships is a result of Jeeter's similar failure to expand outward, to make connections with others. Caldwell's comparison of Jeeter and the blackjack tree contrasts vividly with Hurston's tree symbolism in *Their Eyes Were Watching God* and *Seraph on the Suwanee*. Janie's pear tree and Arvay's mulberry tree are natural symbols of female identity and strength that signal an empowering relationship with a healthy natural world. While these trees blossom and grow, the black-jack tree hardens and turns inward.

The entire family, in fact, seems inert and incapable of any sort of progress: phrases and actions are repeated over and over, and nothing ever seems to "happen" in the novel. The mechanical nature of the characters' behavior emphasizes the loss of humanity caused by debilitating poverty. The chief object of affection in the novel is, fittingly, Sister Bessie's brand-new automobile. Dude's primary reason for marrying this itinerant preacher, who has a grotesquely deformed nose and is twenty years his senior, is so that he can drive the car. The image of the car hurtling along the dusty country roads with Dude at the wheel maniacally blowing the horn (which he tends to do the entire length of every trip) recalls Leo Marx's machine-in-the-garden metaphor in which the machine is an aggressive, masculine intruder on a feminized landscape. And, with Dude at the wheel, this car is an agent of destruction, mowing down Grandmother Lester and an African American man guiding a horse and wagon, symbols of a simpler, bygone era. Yet, unlike in the self-conscious pastoral mythologizing of *I'll Take My Stand,* this machine does not cause a devaluation of humanity. There is no "war to the death between technology and the ordinary human functions of living," as Lytle's essay in the manifesto proposes, because the crushing poverty created by an outdated agricultural system has already dissolved these ordinary functions.[21]

After Dude relates the story of carelessly killing the defenseless wagon driver, Jeeter vacuously comments, "Niggers will get killed. Looks like there ain't no way to stop it." The description of the accident—"When we drove off again, he was still lying in the ditch. The wagon turned over on him and mashed him" (159)—is echoed in that of the appalling death of the grandmother: "Mother Lester still lay there, her face mashed on the hard white sand." Dude and Bessie again drive off after twice running over the old woman; Ada stares at the body briefly, "then she walked inside and shut the door" (215); and Jeeter kicks his mother's body before delivering a fitting eulogy to Lov: "She ain't stiff yet, but I don't reckon she'll live. You help me tote her out in the field and I'll dig a ditch to put her in" (225). The detached narration mirrors the detachment of the characters from one another, from their own emotions, from nature, and from life itself. Dude has far more affection for the car than for his new wife, reflecting the spirit of competition for limited resources that pervades the environment. All energy seems to be slowly dissipating on the Lester farm. Even Bessie and Dude's brand-new car, which at first thrilled the family with its speed and loud horn, is virtually totaled in a matter of days: "Springing the front axle, cracking the wind-shield, scarring the paint on the body, tearing holes in the upholstery, and parting with the spare tire and extra wheel were considered nothing more than the ordinary hazards of driving a car" (199–200).

The only life still clinging to the land is a dreary mix of stunted blackjack trees, turnips full of "damn-blasted green-gutted worms," and the dwindling brood of Lesters. Each family member seems unable to do more than mechanically repeat certain behaviors: Dude throws a baseball against the side of the house over and over; the grandmother collects twigs for the stove three times a day in anticipation of food that never comes; Ada worries constantly about owning a stylish dress to be buried in; Jeeter repeats his vain wish for seed and fertilizer while burning the fields each year in vain preparation for planting; and the harelipped Ellie May voyeuristically watches everything from behind a chinaberry tree. Similarly, the characters' speech is marked by numerous repetitions of particular words and phrases, reflecting the monotony of their lives as well as the barrenness of their environment.[22]

A 1929 editorial in *New Masses* (for which Caldwell sometimes wrote) described its ideal author as one whose writing is "the natural flower of his environment," and this is a perfect way to think about *Tobacco Road*.[23] The lack of intricate plotting and underdeveloped, flat characters make more sense when one considers Caldwell's style as a reflection of his novel's setting. The narrative mirrors the lives of the characters: there is not a progression through a series of interesting events, just monotonous repetition interspersed with a few episodes that seem to promise change but wind up delivering nothing but more misery. Although the novel's episodic narrative structure resembles that of the picaresque and other tales of quest, Jeeter Lester is a parody of the masculine hero, a picaro with pellagra who can never quite get started on the triumphant journey: "Jeeter made a false start somewhere nearly every day" (102).

Rather than a progression, the episodes of *Tobacco Road* either never see Jeeter leave home or they end right where they began with nothing having changed significantly. A car trip to Augusta begins promisingly: Jeeter is going to sell a load of wood and it seems food may finally be on the way. The trip, in essence, is the antipastoral version of the retreat and return motif. Instead of an invigorating sojourn to the country with a subsequent return to the city more wise for the journey, Caldwell presents an excursion to the city from the country. Jeeter, Dude, and Bessie get their hands on some food in Augusta, but although they seem briefly reenergized while removed from the farm, Caldwell shows that they actually worsen their predicament on their visit. The excursion ends with Jeeter and Dude leaving the unsold blackjack on the side of the road, having succeeded only at further destroying Sister

Bessie's prized car and inadvertently putting her to work for the night in a brothel. Time and again any hope of advancement is thwarted by Caldwell's narrative structure, adding to the pervasive sense of frustration and stasis. While the novel opens with Lov Bensey walking steadily forward on the old tobacco road, it ends with Dude going nowhere, figuratively filling his now-dead father's stagnant footsteps and taking his place in a new tradition of Lester men while repeating the hopeless refrain, "Maybe I could grow me a bale to the acre, like Pa was always talking about doing" (241).

Tobacco Road discloses another side of the rosy, agrarian view of the simple farmer living off of the land and avoiding the modern alienation of the urban dweller. The Lesters living on the farm seem as estranged from the earth as do Caldwell's prominent characters who live in towns (e.g., Jim Leslie Walden in *God's Little Acre* or Chism Crockett in *This Very Earth*). My claim that Jeeter is simultaneously linked to the land and alienated from it (materially and symbolically in both cases) may appear contradictory, but I would argue that it indicates Caldwell's halting efforts to envision a different model of human interactions with nature. He seems at times to move toward a more ecocentric view of humans and nature as part of the same network, but he ultimately cannot break away from seeing humans as stewards of the garden who just need a different type of system for ruling and controlling land, not a different relationship altogether.

This attitude is perhaps most clearly revealed through Caldwell's representation of gender. As in the versions of pastoral from plantation school fiction, the natural world is consistently gendered as feminine (although this equation does become more complicated in *God's Little Acre*). Viewing the land in this way justifies its treatment as passive, inert material that needs the imposition of an active, masculine force to give it value. And when monetary value is all that matters, overfertilization and monocrop planting are regularly inflicted on the land despite the negative consequences—consequences that might, in a more interdependent, less hierarchical model of environmental interaction, be read as signs that such techniques are unsuitable for the soil. Although the novel exposes the shortcomings of an anthropocentric worldview and occasionally challenges gendered assumptions about nature, Caldwell seems unable to commit fully to an alternative paradigm. In *God's Little Acre*, the barrenness of the farm is contrasted with the vitality that comes from the collective identity of the mill town. However, nature remains feminine and the hierarchy that subordinates land to farmers and farmers to bankers in *Tobacco Road* is replicated in the relationship of the mill owners to the striking workers in Caldwell's follow-up novel. The compulsion of male characters to access a feminine vitality drives both narratives, but the insistence on feminine passivity undermines Caldwell's ability to envision real and lasting changes in the barren lives of the people he champions.

Only Jeeter, among all the characters of *Tobacco Road*, professes a strong attraction to the earth, compulsively longing to "make plants grow in it," even though he has no way of securing seed and fertilizer and nothing is likely to grow in the depleted soil. His emotional obsession with plowing the earth is not shared by the other Lesters, and Jeeter's fixation is often sexual:

> When the winter goes, and when it gets to be time to burn off broom-sedge in the fields and underbrush in the thickets, I sort of want to cry. . . . The smell of that sedge-smoke this time of year near about drives me crazy. Then pretty soon all the other farmers start plowing. That's what gets under my skin the worse. When the smell of that new earth turning over behind the plows strikes me, I get all weak and shaky. It's in my blood—burning broom-sedge and plowing in the ground this time of year. I did it for near about fifty years, and my Pa and his Pa before him was the same kind of men. Us Lesters sure like to stir the earth and make plants grow in it. I can't move off to the cotton mills like the rest of them do. The land has got a powerful hold on me. (21)

In being denied the opportunity to renew his ritual interaction with the soil, Jeeter is denied the chance to reaffirm his purpose for living and assume his place in a masculine tradition. Plowing the soil and growing crops have defined the Lester men, so his failure to continue farming seems to Jeeter a form of temporary emasculation. Seeing the other farmers plowing only reinforces his impotence and increases his despair. Only by encountering the land as a feminized field for the exercise of male power could Jeeter experience such extreme plow envy.

Yet this passage also shows that the land's hold on Jeeter threatens to invert the relationship and feminize him, making him feel "weak and shaky" and as if he wants to cry. He equates the prospect of working in a mill, however, with the total relinquishment of masculinity: "Them durn cotton mills is for the women folks to work in. They ain't no place for a man to be, fooling away with little wheels and strings all day long. I say it's a hell of a job for a man to spend his time winding strings on spools. No! We was put here on the land where cotton will grow, and it's my place to make it grow" (151). It is not the inability to work and provide for his family that assails Jeeter's masculinity; work is apparently available in the mills. It is, instead, specifically his inability to compel the earth to do his bidding and grow a crop that im-

perils his manhood, and these feelings of frustration and impotence are reinforced by the novel's narrative form. The solitary and questing male hero
of American myth and literary tradition is here confined to the domestic
sphere typically associated with stasis and femininity.[24] Like the land itself,
the house is a feminine place that is barren, diseased, and dying.

While Caldwell's naturalist portrayal of the Lesters may lessen Jeeter's direct blame for their plights, this method also sometimes points a finger at
women through their implicit identification with the ruined land. The numerous physical deformities are perhaps the most memorable grotesque elements for which Caldwell is so notorious, yet they are limited, almost exclusively, to female characters. Ellie May has a harelip that makes her mouth
look "as if it had been torn" (49), and Bessie Rice is disfigured by her nose,
which "had failed to develop properly. There was no bone in it, and there was
no top to it. . . . it was like looking down the end of a double-barrel shotgun"
(58). Youngest daughter Pearl is a beautiful child but refuses to speak a single
word and will not let her husband, Lov, touch her at all. Ada, whom Jeeter
says was similarly silent for years after their marriage, is suffering from pellagra, which is "slowly squeezing the life from her emaciated body," as is old
Mother Lester, withered away to seventy-two pounds and reduced to eating
"wild grass and flowers in the field" (93–94). While Pearl seems an exception
who has "far more sense than any of the Lesters," Caldwell also informs us
that her intelligence, "like her hair and her eyes, had been inherited from her
father," a nameless stranger who happened to pass by one day (40). Her shortcomings, then, implicitly derive from her mother, and her refusal to submit to
Lov's sexual desires after being sold to him as a bride is certainly seen by the
men as one of those unfathomable shortcomings. Caldwell constructs his tale
so that the central, male subject is assailed by diseased, degenerate women
and land whose otherness is signified by their "unnatural" deformities.

Neither Dude nor Jeeter are afflicted the way that the women characters
are; rather, they are afflicted *by* the women, who are burdens that must be
cared for, and by the feminine earth that lacks the fertility to provide for
them. In the end, it seems that the beautiful and silent Pearl is Caldwell's
lasting symbol of estranged feminine nature. Pearl never appears directly in
the novel, and her absence is symbolic of the lost connection between humans and their natural environment. Jeeter has sold his daughter into the
consumer marketplace by trading her to Lov for $7, "some quilts and nearly
a gallon of cylinder oil" (32), but she is completely unresponsive toward her
new husband, never speaking to him and rarely acknowledging his existence. Lov, in fact, talks about her after she runs off to Augusta in almost the
same way Jeeter describes his feelings for the land: "[S]ometimes I used to

sit and shake all over, for wanting to squeeze her so hard. I don't reckon I'll ever forget how pretty her eyes was early in the morning just when the sun was rising. . . . Seeing them long yellow curls hanging down her back used to make me cry sometimes. I'd look at her pretty hair and eyes so long that I thought I'd go crazy if I didn't touch her and see deep down into her eyes. But she wouldn't never let me come close to her, and that's what made the tears fall out of my eyes, I reckon" (223). The shaking, crying, and exclusion from his feminine object of desire all parallel Jeeter's relationship to "his" land. The silent Pearl subverts the text's figuring of her as passive object by escaping her would-be conqueror as Lov tries to tie her to the bed with—fittingly enough—plow lines. Rather than using Pearl's escape as a way of exploring alternative models of living, Caldwell remains fixed on the intertwined demise of Jeeter and a landscape lacking feminine vitality.

The novel does suggest that the pastoral ideal is untenable, but does not see as problematic its underlying gendering of farmer and land. This failure to question the notion of nature as a feminine entity to be dominated precludes any meaningful change in the Lesters' situation. Caldwell, instead, chooses to make pronouncements about the causes of their predicament, with only a cursory stab at offering a solution:

When Jeeter had over-bought at the stores in Fuller, Captain John let him continue, and he never put a limit to the credit allowed. But the end soon came. There was no longer any profit in raising cotton under the Captain's antiquated system and he abandoned the farm and moved to Augusta. . . . An intelligent employment of his land, stocks, and implements would have enabled Jeeter, and scores of others who had become dependent upon Captain John, to raise crops for food, and crops to be sold at profit. Co-operative and corporate farming would have saved them all. (82–83)

Caldwell's prescription for curing the ills of the small farmer in the last sentence posits that humans have simply exerted the wrong type of agency over the land. As he puts it in *You Have Seen Their Faces,* the tenancy system is responsible for "the degeneration of man as well as for the rape of the soil in the South" (76). Rather than envisioning a truly interdependent network of relations, Caldwell remains locked into a conception of the masculine farmer controlling feminine nature, as his gendered language of sexual assault makes clear.

Yet there are brief moments when ostensibly passive objects do, in fact, assert an agency of their own. Pearl is a destabilizing force who lurks on the margins of the text. The land itself, as we have seen, grows plant species on its own that have not been planted by humans. In the novel's conclusion, Jeeter habitually burns the broom sedge again in baseless anticipation of planting season. During the night, the wind shifts and the embers from years of accumulated dried grass and broom sedge blow onto the house, setting it ablaze and killing Jeeter and Ada as they sleep. Here, nature is an actor, ironically joining Jeeter to the land in the end. Nonetheless, the instances of nature exerting agency are few and far between in *Tobacco Road*. Overall, the novel illustrates the devastation that results when human agency and social processes overwhelm place. The Southern farm is no longer a pastoral place at all because there is no longer any balance between culture and nature: the cultural has subsumed the natural. In subsequent chapters, I will examine how Rawlings, Hurston, and Faulkner move the pastoral location from the farm to the wilderness in response. Caldwell, however, investigates in *God's Little Acre* whether the mill town might replace the countryside as the new Arcadia.

Another battered and failing Georgia farm provides the antipastoral counterpoint to the mill town of Scottsville, just across the river in South Carolina. Ty Ty Walden is, like Jeeter, a cotton farmer in name only, for he and his sons Buck and Shaw have been digging deep holes in their land for the last fifteen years in a misguided and hopeless quest for gold. Not much work is happening at the mill, either, which has been shut down for eighteen months by a strike prompted by the owners' imposition of a stretch-out, and the workers, led by Ty Ty's son-in-law, Will Thompson, are quickly running out of food.[25] The dichotomy between the rural setting of the Walden farm and Scottsville is coupled with differences in narration and style: a realistic style for the country setting, where most of the novel's comedic interludes occur, and an expressionistic, sometimes surreal, rendering of the more serious city episodes. The metaphor of hunger connects Ty Ty's reverence for gold, the land, and female sexuality with Will's desire for conquest of both women and the machinery of the mill.

The novel's title comes from Ty Ty's commitment to tithe the proceeds from one acre of his land to God, although the only current farming is done by his two black tenants, Uncle Felix and Black Sam. In order to avoid sharing with the church the proceeds of his expected gold strike, Ty Ty constantly shifts the location of "God's little acre" to an area he is not currently excavating. He is convinced that his "scientific" approach to mining is the best method of extracting value from the earth, and considering Jeeter's experiences with cotton farming, Ty Ty's method is perhaps not as crazy as the other characters derisively suggest. Faulkner's Lucas Beauchamp similarly abandons farming to search for buried gold in *Go Down, Moses,* and both characters retain a bond with nature as they seek a greater financial reward *in* the land than they ever found *on* it. There is also a suggestion of a desired return to the womb of Mother Nature in the image of a man compulsively digging twenty-foot-deep holes in the ground. Ty Ty's wife has died, and he constantly praises the sexuality of his daughters, Darling Jill and Rosamond, and his daughter-in-law, Griselda. Unlike the lecherous Jeeter, though, Ty Ty transfers his sexual energy to his obsessive digging for gold.

Will Thompson is a step further removed from the soil than Ty Ty as a textile mill worker who converts the cotton from the farms into fabric via the powerful machinery that is now idle and silent. His ceaseless womanizing—Rosamond says he has "had every girl in town, once"—is a substitute for his erotic fascination with the energy and power of the mill.[26] Jim Leslie Walden is even more detached from the natural world, living on "The Hill," a rich section of Augusta, and working as a cotton broker, a middleman with no direct contact with raw materials, who profits from the abstract fluctuations of the market. His wife's gonorrhea and emotional frigidity prompt Jim Leslie's frantic attempts to buy or take by force his sister-in-law Griselda. Nature, then, is perhaps most significant in the novel in its absence and its degrees of separation from the lives of the principal male characters. All three men pursue a feeling of vitality, the "secret of living," in Ty Ty's words, which they associate with women and other feminine forces.

As in *Tobacco Road,* the family farm is figured as an inversion of the conventional pastoral paradise, but Caldwell also seems to be searching for a new place that can restore the vitality missing from the depleted cotton farms and regenerate the common man. The dynamic Will Thompson is the one character who repeatedly travels between the two settings, and he seems to be symbolically transporting this vital spirit from the farm to the city at a time when millions of erstwhile Southern farmers were moving in the same direction. Significantly, Will is also taking the females away from the farm, not only his wife, Rosamond, but her sister, Darling Jill, and sister-in-law (and Buck's wife), Griselda, both of whom he later seduces in Scottsville. While Ty Ty continually extols the three young women's sexuality, it is Will who acts on his impulses and urges. Thus, Will is removing a vitality that Caldwell associates with the feminine and (formerly) the land and taking it to the new place of economic opportunity, the mill town.

What Caldwell is doing in this novel, I argue, is positing the mill town as a potential new location for the pastoral ideal: a harmonic blend of culture and nature that can support the rural Southern worker. Although it may seem counterintuitive to look for elements of the pastoral in a mill town, I see Caldwell as doing essentially the same thing that the other writers of ecopastorals are doing: they are all searching for a Southern place that combines the natural and cultural in a way that empowers the individual, ironically by making him or her a part of a larger, interdependent network. The repeated image of the mill covered with ivy symbolizes the pastoral middle ground, and Caldwell's description of his plans for this novel in his Guggenheim application support this reading: "[W]hereas *Tobacco Road* . . . is a study of a group of people existing under an outmoded system of agriculture and economics, I want to write in the book I have in mind something of the direction which the masses must turn to in order to live under the present and forthcoming conditions of life. It is a sort of union of agrarian and industrial societies."[27] Interestingly, in the course of writing the novel Caldwell's enthusiasm seems to have waned because, in the end, the mill town does not provide salvation for the working classes. While Caldwell does locate an empowering sense of collective vitality in the town, the replication in the mill town of the exploitative labor relations of the tenancy system denies a final sense of triumph—and perhaps even progress.

James Devlin identifies the vitality missing from the lives of the men in of *God's Little Acre* as an "ineffable life force" or "*élan vital*" that is "intimately linked with aggressive sexual drive," and says that for Will, "the inaccessible, closed mill is another woman to be overcome and won." Lawrence S. Kubie, in an insightful 1934 psychoanalytical reading, claims a similar "deep inner logic" in the relationship of nature, the mill, and women: "[T]he book is a story in symbolic language of the struggle of a group of men to win some fantastic kind of sustenance out of the body of the earth, the 'body' of factories, and the bodies of women."[28] These readings, while useful, fail to account for the strange masculine power of the mill that threatens to displace men from their position of dominance, as well as for the fact that some of the women, especially Griselda, feel a similar compulsion to access this vaguely defined life force, which is not, for them, gendered as feminine. These critics' reliance on opaque phrases like "ineffable life force" and "some fantastic kind of sustenance" testifies to the difficulty of articulating an idea that is clearly key to the novel but that is never delineated conclusively by Caldwell.

At the risk of merely substituting one nebulous idea for another, I would suggest that the characters are tapping into a collective identity, a communal vitality that transcends but includes the self and is related to a communal spirit fostered by the hardships of the Depression. Caldwell's two novels together show a movement of this life force from the feminine land to the female body to the collective masses of striking workers in Scottsville. Moving the life force off of the land and into the mill town, where women work in the same factory as men, substantially "de-genders" this ineffable vitality.

Thus, while the male characters (and perhaps Caldwell, too) identify this power as feminine, it need not be for everyone (for Griselda, for example, it is masculine). Similarly, access to the collective identity may be through nature or through the machinery of the mill. Once this collective vitality has been tapped, there is a compulsion to return to it over and over.

Although Ty Ty no longer farms, his search for gold still requires him to work the soil and to interact with nature, albeit in a destructive fashion. The devastation of the land in the quest for paradise is not incompatible, however, with pastoral idealizations of the countryside in this context. In this time of great financial hardship, monetary wealth easily becomes the only component of an imagined new Eden. With little money to be made from cotton farming, Ty Ty hopes to remove riches from the earth more directly. After fifteen years of using his "scientific" approach, however, Ty Ty has had no luck finding gold, and he readily embraces the idea of capturing an albino man who lives nearby in order to harness his supposed mystical divining powers. Ty Ty assumes that Dave, the albino, like women and African Americans, is somehow closer to nature because of his otherness. Dave is the same as "a coal-black darky" (117), Ty Ty says at one point, suggesting that Caldwell perhaps includes this bizarre incident in order to mock racist attitudes.

Fittingly, the albino lives on the edge of a swamp, a type of landscape historically associated with the female body, and the Walden clan regards him as a strange object: "With their eyes upon him, Dave felt like an animal on exhibition." The white males of the Walden family regard their hostage as a foreign Other, and Ty Ty treats him as if the albino were part child, part animal, like some sort of magical pet the family can keep and train to divine the location of gold: "Sure, he can do it. . . . He can do it and don't know it. . . . When he grows up, he's going to be some almighty gold-diviner. He's young yet. Just give him time" (124). Although Dave is unable to divine the location of gold in the earth, it is noteworthy that he is immediately drawn to the Walden women, again insinuating that the life force has been transferred to them from the land.

While the albino scenes are clearly comical (Dave quickly vanishes from the novel), they establish a pattern of male characters seeking to fill a void through the conquest of a feminized object or of actual women. Despite his claim that "I don't take any stock in superstition and conjur and such things" (22), Ty Ty is admitting his inability to divine the secrets of the earth when he kidnaps Dave for help. Will, who is frustrated by not being able to work in the mill, and Jim Leslie, who endures similar feelings of impotence because of his wife, both seek recourse in the body of Griselda, whom Caldwell figures as an earth goddess like Faulkner's Eula Varner. The widower Ty Ty fulfills his urges by continually extolling the virtues of Griselda's body parts and by repeatedly assaulting and penetrating the earth in search of its buried treasure: "There were times . . . when he was so provoked that he would pick up a stick and flail the ground with it until he dropped exhausted" (3). Instead of wanting to make things grow from the earth like Jeeter, Ty Ty prefers his self-proclaimed "scientific" method for extracting value from the land, a parody of the "scientific" farming practices that had exhausted the soil of the South throughout the previous century.[29]

As in *Tobacco Road*, Caldwell associates the inability to work with emasculation, and the Great Depression, of course, swells the ranks of the unemployed in big cities, small towns, and country farms. Will feels driven to turn the power on at the mill himself, fantasizing that the workers can run the facility independently of its owners. He consistently rebuffs Ty Ty's suggestion that he dig with them; Will feels no attraction to nature and longs to be back amid the humming machinery: "The sight of bare land, cultivated and fallow, with never a factory or mill to be seen, made him a little sick in his stomach" (148). Will's nausea at the sight of the land opposes the novel's most dynamic and charismatic character to its endearing agrarian philosopher, Ty Ty. Coupled with Caldwell's jaded depictions of fruitless farm labor, the result is a thorough dismantling of pastoral myths. The mill town emerges as a more viable site for productive Southern labor, but as the strike makes clear, exploitative class relations threaten to make the "lint-heads" no better off than the tenant farmers of *Tobacco Road*. Even as the mill town facilitates a collective vitality, the mill itself is designed to exploit nature (both human and physical) for profit. The specter of domination and ownership looms over this company town throughout the novel. It is the mill that dictates monocrop planting, the exploitation of tenant farmers, and the destruction of both the farmer and the soil. Caldwell suggests there is a price to pay for the collective identity forged by the workers: the vitality of the mill town comes from the life force extracted from the farmers and even nature itself.

Caldwell constructs the mill as a contested site, both in terms of labor relations and in terms of gender. It is neither exclusively masculine nor feminine, suggesting the possibility that machines can dominate men the way that men have historically dominated nature. Even when the Scottsville mill was operating, Will remembers that "the girls were in love with the looms and the spindles and the flying lint" (99–100). Caldwell blends realistic and expressionistic techniques as Will imagines the women workers, who have been hired across the valley because they accept "the harder work . . . the longer hours [and] the cutting of pay," as unfaithful to their men: "[W]hen evening came, the doors were flung open and the girls ran out screaming in laughter.

When they reached the street, they ran back to the ivy-covered walls and pressed their bodies against it and touched it with their lips. The men who had been standing idly before it all day long came and dragged them home and beat them unmercifully for their infidelity" (98–99). The men's estrangement from nature appears less important than their estrangement from labor. Although contact with the land can sustain men like Ty Ty, Will has broken with the agricultural traditions of the past, and he needs the sustenance of work more than the paltry rations provided by the union.

Industrial machinery is not as easy for the men to conceive of in feminine (and therefore submissive) terms as is the land. On the farm, men are thought of as the providers of the family; the machinery of the mills, however, can be operated by women as well as men. Will imagines that the machines are idolized as the source of power by the women who press their bodies to the ivy-covered walls, and he is therefore in danger of being feminized, displaced into a subservient role. When the aptly named Will is able to seduce Griselda and make her submissive to his masculine desire, he is subsequently able to enter the mill and turn on its power himself. Sexual acts allow him to overcome the powerlessness and idleness symbolized by the silent machinery of the mill. Will's sexual exploits, his desire for collective appropriation of the mill, and his holding a dying rabbit in his hands enable transcendence of solipsism through a palpable sense of collective vitality.

Just before his seduction of Griselda, Will explains his affection for the mill towns of the valley: "You don't know what a company town is like, then. But I'll tell you. Have you ever shot a rabbit, and gone and picked him up, and when you lifted him in your hand, felt his heart pounding like—like, God, I don't know what!" (220). For Will, feeling the rabbit's pulsing body provides an unmediated connection to life outside his own. Ironically, it is a dying life, one that he has destroyed. This irony is paralleled by the fact that the collective vitality that emerges among the workers comes from the environment of a company-owned town. The communal nature of the mill town (where the houses are so close together that a tryst between Will and Darling Jill is interrupted by a neighbor beating her dust mop on the wall beside the bed) allows Will to feel the pulse of life in the network of families, too: "Murmurs passed through the company streets of the company town, coming in rhythmic tread through the windows of the company house. It was alive, stirring, moving, and speaking like a real person" (219–20). In these passages, Will is overcoming his feelings of alienation through recognition of and connection with the life around him. His reticence yields to thundering soliloquies in which he attempts to reach out to his audience of Rosamond, Griselda, and Darling Jill and make them understand his thoughts and motivations. While

he never seems capable of truly egalitarian exchange or dialogue, he succeeds
in tapping into what Ty Ty refers to as "the God inside of a body" (268) and
"something you've got to feel" that cannot be expressed in words (271). Interestingly, though, the feelings of collective identity and purpose that al-
leviate individual alienation are strongest during the strike, not when the
people are actually working in the mill, a detail indicative of Caldwell's view
of Southern labor relations as stifling and oppressive to the human spirit.

Griselda experiences an epiphanic moment, just before the climactic scene
of her seduction, when she, too, feels the pulse of collective life joining her to
the community of beleaguered strikers, a sensation unknown to her on the
Walden farm: "She could hear sounds, voices, murmurs that were like none
she had ever heard before. A woman's laughter, a child's excited cry, and the
faint gurgle of a waterfall somewhere below all came into the room together;
there was a feeling in the air of living people just like herself, and this she had
never felt before. The new knowledge that all those people out there, all those
sounds, were as real as she herself was made her heart beat faster" (215). When
Will strolls into the house, Griselda feels like running to him and embracing him, and she knows that "[h]e was one of the persons she had felt in the
night air" (216). For both Griselda and Will, the empathetic bond they feel
leads paradoxically to an empowering sense of individuality, echoing the sentiment of cooperative individualism on the rise among the lower and middle
classes of the 1930s. Will explains to his "enthralled" audience that only the
atmosphere of the company town provides him with both the sense of a collective life force and the sense of individual power that will allow him to re-
open the mill:

> Back there in Georgia, out there in the middle of all those damn holes
> and piles of dirt, you think I'm nothing but a dead sapling sticking up
> in the ground. Well, maybe I am, over there. But over here in the Val-
> ley, I'm Will Thompson. You come over here and look at me in this yel-
> low company house and think that I'm nothing but a piece of company
> property. And you're wrong about that, too. I'm Will Thompson. I'm as
> strong as God Almighty Himself now, and I can show you how strong
> I am. . . . I'm going up to that [mill] door and rip it to pieces just like
> it was a window shade. (221)

Reviving the image of a withered tree from *Tobacco Road*, Caldwell continues, in passages like this one, to suggest the obsolescence of living off the
land in the Depression-era South. For Will it is, instead, the collective humanity of Scottsville that gives him the power to act for the betterment of the

community of individuals to which he belongs. Yet his status as something more than "a piece of company property" is not so certain for readers or for Caldwell. The novel's ending implies that he is owned by someone else, like the land of tenant farmers, and that this fact saps him of "life force," leaving him a "dead sapling" once again.

Will's reference to ripping the door as if it were a window shade reasserts the masculinity that he imagines has been taken from him. He prepares for his reclamation of the mill by ritually and obsessively shredding Griselda's clothes in a frenzied display of virility: "I'm a loomweaver. I've woven cloth all my life, making every kind of fabric in God's world. . . . We're going to start spinning and weaving again tomorrow, but tonight I'm going to tear that cloth on you till it looks like lint out of a gin" (224). When he fulfills his promise, Caldwell describes him as "a madman," "tearing it insanely," "tearing, ripping, jerking, throwing the shredded cloth . . . frantically . . . [and] savagely" (225). The shredding of the fabric undoes the work of the machinery that he operates and suggests that his attack on the closed mill is an indirect reassertion of his masculinity, making a woman of the mill that had taken his place. Taking matters into his own hands, Will removes a level of mediation between himself and Griselda, and like Ty Ty, he searches for a treasure buried somewhere beneath the external surface. Unlike Ty Ty (and Jeeter), Will successfully conquers the feminine body, restoring his sense of (dominant) masculinity.

Will's role as the agent of Ty Ty's desire becomes evident as he explains himself to a now-naked Griselda: "Ty Ty was right! . . . he said you were so God damn pretty, a man would have to get down on his hands and knees and lick something when he saw you like you are now. . . . And I'm going to lick you, Griselda. Ty Ty knew what he was talking about. . . . He's got more sense than all the rest of us put together, even if he does dig in the ground like a God damn fool" (226). When Will takes Griselda from the room to perform "the first act of cunnilingus in serious American literature," in Devlin's memorable phrasing, we can see that Caldwell has fashioned a somewhat crude parallel to Ty Ty's forays into the womblike craters of the earth. Cook points out that the frequent oral imagery associated with sexual craving "suggests a strong connection between women and nature as literal sources of sustenance."[30] Yet since Griselda symbolizes the mill rather than (or as well as) nature, Cook's formula must be amended to include the factory itself, or at least the collective vitality it generates when idle, as a source of sustenance. Caldwell makes these connections clear when Will eats a full breakfast of ham, grits, and coffee before heading to the mill. The three women, whom we might expect to be hostile toward one another since Will has now had sex with both of his sisters-in-law, display a collective unity and cooperative spirit: "Darling Jill brought a plate, a cup, and a saucer. Griselda brought a knife, a spoon, and a fork. Rosamond filled a glass of water. They ran over the kitchen, jumping from each other's way, weaving in and out in the small room hurriedly, easily, lovingly" (234).

Will's sexual prowess makes him feel "as strong as God Almighty himself," and he sets off to repeat his action of "turning on the power," this time at the mill. Overlooking the townsfolk who have gathered as one outside the mill, Will stands in an open window and repeats his shredding action, ripping his shirt and throwing it to the women below, who fight for the pieces as Rosamond, Darling Jill, and Griselda are "pushed forward with the mass." Will leads the way but inspires a collective sense of purpose and power in the crowd, as the men rush in after him and fling their shirts out the windows to the "crowd of women and children" below (240). This collective vitality, however, is always tainted by Will's domination of women, especially the now-passive Griselda: "She stood up immediately, rising eagerly at his command. She waited for anything he might tell her to do next. . . . When he told her to sit down, she would sit down. Until then she would remain standing for the rest of her life" (222–23).

Although he may be the "male man," as Black Sam and Uncle Felix call him, Will assumes that he can also lead the striking workers to victory and dominate "the body of the mill" the way he dominates the bodies of women. However, when he successfully turns on the power in the mill, his illusion of himself as one "as strong as God Almighty" is shattered by three bullets in the back from the guards hired by the mill owners. It is never quite clear what the workers hope to achieve by occupying the mill nor what the plan is after turning the power on, making the endeavor appear, in retrospect, as delusional as Ty Ty's search for gold. Will's death means that the strike will end soon and the workers will be forced to accept lower wages because Will was the galvanizing force, creating a collective entity from a group of individuals. "I don't reckon there'll be any use of trying to fight them without Will," an unnamed worker comments to no one in particular. "They'll try to make us take a dollar-ten. If Will Thompson was here, we wouldn't do it" (250). In his relationships with women, Will reproduces the dominant power relations of the mill owners with the workers, of the cotton brokers with the tenant farmers, and of farmers like Jeeter with the land itself. Will places himself over and above the striking workers he helped to unite in collective action, and his murder is a harsh reminder of his true place in this hierarchy. In other words, Caldwell shows once again that life cannot flourish and people cannot prosper within a hierarchical model of relations.

In the final three chapters, Will's status as savior of the masses is further undercut by the parallels Caldwell draws between him and Jim Leslie Walden, a stylized villain who profits by evicting families from their homes and selling their meager possessions. He is also a cotton broker, a profession that got its name, according to Will, "[b]ecause they keep the farmers broke all the time. They lend a little money, and then they take the whole damn crop. Or else they suck the blood out of a man by running the price up and down forcing him to sell" (109). Alienated in his mansion on The Hill with only his gonorrheal wife, Jim Leslie is completely cut off from a sense of collective life he might experience with his family, nature, or the community. Spurred by another of Ty Ty's speeches about the virtues of Griselda's "pair of rising beauties," Jim Leslie sets his sights on his brother's wife and appears at the Walden farm after Will's death in order to take her by force.

The same sexual longing that is a source of power for Will is portrayed as degenerate and hostile in Jim Leslie. The difference for Caldwell appears to lie in the motivations for the two men's actions. As Ty Ty says to Griselda, she and Will come to understand "a secret of living" from their mutual desire: "It's folks who let their head run them who make all the mess of living. Your head can't make you love a man, if you don't feel like loving him. It's got to be a feeling down inside of you like you and Will had" (262–63). Caldwell constructs Jim Leslie as a representative of the greedy mill owners who are responsible for Will's death and of the entire market system that cheats farmers and starves workers and their families into submission. As readers, we are supposed to differentiate between Jim Leslie's attempted abduction of Griselda and Will's unleashing of her "natural" feelings. For Ty Ty, this difference is no less than that between a person who is "dead inside" (262) and one who has "the God inside of a body" (268).

For Caldwell, the difference is one of the desire for possession. That is, Jim Leslie's lust for his sister-in-law appears quite similar to Will's, as if he, too, has realized the connection to a collective sense of life through Griselda's archetypal female form. Rather than seduce her into a willing affair, however, Jim Leslie can only bark commands like, "Come out of that corner and get into the car before I have to come and pull you out" (280). Griselda is simply another possession to acquire, an upgrade from his diseased wife. Will is never interested in possessing her, or any one woman for that matter; instead, fulfilling his desire once lets him tap into the energy he needs to turn on the power. When Buck shoots Jim Leslie in the yard and then walks off to commit suicide before the sheriff arrives, his actions seem as much a revenge for Will's seduction of his wife as a response to his brother's immediate threat. Jim Leslie runs to his car, apparently ready to leave at the sight of the shotgun, and, since Will is already dead, Buck finds a fitting surrogate in his greedy brother. This substitution suggests that Will and Jim Leslie are not so

different after all and even, by extension, that the sentiments of collective individualism and acquisitive individualism are quite similar as well. One can
easily bleed into the other, as the violent deaths of both men attest.

The collective individualism felt by the workers of Scottsville is based on a
need to earn a wage and thus pursue the acquisition of wealth. The communal vitality that emerges briefly in the town is based on principles of interdependence and cooperation, but ultimately the hierarchical model is reinscribed. It is important to recognize that this sense of vitality exists among
striking employees, people acting together to improve their conditions and
become more autonomous. Ironically, without the mill there to exploit and
galvanize the workers, there would likely have been no communal identity
in the first place. Restarting the machinery of the mill in preparation for actual work, however, brings this empowerment to a thundering halt. The goal
of the workers running the mill themselves is revealed as a mere fantasy—
reflected in the often surreal narration of the Scottsville scenes—and one that
quickly ends. Caldwell suggests that widespread and significant changes in
labor conditions must occur for there to be a true and long-lasting return of
vitality to the Southern landscape.

The mill town does not provide a replacement for the pastoral farm in
Caldwell's presentation. Instead, the patterns of exploitation are repeated
and life is extinguished because of the failure to discover a sustainable model
for living. Caldwell recognizes the interrelatedness of humans and their environment, but he appears unable to embrace a network-based model that
would not rely on total human domination of the natural. Nature remains
largely passive in Caldwell's antipastoral fiction, and his consistent feminization of the land implies a natural submissiveness of women as well. Thus,
while Caldwell's novels make a compelling case for the death of the traditional pastoral dream, he does not acknowledge the role of the hierarchy of
gender relations inherent in the traditional pastoral model. These novels are
ecopastorals in the sense that they vividly illustrate the importance of the
natural environment in the lives of humans. Caldwell demonstrates the inherent interdependency of humans and nature but does not develop an alternative vision of nature that might suggest a similar social structure: more
flexible, more variable, more egalitarian. The passivity imposed on nature
by humans and social processes creates an imbalance that weakens the entire network. The writers examined in subsequent chapters look elsewhere,
to the wilderness, in order to investigate whether the communal vitality
glimpsed in *God's Little Acre* is sustainable without the subjugation of workers to bosses, women to men, and nature to culture.

2
Cross Creek Culture

Marjorie Kinnan Rawlings's Wilderness Pastoral

Marjorie Kinnan Rawlings owes her career to the pastoral retreat she made from New York to Cross Creek, Florida. Had she not moved from Rochester in 1928, it is quite likely that Rawlings would have never found success as a fiction writer, and almost certainly she would not have been nominated for two Pulitzer Prizes, winning for *The Yearling* (1938). While Rawlings was uncomfortable with the label of "regionalism" often applied to her writing,[1] she was fascinated by the connection between people and place, particularly that of the poor "crackers" and the lush, isolated landscapes of Alachua, Putnam, and Marion counties in north central Florida. In the opening pages of *Cross Creek,* her 1942 memoir about life in the Florida backwoods, Rawlings proclaims that "the consciousness of land and water must lie deeper in the core of us than any knowledge of our fellow beings. We were bred of the earth before we were born of our mothers.... We cannot live without the earth or apart from it, and something is shrivelled [*sic*] in a man's heart when he turns away from it and concerns himself only with the affairs of men."[2] A large part of the allure of Cross Creek for Rawlings was its remoteness from the "civilized world" to which she belonged until purchasing seventy-four acres of orange groves in 1928.[3] Rawlings's adopted home in north central Florida is geographically close to Caldwell's of south Georgia, and her characters are also usually poor farmers isolated from and ignored by the economic mainstream. While Caldwell's sharecroppers tend to have an antagonistic relationship with barren earth and bleak landscapes, Rawlings's work is populated by industrious yeomen protagonists who experience an intimate bond with their natural surroundings, the sort of bond Jeeter Lester nostalgically imagines his father and grandfather having prior to the depletion of the soil.

In numerous letters Rawlings remarks that she is especially compelled by the "elemental" and "primal" quality of life in her new home. Gordon

Bigelow's 1966 biography, *Frontier Eden,* notes that "this pull she felt toward elemental things . . . was something she shared with many other American writers of her generation," notably Faulkner, Hemingway, Robert Frost, and Thomas Wolfe. This quest for the elemental and the desire to retreat from the modern, urban world is, at least partially, a reaction to the horrors of World War I, the panic following the Wall Street crash of 1929, and the onset of the Great Depression. Bigelow further observes: "Economic catastrophe and social unrest produced a widespread renewal of interest in the regions, so that life in the village began to receive new scrutiny as a source of those virtues which could heal the ills brought on by too much city and too much big business."[4] In Caldwell's fiction, these villages, too, are suffering from the trickle-down effects of "too much big business," but Rawlings's settings are even more rural and further removed from the economic and cultural centers whose influence remains tangible in Caldwell's Southern Georgia farms and mill towns.

If Caldwell's landscapes of desolate wastelands in *Tobacco Road* and *God's Little Acre* stem from his despair at the prospects faced by poor Southerners during the Depression, then we might expect similar portraits from Rawlings in nearby Florida. But Rawlings admittedly shies away from a head-on confrontation with the political, social, and economic problems of the era. Instead, Rawlings claims to seek a metaphorical return to childhood in the Edenic sanctuary of wilderness that she depicts in her work, where the problems of modern civilization melt away: "[T]ime frightens me, and I seek, like a lonely child, the maternal solace of timelessness" (243). Caldwell laments the loss of the American and Southern pastoral garden, but Rawlings finds that it still exists, not in the traditional locations of farms, plantations, or country estates, but in the wilderness and frontier settlements of the north Florida scrub country.[5]

However, Rawlings finds this paradise under assault from the forces of modernization, the inexorable counterforce to pastoral harmony. In the 1930s, Florida was still in the early stages of a population boom that continued into the twenty-first century. In 1900 the population of the entire state was 528,000, while by 1950 Dade County alone was home to 495,000 residents. By 1930 the state's population was about 1.5 million, and it had become the first Southern state with a predominantly urban population, which took its toll on the state's natural resources: "The reason for Florida's environmental decline [in the 1930s and 1940s], simply put, is millions of people and their concentration in cities and resorts along the coasts and around the lakes and rivers of Orlando and central Florida."[6]

While many new arrivals were drawn by the state's natural beauty, established citizens were already decrying the human damage to the environment. Edenic imagery continued to be used for Florida in writings from that era, as it had since its discovery, but now the context was more likely to be a lament for a lost garden of plenty. Thomas Barbour, a Harvard-educated paleontologist and naturalist who was raised in Florida, describes his 1944 book *That Vanishing Eden: A Naturalist's Florida* as a follow-up to Dr. John K. Small's *From Eden to Sahara: Florida's Tragedy* (1929), and Barbour's tone is elegiac and mournful throughout: "A large part of Florida is now so devastated that many of her friends are disinclined to believe that she ever could have been the Paradise which I know once existed."[7] As a new arrival to Florida, Rawlings picks up this motif of a vanishing paradise, writing about threats to local nature and culture in work that defends the land and people as well as chronicling the particulars of their existence before they disappear.

Rawlings herself undertakes a pastoral retreat, and her work after the move represents a new kind of pastoral, an ecopastoral that revises key concepts of the traditional forms even as it retains others. Specifically, Rawlings challenges traditional pastoral notions of gender, property, and individuality facilitated by her relocation of the pastoral site from the country farm to the wilderness. The idyllic aspects of the pastoral genre are evident in the Edenic qualities that Rawlings's wilderness landscapes exude: timelessness, natural abundance, and a sense of spiritual communion with fellow creatures. As Caldwell's work shows, the ideal of the improved garden has become untenable in light of the state of Southern farms. In wild nature, Rawlings locates values of freedom and equality, presenting those concepts as natural foundations for an improved society: the wilderness becomes a pastoral counterpart to the corrupted farm and city.

The improved garden of the traditional pastoral middle ground is very often not so much a harmonious blend of culture and nature as it is an ideologically loaded transfer of culture into a rural setting. For instance, pastoral identifications of (white) women with the Southern garden itself, and of slaves and black laborers with the other property of the plantation, reinforce cultural hierarchies and even justify them as natural in this setting.[8] While issues of race and gender are often linked in pastoral representations of nature, Rawlings's writing largely avoids race and, in addition to the urge to celebrate nature, is concerned with freeing women from the narrow and limiting gender roles that are often reproduced in the traditional pastoral context. She therefore offers a reformulation of the pastoral equation by rejecting the orderly, improved garden in favor of an open, free, and chaotic wilderness that, in her presentation, embodies "real" nature.

In essence, Rawlings presents a conception of nature as a network of relations in which humans participate as more accurate than a Newtonian, mechanistic view that deepens the divide between nature and humans by assuming an ideal of scientific detachment. The issue of accuracy is debatable but also, I think, irrelevant.[9] What is most interesting is that nature is made the arbiter of social systems in order to promote a particular ideology as more natural, and therefore more correct, than another. Rawlings uses an interdependent concept of humans and nature to promote principles of egalitarianism and cooperation and to critique the absence of those values in modern society. Conversely, someone like Thomas Nelson Page or Andrew Lytle can celebrate the orderliness of nature on a farm or plantation in order to lament and decry the perceived loss of "proper" stability in the social order of the post-Reconstruction New South. Thus, Rawlings attempts to move her characters beyond the restrictive pastoral garden and into the liberatory landscape of wilderness where artificially constructed gender roles are replaced with more relative and flexible identities.

Yet her work remains pastoral in the sense that she envisions these communities on the edge of the wilderness as combining the best of culture and nature. Elizabeth Jane Harrison, although she does not include Rawlings in her study, examines this same pastoral revision in the literature of other twentieth-century Southern women. The "female pastoral," she argues, is created through a concomitant restructuring of landscape and society in their fiction: "Despite difficulties in overcoming the barriers to sex and race equality, female friendship and cooperative communities become an important part of the new Southern garden for these women authors. Their explorations of ways of achieving female autonomy and changing interactions among characters of different class, race, and gender depend upon the invocation of land not as 'property' but as an empowering life source."[10] Working in the same way Harrison describes, Rawlings appropriates the pastoral tradition but alters its conventions in significant ways. She replaces the passive, feminized landscape of the depleted farm with an active, vibrant nature, and she finds in her less developed, more wild settings those elements of the pastoral that Caldwell shows to be missing from the contemporary Southern farm.

This less civilized natural realm of the Florida scrub, instead of being a hostile environment for its scant human population, is more hospitable to those in tune with its natural processes than are the towns across the river. Even though her characters are often just as destitute as the Lesters or the Waldens in south Georgia, Rawlings never portrays nature as a cause or reflection of impoverished lives. If anything, the opposite is true. The natural environment is quite often the only significant source of hope, beauty, wealth, and sustenance, and consequently, her characters do not at all resemble the starving, forsaken souls of Caldwell's stories.[11] Rawlings settings are, by virtue of their isolation, places of refuge where she seldom permits the harsh realities of Depression-era American life to enter. Perhaps since she is not a native Southerner, Rawlings also does not feel compelled to grapple with the ghosts of Southern traditions and the legacy of slavery. Therefore, her landscapes are relatively free of the burden of Southern history, and she chooses to explore more "elemental" questions of human beings' attachment to specific natural places, as well as issues of gender, in a fairly hermetic environment.

Her isolated home allowed Rawlings to retreat from the modern world and, somewhat paradoxically, to grapple with the problematic oppositions of the culture she left behind, including those between civilization and wilderness, men and women, and the individual and community. She felt particularly drawn to write about the seemingly simple people who lived around her in the Cross Creek area: "[C]ivilization had remained too remote, physically and spiritually, to take something from them, something vital. . . . The only ingredients of their lives are the elemental things."[12] This withdrawal in order to criticize society from a distance by a set of supposedly purer, more natural standards is a staple of the pastoral mode, which, as Jan Bakker explains in his study of antebellum Southern literature, "characteristically deals with the complexities of life against a background of apparent simplicity."[13] Rawlings therefore may overestimate her own evasion of modernity in a 1936 letter to F. Scott Fitzgerald: "I have probably been more cowardly than I'd admit, in sinking my interests in the Florida backwoods, for the peace and beauty I've found there have definitely been an escape from the confusion of our generation. You have faced the music, and it is a symphony of discord."[14] Historian Richard Pells attributes the "extraordinary interest in folk cultures, agrarian communities, and peasant life," especially among intellectuals and writers, to their attraction to societies that seemed "outside the pale of capitalist civilization" of 1930s America: "[M]any writers felt more justified in offering a symbolic reproach to American materialism and greed than in outlining programmatic solutions to the depression."[15] In choosing a pastoral retreat into the sparsely populated Florida scrub, Rawlings engages in the traditional pastoral critique of modern, urban culture, while she also critiques the traditional pastoral mode itself, reworking it to create a version that empowers instead of reifies women.

Rawlings's greatest success as a writer prior to her move to Florida was a daily series of poems called "Songs of the Housewife," initially published in the Rochester *Times-Union* and eventually syndicated in over fifty newspapers. These unremarkable poems, which appeared six days a week from May 24, 1926, to February 29, 1928, tended to be sentimental celebrations of the domestic sphere with titles like "This Morning's Pancakes," "Making the Beds," and "Washings on the Line."[16] She moved to Cross Creek in November of 1928 with her husband of nine years, Charles Rawlings, himself an aspiring writer, and she immediately realized that she had found a place and people rife with stories waiting to be told. The couple's already strained marriage could not be salvaged by the change of locale, and they separated early in 1933, just after the publication of her first novel, *South Moon Under,* with the divorce to be finalized several months later.

In a letter written just after the divorce, Rawlings characterizes her marriage as fourteen years of hell from which she was all too ready to be liberated: "It was a question, finally, of breaking free from the feeling of a vicious hand always at my throat, or of going down in complete physical and mental collapse."[17] It is perhaps not surprising, then, that a central concern of *South Moon Under* is revealing the artificiality of societal gender roles that are commonly justified as natural and therefore unquestionable and immutable. The chief female protagonist, Piety Jacklin, née Lantry, is, like Rawlings, a mentally and physically strong woman who is able to resist and ignore traditional notions of proper gender roles because she lives in the sparsely populated wilderness that abuts the scrub region. Piety's identity is integrally tied to the natural environment in which she lives, but Rawlings does not reduce this to "a narrow association with the southern garden," which Harrison notes is characteristic of the male pastoral tradition in the South.[18]

In *South Moon Under,* the wilderness of the scrub country facilitates a fluid and dynamic conception of gender roles, which Rawlings portrays as more natural than typical notions of femininity and masculinity. She also examines how the expanding powers of the government threaten the local culture of the vanishing Florida frontier. In *The Yearling,* Rawlings focuses more narrowly on redefining masculinity, again using the natural environment as a guide to a more nurturing, less individualistic type of manhood. The novel also employs its prepubescent protagonist to expose pastoral notions of permanence and isolation as childish fantasies. *Cross Creek* is a partly fictional, partly autobiographical book in which Rawlings uses portraits of people and wildlife to posit the natural superiority of a community on the cusp of the wilderness. She makes a case for the instructive power of nature as a model for human societies and for the benefits of recognizing the interconnectedness of humans with other life.

In the Southern pastoral tradition of the nineteenth century, the land inside the boundaries of the plantation is figured as the ideal middle state, a stable and static refuge from the chaos of time and the outside world. The act of fencing helps people to symbolically domesticate land and nature by delineating boundaries and imposing a sense of order on previously "wild" terrain. Rawlings, however, repeatedly shows us the double nature of fencing in *South Moon Under:* fences disrupt an existing order while signaling the creation of a new order that threatens the wildness of the scrub as well as the communal values of its inhabitants. Fences symbolize the modern society that Rawlings seeks to escape, and their encroachment into the virtually uninhabited scrub region entails, in her view, the threat of subjugation for nature and women alike. The fences erected by a new wave of cattle ranchers threaten to disrupt the free-range tradition of the locals, and Rawlings links women to land, as well as fencing to the imposition of limiting gender identities. She reveals that, though these limitations are justified by some as naturally ordained, they are, as much as the idea of property, social constructions. By positing a nonhierarchical conception of nature, Rawlings suggests that the principles of egalitarianism, interdependency, and cooperation found in wilderness ecosystems are actually more natural models for human social relations than the classificatory traditions that tend to isolate and rank individual parts of communities.

The identification of women with nature (and of nature with women) has been examined in its historical and scientific contexts by Carolyn Merchant, traced from its New World origins by Louise Westling and Annette Kolodny, and analyzed as a staple of Southern pastoral fiction by Elizabeth Jane Harrison.[19] As these critics note, to view nature mechanistically, as fundamentally passive raw material to be shaped and used by masculine culture, is also to justify as natural a social hierarchy that subordinates women, African Americans, and Native Americans—those people deemed closest to nature. In *South Moon Under,* Rawlings seeks not to deny outright the perceived connection between women and nature but to reveal that association as dependent on historical and cultural factors. Viewed in this light, the novel is a proto-ecofeminist text in its illustrations of the standpoint[20] claims of an ecofeminist critic like Ariel Salleh, who writes:

It is nonsense to assume that women are any closer to nature than men. The point is that women's reproductive labor and such patriarchically assigned roles as cooking and cleaning bridge men and nature in a very obvious way, and one that is denigrated by patriarchal culture. Mining and engineering work similarly is a transaction with nature. The difference is that this work comes to be mediated by a language of domination that ideologically reinforces masculine identity as powerful, aggressive, and separate over and above nature. The language that typifies a woman's experience, in contrast, situates her along with nature itself.[21]

In her attempt to counteract this dominant ideology that aligns woman/nature against man/culture, Rawlings envisions fences as representative of a hierarchical society that tends to establish a sense of order by defining nature (and therefore women) as raw material without any identity outside of their relation to masculine culture. Her attempt to refute these reductive versions of women and nature in *South Moon Under* is twofold: she shows that men can be situated as a part of nature, rather than over and above it, and she reveals that the assumption that women and nature are fundamentally passive objects to an active, masculine subject is as much a purely human creation as a split-rail fence.

As the novel opens, the Lantry family has just moved to the Florida scrub, and Pa Lantry feels uneasy in the darkness of his new home, musing to himself, "Time I get me a fence raised tomorrow, maybe 'twon't seem so wild, like."[22] As Lucinda MacKethan says in *The Dream of Arcady*, "the pastoral quest is always basically a search for order,"[23] a sentiment echoed by the narrator of *South Moon Under* who, after the fence is raised, comments: "The mark of order was on the Lantry land" (20). It is also significant that the fence is constructed through the collaborative efforts of neighbors and relatives who rarely converge as a group. Their interaction is an example of how gender is constructed socially, even in a far-flung and loose-knit community. The novel's female protagonist is Piety, then fifteen and the youngest Lantry daughter, and she notices the patterns and forms that govern the group's social behavior. Rawlings shows how Piety's adolescent conception of proper gender roles is being shaped as she is, quite literally, being fenced in to a socially acceptable notion of the woman's sphere—the clearly delineated space around the homestead.[24] Piety's distaste for domestic work and her antagonistic relationship with her mother are clear indications that she will not inherit the traditional gender roles that her mother embodies.

Rawlings shows Piety already resisting these patterns by leaving each day to work in the fields with her father instead of remaining around the house with her sister and mother, who complains to the other women about her daughter's fondness for field work. Piety is closer in spirit to her aunt, Annie Wilson, who, in response to taunts from the men, compares building the fence to sewing, runs across the yard, and good-naturedly throws an armful of fence rails at the men. Piety's mother, whom Rawlings refers to only as Mrs. Lantry, scolds her cousin, saying, "'Tain't mannerly no-ways to go

scaperin' acrost to the men-folks that-a-way" (18), but Rawlings's sympa-
thies are clearly with Annie as a free-spirited role model for Piety. When her
mother dies, Piety is less than overwhelmed by grief: "The house was no emp-
tier than before. No place would be empty, she thought, with Lantry in it. The
man's bulk, the fire of his presence, filled the room so certainly that his wife,
returning from the grave, would have crowded it. Piety stared at the hearth,
missing the accustomed sight of her mother sitting near the fire. It was as
though a sharp-nosed, snappish bitch of long association was gone" (41). This
rather brutal eulogy indicates Piety's disdain for the confining role of wife/
mother and may also suggest Rawlings's own desire to escape the confines of
traditional domesticity. The hearth may have been the place for her mother,
but Piety prefers to be behind the plow. She continues the "men's work" of
farming and hunting while reluctantly assuming her mother's domestic du-
ties as well.

Of course, farming and hunting are no more fundamentally masculine
than other types of labor, nor does Piety see them as such. In her eyes, these
tasks are simply more enjoyable than the housework her mother performs,
and they allow her to be with the father she adores. Rawlings, however,
realizes that activities like trapping, hunting, plowing, and logging have been
traditionally coded as masculine, and she demonstrates that these and other
gender-based divisions are very often illogical, impractical, and arbitrary notions that are passed off as infallible laws of nature. Life in the wilderness dictates divisions of labor based on necessity and ability rather than social convention, and Rawlings presents this as a more natural arrangement in order
to propound a more expansive and flexible role for women.

Two years after his wife's death, Lantry has a near-fatal heart attack and
consequently begins to seek security for his daughter within the comforts
of traditional gender roles: "[H]e could not endure to leave her here alone.
She would have to live with Martha, or keep house for widower Zeke. That
was no life for a woman. He saw in a new light the stupid Jacklin boy, Willy"
(49). Lantry's argument for his daughter's marriage rests on the premise that
the societal convention is, in fact, a mandate of nature: "A man o' your own's
natural. Seems like ever' thing go along better when you do what's natural"
(52). Piety's bewilderment with her father's sudden fixation on marriage—
"For the first time she did not understand him"—gives way to resigned acceptance: "He suits me good as ary feller, I reckon" (51–52). Sleeping in her
parents' old bed with her new husband, Piety feels uncomfortable and bewil-
dered by the prospect of suddenly inheriting the place of her mother: "She
felt a detached affection for her husband. . . . It seemed to her that she was
picking up in the middle something that had been interrupted. But if there

was a meaning, she could not find it" (54). The idea of conforming to the pre-defined, culturally determined roles of wife and mother appears to Piety to be quite *un*natural, and Rawlings subtly links this situation to the imposition of masculine will on nature.

Lantry's first conversation with Willy Jacklin about the possibility of marriage is also the first mention of the lumber company that Willy will work for and that will soon descend on the scrub, removing thousands of trees before abruptly pulling out again. The connection between Willy's impending marriage to Piety and the lumber company's ravaging of the land is clear: both are self-defined masculine forces that threaten to impose a passive femininity on the "possessions" of woman and land. In Rawlings's novel, though, neither the land nor Piety assumes the passive role of inert raw material or of the defenseless woman in need of protection from active, masculine subjects. Rawlings, as a woman and a nonnative Southerner, avoids reducing Piety to an idealized symbol of virgin land, echoing Harrison's description of female pastoral: "[Landscape] is 're-visioned' as an enabling force for the woman protagonist. Her interaction with land changes from passive association to active cultivation or identification."[25] It is actually Willy Jacklin whose role in the novel is primarily symbolic, representing the hubris of a patriarchal culture that envisions men as rulers of nature rather than part of it.

Willy's "slow usefulness was ended" (55), Rawlings tells us, as soon as Piety's son, Lant, is born. When Lant is ten years old, Willy is crushed by one of the falling trees that he was helping to remove as a dronelike employee of the lumber company. Piety, who naturalizes her husband (like her mother) as "a good dog, that fetched and carried as she told him" (54), is hardly devastated by Willy's death. Her father, however, imagined Willy as security for his daughter and is so distraught by "the fool [making] a pore widder-woman o' Pytee before her time" (75) that he suffers another heart attack. Still clinging to the notion on his deathbed that Piety needs a man for security, he tells his daughter that young Lant will be able to make a living and care for her. But Piety provides her own security; her femininity is not symbolized by the hearth or by the fertile land that submits to the plow, but by the plow itself and by that side of nature that occasionally flattens those who abuse it. Lantry relies on the pastoral conception of woman-as-land in his belief that she requires a masculine force to guide and protect her, but Rawlings suggests in the course of the novel that the individual and nature can nurture one another free from a relationship of dominance.

The fences that symbolize the restrictive gender identity of civilization later reappear in the novel as symbols of outside forces that threaten the pastoral sanctuary. When "the Alabamy feller" moves into the area and fences in "two square mile o' worthless scrub" (141), he violates local custom in favor of his individual interests. Leonard Lutwack, in his study *The Role of Place in Literature,* offers a useful and succinct formulation of the attitudes that fences produce: "Enclosure automatically bestows special value on places and things. . . . But there is a price to pay for their worth: because of their concentrated richness and exclusiveness, paradisal places require constant protection and create feelings of guilt and fear of loss instead of the free, expansive feelings inspired by the spaciousness and openness of cosmic places."[26] Lutwack's summary is helpful for understanding the particular order that fences impose on undefined terrain, but I think the arbitrariness of the "special value" he mentions must be emphasized in order to comprehend why Rawlings's fences seem so out of place, so "unnatural," in the landscapes of *South Moon Under.* The land that was "worthless" as unfenced scrub is now meaningful and valuable to Lant and the group of men from his extended family who confront the Alabaman, ordering him to dismantle the fence. They explain the community customs of allowing stock to roam across all land while fencing in only their yards and crops. The fences that traditionally help create pastoral order on the plantation instead disrupt the less visible order of this wilderness pastoral by turning shared land into private property. The action is taken by the local men as a serious threat to the community, and they work together to drive the interloper out of town.[27]

As this incident demonstrates, a complex culture exists in the scrub. It is not simply a wild, primitive antithesis to modern civilization. In this respect, it is quite similar to traditional pastoral locales, rustic places just far enough from the city to permit critical reflection on that world. The society of the scrub is presented by Rawlings as closer to nature, more in touch with nature, and thus more natural in order to promote certain values and castigate others. In this case, Rawlings prefers the cooperative model of the scrub denizens to the acquisitive individualism of the outsider. This vision of collective solidarity is surely a reaction to the realities of the Depression that both Rawlings and her characters hope to shield themselves from in the wilderness. As Richard Pells explains, many young artists of the 1930s were attracted to folk cultures as they became disenchanted with a capitalist system that seemed to have lost any sense of purpose: "The depression confirmed their belief that American ideals were dangerously distorted and unreal, that competition and acquisitiveness were eroding the country's social foundations, that the quality of human life under capitalism offered men no sense of community of common experience."[28] It is this sense of community that Rawlings presents as under attack from the "distorted" values of the outside world.

When "a distant legislature" decrees that all cattle must be kept "under fence," state law is pitted against the customs that the locals view as a natural order. Increased automobile traffic has led to an "urban outcry . . . complaining of the savagery of cattle loose on the highways" (255), and the legislature assumes the responsibility of stewardship, seeking to promote urban interests over those of the local population. Despite the Depression, this was an era of booming car ownership and road construction. In 1900 there were 8,000 registered cars in America; by 1913 there were 1 million and in 1929, 23 million.[29] The reach of paved roads and of the government—both state and federal—expanded at similar rates. The Works Progress Administration alone built more than 6,000 miles of roads in Florida (with the state adding another 3,000), the Civilian Conservation Corps gave work to more than 50,000 Floridians with a wide array of projects, and the state in the mid-1930s "evolved past its traditional status as a small government state."[30]

Paul Sutter demonstrates that the Wilderness Society—formed in 1934 by, among others, Aldo Leopold and Bob Marshall—was created primarily because of its founders' antipathy to the proliferation of autos and roads: "For the founders of the Wilderness Society, modern wilderness advocacy sprang from a sense that as roads and the automobiles carved up the nation's remaining wild spaces, the American desire to retreat to nature, traditionally a critical gesture, was becoming part of the culture's accommodation to the modern social and economic order."[31] Not only do the new roads (and the government influence that comes with them) threaten to disrupt the pastoral landscape, but they also threaten to co-opt the entire pastoral experience, turning Rawlings's critical gesture into a recreational commodity. It is little wonder that she sets up the small group of locals as a natural community to contrast the ever-expanding, "artificial" restrictions of the government. The government seeks to impose limits and more clearly define individual ownership of land and animals through these new laws. While the locals certainly do not shun the idea of private property, they also value commonly held resources. Sometimes, they can accomplish more by working collectively. The changing laws and changing landscapes threaten a local way of life, what Martyn Lee calls "cultural character," which is formed by the relationship among human agency, social process, and spatial location: "[P]laces (towns, cities, regions, nations) have cultural characters which transcend and exist relatively autonomously, although by no means independently, of their current populations and of the consequences of the social processes which may be taking place upon their terrain at a given historical juncture."[32] Lee's formulation helps to expand the ecocritical perspective in that it recognizes that not only are humans, flora, and fauna parts of the interconnected network of a given environment, but so are cultural institutions.

New laws and new fences also bring a new type of people into the scrub country. Rawlings introduces the Streeters, a family of recent emigrants from Arkansas, who exploit the new law by rounding up cattle, driving them within their fences, and claiming the impound fees mandated by the legislature. Spurred by the potential for purely personal profit, the Streeters' actions illustrate how the new regulations are antithetical to the well-being and survival of this folk culture. The tradition of cooperation through sharing land for collective benefit is replaced, practically overnight, by an atmosphere of jealousy and possessiveness caused by fences. What seems particularly unnatural to Lant and his kinfolk is the arbitrary and illogical creation of monetary value: cattle that are practically worthless on one side of a fence are suddenly worth much more on the other side because of the new impound fees offered by the state. Piety is similarly defined earlier in the novel as appropriately feminine when inside the fences of the homestead, but not when she is outside these boundaries, farming or hunting. Rawlings is not advocating a return to traditional rural values as the Nashville Agrarians do. Rather, she envisions a more radically different society where women are not bound by cultural conventions and stereotypes, and where land and animals are not merely possessions to be exploited for individual profit.

Abner Lantry explains that the residents adhere to their own code of behavior that supersedes that imposed by the state: "The law's the law, and the law's always changin', but they's things beyond the law is right and wrong, accordin' to how many folks they [the Streeters] he'ps or harms" (257). Rawlings structures this conflict as one between natural law and man-made law, although it is more accurate to describe it as one set of customs versus another: culture versus culture, not culture versus nature. In the novel, however, allegiance to one culture means breaking up families and traditions for profit, while its counterpart is linked to the naturalness of the wilderness, which lends the scrub society and its customs a degree of authenticity that outsiders and politicians can never achieve.

The illegal activities of the locals actually further enhance their credibility in the context of the novel, establishing them as untainted by urban society, living by their own, more authentic code. The state begins offering cash rewards for information about illegal moonshine stills, like the one Lant helps his Uncle Zeke run in the protective wilderness along the river. Cleve Jacklin is Lant's shiftless cousin who occasionally helps out at the still and whose wife, Kezzy, is obviously constructed by Rawlings as Lant's soul mate. It is hardly surprising when Cleve betrays his relatives by reporting their illegal corn liquor operation to the government revenuers in order to claim a promised reward. His actions leave Kezzy with a choice between the official law of the state and the communal standards of the scrub.

Neither option is a good one because the rigid dualism forces Kezzy to either betray her husband by disclosing his actions to Lant or to betray her moral sensibilities through silent complicity with Cleve's backstabbing of his kinfolk. Forced to choose between mutually exclusive opposites, Kezzy selects Lant over Cleve, justifying her action, as Abner did, by asserting her allegiance to a higher code: "Hit ain't natural for a woman to go agin her husband, whatever he do. But 'tain't natural for Cleve to do what he's a-doin'" (308). The dominant, external culture's idea of the natural is allegiance to the civil bonds of marriage, while the minority culture of the scrub considers fidelity to blood relatives and opposition to government intrusion to be the (more) natural course of action. What I think Rawlings is trying to do in these types of episodes is to show the limitations of dualistic thinking. She shows, for instance, that strict boundaries between "appropriate" masculine and feminine behavior melt away in the context of the wilderness. Similarly, the incident under discussion represents an either/or dilemma in which neither alternative is desirable. Rawlings wants, instead, to have the pastoral blend of culture/nature, city/country, civilization/wilderness that combines oppositions rather than making them mutually exclusive choices. Yet the pattern of binary opposition is intrinsic to the pastoral impulse, as seen in the insider versus outsider, us versus them mentality of *South Moon Under,* and Rawlings at times lapses into these dualistic modes despite her intentions to reform that aspect of the pastoral tradition.

When the government takes over most of "the almost virgin wilderness" of the scrub and designates it a game refuge where hunting and trapping are forbidden, the symbolic enclosure creates the same fear of loss that is symptomatic of literal fences: "[T]he law had come into the scrub and lay over it like a dark cloud. . . . it had seemed at first, with one section shut off by invisible lines, as though there were no other section worth hunting" (233). The designation of the land as a National Forest[33] appears particularly arbitrary and capricious to the residents who regularly hunt on those lands for subsistence and trap on them for furs. That such activities are now crimes seems to Lant and many of the other locals a foreign imposition of regulations that are in no way responsive to local culture or to nature's rhythms: "The varmints came obligingly to the swamps to be trapped as before. The deer still came to the river to drink" (234). The government's creation of a refuge where animals can breed redefines the scrub as wilderness, an idea that is a human construction that William Cronon has critiqued as "the fantasy of people who have never themselves had to work the land to make a living."[34]

Cronon's argument is that the category of wilderness is an anthropocentric creation meant to represent the antithesis of an unnatural civilized realm, but that the designation of land as wilderness actually reinforces the primacy of culture and fosters an alienated relationship with nature: "[T]he romantic ideology of wilderness leaves precisely nowhere for human beings actually to make their living from the land. This, then, is the central paradox: wilderness embodies a dualistic vision in which the human is entirely outside the natural. . . . we reproduce the dualism that sets humanity and nature at opposite poles. We thereby leave ourselves little hope of discovering what an ethical, sustainable, *honorable* human place in nature might actually look like."[35] To put Cronon's statement in the terms I have been using, the ideology of wilderness precludes the possibility of an ideal middle state between culture and nature. To Lantry and his family the scrub is not wilderness; it is home, and they ignore the illogical government boundary, continuing to hunt and trap while being more wary of game wardens and government agents. The government's designation creates an artificial and arbitrary distinction between wilderness and not-wilderness. Although one goal of designating the scrub a wilderness refuge is to "keep away the devastating fires" (244), a huge off-season fire rages a few years after the government's appropriation of the land, fed by unmaintained fire lines intended to halt its path. As for the other goal of creating a refuge for animal breeding, Lant's assessment is, "They was more game in the scrub when they wa'n't no laws, than they is now, with 'em" (213). Thus, the enclosure ostensibly meant to protect the "wilderness" of the scrub kills more of nature than it preserves. Rawlings shows that only by moving beyond simplistic dualisms like nature/ culture and masculine/feminine is it possible to realize Cronon's hope of discovering "what an ethical, sustainable, *honorable* human place in nature might actually look like." The implication is that the people who actually live among nature, and who do not view themselves as stewards of something called "the wilderness," are better equipped to preserve the environment that is their home.

When the residents of the scrub and surrounding areas are employed to help battle the fire, they adhere to divisions of labor based on a tacit acceptance of communal gender roles: "The men loaded axes and hoes and shovels. The women would go along and drive the wagon back again" (236). The propriety of this arrangement is not questioned by the text, but its status as a natural division is. Kezzy, for one, views her role as changeable rather than essentially determined and immediately joins the men beating back the flames on the front line, saying, "Well, I cain't see a mess like this un and not git into it" (238). On the other hand, the traitorous Cleve sleeps under a bush for most of the ordeal, which prompts Lant to compare him to a woman. Rawlings demonstrates in these scenes that loosely maintained, communally created boundaries work well, while rigidly enforced, externally imposed ones create more problems than they solve. The division of labor between men and women is effective because Kezzy can transgress the permeable boundaries when it is better for the community. The unyielding boundaries and regulations of the government, on the other hand, lead to an unintended depletion of game and the worst fire that the locals can remember.

Rawlings metaphorical understanding of nature as a fluid, interwoven web of life not only supports a more flexible conception of gender, but also becomes a model for a less hierarchical society based on cooperation of its members. This longing for a more egalitarian society was a popular one in the midst of the Great Depression, especially among the disaffected, who flocked in large numbers to support dissident leaders like Huey Long and Father Charles Coughlin. Millions found great appeal in their notions of collective property ownership and wealth distribution: "A community, they [Long and Coughlin] suggested, was less a particular place than a network of associations, a set of economic and social relationships in which the individual played a meaningful role and in which each citizen maintained control of his own livelihood and destiny."[36] Rather than envisioning this type of society as a possible future reality, however, Rawlings presents it as the final throes of a fading community, a vanishing Eden where cultural and environmental changes go hand in hand, as Rawlings explains in a letter that outlines her plans for *South Moon Under:* "The old clearings have been farmed out and will not 'make' good crops any more. The big timber is gone. The trapping is poor. . . . the old-timers have recently heard their doom pronounced. The cattle must be fenced, which means the end of the old regime."[37] Rawlings uses a somewhat evasive tactic, avoiding dealing directly with "the confusion of our generation" in favor of a pastoral retreat to the wilderness. She suggests that, in nature, all divisions may be erased and the self joined to a larger web of life, a cosmic vision that erases particular political and social problems.

As the plot works toward the inevitable coupling of Lant and Kezzy, Rawlings uses the character of Ardis Mersey as a potential love interest for Lant and a foil for the unsophisticated and rugged Kezzy. Significantly, Ardis is the cousin of the game warden, and her introduction into the novel is followed immediately by the revelation that the government has created a National Forest in the scrub. Having only recently returned to the area, Ardis is a product of the more urban world across the river, and her "pretty and soft-like" (268) femininity is equated with enclosure and the fencing of the scrub. In a letter to her editor, Maxwell Perkins, Rawlings calls Kezzy a "harbor of refuge" for Lant and explains that Ardis is too much a part of "the civilized world he does not know" for Lant to trust her: "Everything about her, except her physical appeal for him, will chill the very marrow in his bones, and make it impossible for him to do anything but run from her and from his desire."[38] When Lant discovers Ardis fraternizing with his enemies—the Streeters, the sheriff, and the game warden—she becomes to him as unnatural and unpalatable as the fencing and game laws of the society she represents: "[S]he was something he had bolted whole in his hunger and had spewed up" (282).

The choice between Ardis and Kezzy is simplified into a choice between the artificial and imposed regulations of civilization and the natural freedom of the scrub. Rawlings does not have Lant choose between a masculine and feminine world. Instead, there are two types of femininity: one she associates with governmental authority and the other with a more rugged, less constrained existence. Both sides of the river actually offer a combination of culture and nature. But on one side, culture dominates, while closer to the wilderness, Rawlings suggests, the pastoral ideal of balance can still be found. Like Caldwell, she sees the cultural subsuming the natural, but unlike him, Rawlings finds a place where these opposing forces can be blended harmoniously. Marrying Ardis would mean fully accepting the limits represented by game wardens, sheriffs, cattle rustlers, legislators, and all the rest of society's regulations: a false paradise represented by the Eve/snake temptress, Ardis. Lant runs as fast as he can "toward the river" (283), and his ensuing river trip illustrates his ability to live harmoniously, honorably even, within nature without fetishizing wilderness as a morally pure corrective to an immoral civilization.

Lant, unlike his father, Willy, wants no part of the logging work that exemplifies the stereotypical notion of masculine identity as "powerful, aggressive, and separate over and above nature."[39] His brief foray into logging, therefore, involves methods quite different from those of the lumber companies, which are described by Rawlings in the "language of domination" that so often defines the relationship of masculine ideology to nature and anticipates Leo Marx's machine-in-the-garden metaphor: "The noise of the timber outfit hummed in Lant's ears. He heard the shouts of men above distant axes and cross-cut saws. The drum on the pull boat chattered, the gears ground and creaked. A steam whistle blew, the engine puffed and chugged. The great cypress began to fall. Three hundred feet away he saw a trembling in the dark canopy that was the tree-tops over the swamp. There came a ripping, as woody cells, inseparable for a century, were torn violently from one another" (62–63). To Lant, the loggers seem like puny and insignificant creatures compared to the trees he calls the "giants of the swamp." His relationship with his environment is based on an ecological model of interdependence, and he consequently chooses to raise the immense cypress logs discarded at the bottom of the river by the lumber companies. Just as he has seen the plants and animals of the scrub utilize decaying trees and rotting carcasses, Lant converts the waste products of the loggers into a marketable commodity.

Rawlings uses Lant's approach as an example of a male relationship with nature that is mutually beneficial rather than exploitative, characterizing his work as part of an organic cycle instead of a mechanical assault on the land. Thus, the lumber companies are a threat to this Edenic garden not just because they are cutting down trees, but because their methods are unnatural, even sinful. As in most Southern states, Florida's forests were heavily logged in the first decades of the twentieth century: "By the 1930s naval stores and logging firms had practically depleted longleaf yellow pine forests."[40] The clear-cutting, skidding, and other destructive logging practices often left the land unable to support new growth: "Some 30 percent of the clear-cut pinelands were no longer capable of producing trees because of soil depletion, drainage, and repeated assaults by ax and fire."[41] Lant's methods, by contrast, take into account the interests of the forest, and by extension the entire scrub environment, in addition to his immediate need for money.

Rawlings does not advocate a strict conservationist approach to nature; she suggests there are ways of living that allow for financial profit while still working in accord with the environment. She reintroduces the symbols of the hearth and the kitchen, traditionally coded as feminine but rejected by Piety earlier in the novel, and this time associates them with Lant's primary source of income, his illegal corn liquor still. In several passages, Rawlings describes how the still blends man-made, store-bought components with the nature that surrounds and protects it. The flame that heats the copper kettles is protected by a roof of thatched palm fronds, creating a small kitchen in the midst of the natural beauty of the scrub. The split-rail fences that signify the confinement of the kitchen and the homestead to Piety are replaced by the natural barriers of the creek and thicket, which emphasize continuity with the landscape rather than division from it. His work at the still allows Lant to feel enmeshed in the natural environment: "[H]e liked the blue flame of the burning ash in the black of night, and the orange glow in the sweet-gum leaves. Here he liked the intimacy with the hammock. Its life washed over him and he became a part of it. . . . he and the scrub were one" (224). Again, Lant does not see himself as separate from nature, which would make it only an object or commodity, but he is nonetheless able to responsibly use the environment for monetary gain.

While Rawlings herself was an accomplished cook and gourmet—she even wrote a cookbook based on the cuisine of north central Florida, *Cross Creek Cookery* (1942)—practically the only cooking scenes in this novel describe Lant's recipes and meticulous preparation of moonshine. In the scenes of Lant at his still, Rawlings effectively questions conventional assumptions about gender identity. Does Lant's love of cooking somehow feminize him? Is his desire to commune with nature a masculine trait when hunting yet feminine when cooking? Are his acts of cooking more masculine because of where his kitchen is and what he makes? Is corn liquor more masculine than corn bread?

If fences symbolize the artificial society of the outside world, Rawlings's counterpoint is the river, with its constant motion and its ability to divide and unite simultaneously. As Lant travels on this fluid, living boundary, history and culture seem to disappear and his subjective identity disintegrates into the oneness of the river: "The river flowed interminably but as though without advance. The boy thought that he had been always in this still, liquid place. There was no change. There was no memory and no imagining. The young male restlessness that had begun to stir along his bones was quiet. If Piety and Cleve and Kezzy were really persons, instead of names, they lay drowned behind him. Nothing existed but the brown, clear water, flowing in one spot forever" (164). The very concept of opposites is swallowed up in water that is both brown and clear, always flowing but never advancing. Lant's "young male restlessness" is also subdued on the river, where the duality of gender is washed away. The distinction between male and female in a general sense, and between masculine culture and feminine nature particularly, loses its meaning outside of anthropocentric structures that "lay drowned behind him." Even the ostensibly fundamental split between humanity and nature is fused (at least temporarily) in a denial of nature's essential otherness: "The river flowed, a dream between dreams, and they were all one, the boy and the river and the banks" (165).

In the novel's final chapter, Lant and Kezzy are finally coupled, and Rawlings voices their view of the scrub as free from boundaries and restrictions: "'Man, the scrub's a fine place to be,' she said. 'If things ever gits too thick, you and me jest grab us each a young un and a handful o' shells and the guns and light out acrost it. I'd dare ary man to mess up with me, yonder in the scrub'" (333). The deepest interior of the scrub has never been populated, and much of it has never even been seen by human eyes. Ultimately, then, Lant's remote dwelling on the borders of this wilderness retains something of a pastoral identity as a location between the extremes of culture and nature. However, Rawlings moves this site, both spatially and conceptually, away from a middle state to the very fringes of total wilderness. Its distance and independence from society, she hopes, will allow it to remain a place outside of restrictive anthropocentric dualisms.

Yet we can see Rawlings herself lapsing into such binary patterns, as when she occasionally asserts that the scrub exists independent of human consciousness and impervious to humankind: "It was there, the scrub, immense, aloof and proud, standing on its own ground, making its own conditions, like no other . . . within, it was inviolable" (125). Though she is here rejecting the idea that nature has meaning only through its relation to culture, this claim is inconsistent with the network model of interdependency: it places humans entirely outside the natural. In wanting to show nature as an active participant in the world, she characterizes it as an unknowable "other," similar to traditional Southern pastoral's distinction between the improved garden inside and the dangerous, chaotic nature outside the plantation fences. Rawlings wants to embrace the network model and break down the barriers between self and nature, creating a new type of wilderness pastoral. But her own pastoral ambitions of a retreat from the modern world sometimes show up in the form of the dualistic thinking she tries to combat. In *Cross Creek,* this tendency to waver in her presentation of nature is more significant, but I first want to discuss *The Yearling*, a novel that further grapples with gender issues and questions the viability of the pastoral impulse itself.

Rawlings always maintained, and Max Perkins agreed, that *The Yearling* was not merely a book for boys but, first and foremost, a novel that happened to have a young boy as the main character. In spite of her protests, the book has become nearly exclusively identified with juvenile or adolescent fiction. Despite its coming-of-age theme and sometimes obvious symbolism, I would agree with Rawlings that *The Yearling* should not be read as "merely" a children's book, for it is certainly much more than that, both in intention and execution. There is much to admire in Rawlings's writing, including the pared-down, elemental quality of the narrative, which provides the story with much of its power and intensity. F. Scott Fitzgerald wrote to Perkins that he was fascinated by this instant best seller: "I thought it was even better than 'South Moon Under' and I envy her the ease with which she does those action scenes, such as the tremendously complicated hunt sequence, which I would have to stake off in advance and which would probably turn out to be stilted business in the end. Hers just simply flows."[42]

Rawlings is able to capture the youthful viewpoint of Jody Baxter, who finds wonder in virtually everything new that he encounters, creating a compelling novel for all readers. All of Jody's activities and adventures gain additional significance and poignancy for adult readers who, like Rawlings, empathize with the desire for the "maternal solace of timelessness" represented by the pastoral garden of childhood that we see Jody preparing to leave forever. The wilderness and natural world of *The Yearling* are not, however, employed only as symbols of pastoral refuge from the complexities of the "outside world" of modern society and of adulthood. Rawlings instead shows that the desire for a static garden of the middle landscape, permanently insulated from exterior threats, is a childish wish that must be abandoned in maturity. Yet, to some extent, this novel represents an indulgence of that wish in its avoidance of the larger social issues of the time, illustrating the double-edged character of the pastoral, both complex and sentimental at once.

As in *South Moon Under,* the remote setting provides Rawlings with a place relatively unfettered by artificial, human-imposed restrictions in which to examine issues of gender. Although her first novel employed a female character, Piety, almost as much as the central male figure, Lant, in its explorations of the social construction of gender, *The Yearling* includes only one female character of note, Jody's mother, Ora Baxter, and relegates her to a minor role. This authorial choice is a major factor in the novel being pigeon-holed as a boy's rite of passage story and in Rawlings's exclusion by most critics from the canon of Southern female writers. Rhonda Morris has suggested that because her most acclaimed work does not tell a "woman's story" similar to that of other Southern women's texts, Rawlings has often been overlooked as a constituent of "a female tradition."[43] Morris points out that, in order to achieve the type of critical success she was seeking, Rawlings may have had good reason to eschew ostensibly feminine issues, especially since she was already battling the derisive "regionalist" appellation: "[R]egionalist writing by a woman which explored women's situations seemed destined for critical rejection."[44] As we have seen already, Rawlings was trying to escape her "Songs of the Housewife" days, so it is hardly surprising that she may have assumed that a vigorous, "masculine" style would be more in tune with the critical atmosphere of her day.

I agree with Morris's point that despite a sometimes glaring lack of representations of women in her work, Rawlings merits inclusion in a larger Southern female tradition of writers because she "recognized that gender was not just a self-construction but a social construction" and because she was concerned about the limiting effects of gender roles, particularly on women.[45] Although *The Yearling* focuses on male characters, Jody and his father, Penny, like Lant in *South Moon Under,* reshape traditional notions of masculinity by transgressing conventional societal boundaries of gender identity. By portraying their seemingly feminine maleness as entirely natural—that is, in harmony with their inner selves (with human nature) and with their environment—Rawlings again seeks to subvert the polarizing structures that restrict conceptions of gender to mutually exclusive opposites. The male Baxters share a bond with one another and with their natural environment, but female characters are portrayed as disruptive of male companionship, undermining the stereotype of women as closer to nature.

In the first chapter of *The Yearling*, Penny announces that Jody's propensity for "ramblin," abandoning his work and his mother's authority in order to play in a nearby glen, is a sure sign of masculinity: "Most women-folks cain't see for their lives, how a man loves so to ramble."[46] Less obvious as a sign of adolescent male identity is Jody's intense longing for "something with dependence to it" (98), after seeing the numerous semiwild pets of his friend Fodder-wing Forrester. When Jody finally gets his wish, it is because Penny has been bitten by a rattlesnake and killed a fawn's mother in order to use her liver to suck the poison from his body and save his own life. Still unsure if his father will survive, Jody is driven by guilt to find the fawn that has already lost his primary parent. This desire to nurture the deer has been read as a maternal instinct, but it is also Jody's attempt to imitate the behavior of his caring father.[47]

Jody clearly feels a closer kinship with his father than his mother, who "was outside the good male understanding" (199), and on the night of the rattlesnake attack, Jody does not even remember the orphaned deer in the woods until he first imagines his father's death: "He could not help but feel a greater security here beside his father, than in the stormy night. Many things, he realized, would be terrible alone that were not terrible when he was with Penny" (159).[48] Consequently, remembering the fawn alone in the woods, hovering near its mother's carcass, Jody cries himself to sleep and has a "tortuous dream" of battling a gigantic rattlesnake that is slithering over the bloated corpse of his father. When the snake and Penny suddenly vanish, Jody is standing "alone in a vast windy place, holding the fawn in his arms" (160). Faced with the prospect of losing his father, Jody recognizes a counterpoint in the abandoned, grieving fawn.

Upon retrieving the fawn from the woods, Jody feels he can possess the deer (named Flag by Fodder-wing) and thus ensure its constant companionship: "It belonged to him. It was his own" (171). This belief that humans can own nature (because they are outside or above it) is one that Rawlings critiques throughout her writing, and in this context, she reveals the idea as a childish fantasy. The lesson is a harsh one for Jody, who learns that he cannot control the deer's behavior any more than he can the weather.[49] When

Flag's destruction of crops threatens the Baxter family's survival, the yearling must be killed. However, it is not the seemingly climactic act of killing his pet that symbolically ushers Jody into adulthood. Rather, it is the entire experience of caring for and nurturing the animal until its death as well as Jody's reaction to the shooting, which signify that the boy is "moving into that mystic company" of men (201).

Rawlings is able to include values of caring and nurturing in her definition of Jody's manhood without stigmatizing them as stereotypically feminine attributes because she incorporates those same qualities in the character of Penny, Jody's model of masculinity. John Lowe describes Rawlings's construction of masculinity in a way that highlights her combination of opposites: "Penny and Jody will demonstrate and sometimes discuss modes of masculine behavior that involve toughening, stoicism, bravery, and silence. On the other hand, these scenes are always balanced by ensuing ones that provide for the development of sympathy, loyalty, gentleness, and respect. Rawlings, more so than any other woman writer of her time, appears to understand the ambiguous nature of American manhood—how the world insists on one quality one minute and its opposite the next." Similarly, Carol Anita Tarr describes Penny as "kind, sympathetic, strong [and] ecology-minded,"[50] and Rawlings portrays him as a doting, nurturing father and an expert woodsman. Penny tolerates his son's frivolity during working time, delivers a heartfelt eulogy when Jody's friend Fodder-wing dies, visits regularly an elderly friend, Grandma Hutto, who lives across the river, and refuses to use poison to kill a pack of marauding wolves because it "jest someway ain't natural" (287) and might harm other, innocent animals. Rawlings also demonstrates repeatedly that Penny is more than equal to the rough-and-tumble Forrester men when it comes to marksmanship, hunting, fighting, and trading, traditionally more masculine endeavors. Rawlings seems deliberate in her efforts to create in Penny a strong male character who is also a sensitive, loving parent. I would not say that Rawlings feminizes Penny because I think what she is doing in *The Yearling*, as well as in *South Moon Under*, is insisting on the need for revising, if not abolishing, the limited (and limiting) conceptions of gender that have come to seem natural because they are so institutionalized.

Jody's final adventure of the novel occurs on the river as he determines to flee his home after he kills Flag. He plans to head to Boston to pursue a romanticized vision of life at sea with the older friend he idolizes, Oliver Hutto. Unlike the river scenes in *South Moon Under* and *Cross Creek*, the water does not provide solace or liberation, but it is still a place where the certainty of fixed categories disintegrates. In the aftermath of Flag's death, Jody sees only that his father has betrayed him, undermining the sense of safety and order Jody associates with home: "Without Penny, there was no comfort anywhere. The solid earth had dissolved under him" (415). As Jody paddles a small canoe toward the middle of Lake George in search of a passenger ship that will pick him up, the vast expanse of water symbolizes the terrifying and solitary world of adulthood: "He was out in the world, and it seemed to him that he was alien here, and alone, and that he was being carried away into a void. . . . the open water seemed to stretch without an end" (416–17). Jody's panic increases as the waves intensify and his canoe starts taking on water, and he madly paddles back to the relative comfort of the shoreline.

Finally exhausted and weakened by hunger, Jody faints and is plucked from the lake by a passing government ship. The crew members scoff at his plan to travel to Boston, and the captain's patronizing dismissal of him as only a child conflicts with Jody's notion that he has already entered the company of men: "Well, if I was a scrawny little big-eyed booger like you, I'd stay home. Nobody but your folks'll bother with a little ol' shirt-tail boy like you. Swing him down to the dock, Joe" (420–21). And with that, Jody is lifted like a baby back onto solid ground. Chastened by his experiences, Jody heads for home, but he realizes that nothing will be the same again. Baxter's Island is no longer an idyllic haven from the rest of the world, but a place where Jody must assume the responsibilities of his incapacitated father. Penny explains to his son that uncertainty and doubt—like that felt by Jody on the fluid currents of the river—are permanent features of life.

Most significant for Jody is his experience with real hunger, as he goes days with nothing to eat on his circular journey. His hunger connects his home to the world at large, disabusing him of his childhood conception that "Baxter's Island was an island of plenty in a hungry sea" (142). He understands that Flag's destruction of their food supply is a serious threat to their survival: "This was what his mother had meant when she had said, 'We'll all go hongry.' He had laughed, for he had thought he had known hunger, [but] . . . it had been only appetite. This was another thing" (418). Jody feels that the trial of his trip and his acceptance of his duty to return home confirm his entry into the adult world. But as his condescending treatment at the hands of the sailors shows, his status as child or adult also depends on external social constructions of those categories.

The close affinity he feels with Flag from the time of his dream about the helpless fawn introduces the reality of death to Jody's idyllic world and exemplifies a literary tradition of associating children with animals. Children's literature critic Karin Lesnik-Oberstein, who traces the modern invention of this idea of the child as truly natural to John Locke and Jean-

Jacques Rousseau, explains that the concepts of "child" and "nature" are related "through their joint construction as the essential, the unconstructed, spontaneous and uncontaminated."[51] The linking of children and animals in children's and other literature reinforces the assumption that both the "child" and the "natural" are outside of language, history, and culture. Although Lesnik-Oberstein notes that children's books participate in "a fundamental and crucial resistance" to the idea that the "child" and the "natural" are "constructed, variable and changeable discourses,"[52] *The Yearling* explores the possibility that these categories are not necessarily any less socially constructed than gender roles. Setting up Jody and the deer as counterparts (a pair of yearlings), Rawlings demonstrates the mutability of Jody's identity as a child and the fawn's as a wild animal.

Jody's transition to manhood is not effected by a single rite, but by his assumption of adult roles that require responsibility. As Penny recovers from the snakebite, Buck Forrester does most of the labor around the Baxter house. Jody assists with some of the "man's work" that must be done, but he also has time to revert to playing games with Flag. Thus, the circumstances of his society—basically, a one-family society in the remote wilderness—compel a repeated switching of roles from carefree child to adult laborer. Penny knows that childhood is not necessarily a natural state since "he himself had had no boyhood" (16). His strict father and poor family had necessitated that he work on his parents' farm as soon as he could walk. Economic conditions precluded a "natural" childhood, and he therefore works himself to the point of exhaustion to create a "proper" childhood for Jody. When Penny is incapacitated by rheumatism and an apparent hernia from the strain of his constant labor, Jody is forced to assume a more adult role. The boundary between child and adult is not definitively crossed through ritual hunting or the passing of a ceremonial birthday, but by a redefinition or shifting of one's status and roles in a social group.

Both Jody and Flag are "betwixt and between" childhood and adulthood, "like a person standin' on the state line . . . leavin' one and turnin' into t'other" (380). That is, the passage from one state to the other is not a single, irreversible movement, but one that can be undone and repeated, like Flag jumping the fences meant to keep him out of the family's crops. After Flag first destroys a crop of newly planted corn, Jody works tirelessly to raise the height of the split-rail fence to six feet in order to keep the yearling from destroying the food supply. Although the fences have been successful in keeping other animals out, Flag's identity has been reconstructed by his inclusion in the family and he is "betwixt and between" a pet and a wild animal. Even after the fence has been raised, Flag playfully leaps the boundary at will and

eats the neat rows of crops rather than forage in the forest as his "natural"
instinct should compel. Ordered to shoot Flag, Jody makes a final appeal to
Pa Forrester, who agrees that the deer must be shot. Thinking that "he had
not made the matter clear," Jody tries to invoke the "natural" connection between animals and children to elicit a different response: "Supposin' it was
a yearlin' you loved like you-all loved Fodder-wing?" Pa Forrester's response
shows that rigid conceptions of love and naturalness have no place in this
demanding wilderness setting: "Why, love's got nothin' to do with corn. You
cain't have a thing eatin' the crops" (406).

The wilderness is not a foreign entity nor is it necessarily hostile; it is
a home that can be unforgiving to all its residents, human or otherwise.
Jody's childhood conception of Baxter's Island is of a "fortress ringed around
with hunger" (43) or a safe refuge from the perils of the outside world, quite
similar to the traditional pastoral ideal of an orderly, simple refuge from both
the chaotic wilderness and the complex city. However, Rawlings equates this
ideal with childish naïveté as Jody comes to realize that his home is inseparable from the hunger, destruction, and death of the world at large. Growing up necessitates the assumption of a place in the complex, interdependent
network of nature, which entails conflicting allegiances and difficult deci-
sions. To view Flag as a pet is to place oneself outside of nature, as a master
of it. Jody's recognition that he is a part of a natural ecosystem is depicted as
a part of his maturation into a man with a responsible environmental ethic.
Rawlings shows that, despite its occasional harshness, this natural community provides for its members in ways that Depression-era American society
may not. Wolves prey on the weakest animals, buzzards recycle the carcass of
Flag's mother, Penny takes honey from beehives but leaves enough for "their
own winter store" (181), and families find a use for every part of the animals
they kill (274). As Lowe says of the novel, "Over and again, however, out of
death comes life."[53]

Similarly, out of the destruction of nature can come a bond with nature,
knowing it intimately through the sort of close contact that only living off
and with the land can inspire. Things are destroyed and killed in nature in-
cessantly, but they are also reused, recycled, and regenerated, especially in
the context of the network model of nature that pervades the ecopastorals
of this time period. Although it may be difficult to say just where responsible
use ends and wanton destruction begins, the network model (and the pastoral ideal of balance) suggests that there is a tipping point when too much
is taken out and not enough put back in. The lumber companies in *South
Moon Under* and in Faulkner's *Go Down, Moses,* as well as the farmers in *Tobacco Road,* take all that they can from the natural environment without re-

turning anything. Hurston, especially in *Seraph on the Suwanee* (discussed in the next chapter), makes it difficult to tell just when that line between exploitative and sensible work in nature has been crossed. The protagonists of Rawlings's ecopastorals, though, tend to exemplify responsible and ethical work in nature while still making a living (even a profit) for themselves and their families.

Penny is Jody's teacher, and Rawlings links his instruction about how to read nature's signs to his modeling of responsible masculinity. Penny is acknowledged by the locals as an expert tracker and hunter, so his ability to interpret nature lends authority to his version of masculinity. As in *South Moon Under,* Rawlings uses a wilderness setting and the network model of nature to reimagine traditionally limited conceptions of gender, making uncivilized nature a landscape of freedom and change. Although *Cross Creek,* her semifictional, semiautobiographical memoir, does not return to gender as a major theme, it does offer Rawlings's most explicit affirmation of the advantages this isolated, "natural" community has over the "artificial" society from which she has fled. In this sense, *Cross Creek* is an indulgence of the pastoral impulse she depicts as immature in *The Yearling.* More so than her novels, *Cross Creek* reveals how moving the pastoral location to the wilderness does not mean that the traditional pastoral mode is completely left behind. Yet the book also contains some of her most impassioned and eloquent pleas for the need to allow the self to be subsumed into a greater web of life, thus rejecting traditional pastoral configurations of humans as essentially outside of nature.

Rawlings explains in the book's opening that the lack of a significant human population in "the Creek" creates a more harmonious community than those of crowded towns and cities: "We know one another. Our knowledge is a strange kind, totally without intimacy, for we go our separate ways and meet only when new fences are strung, or some one's stock intrudes on another, or when one of us is ill or in trouble. . . . And when the great enemies of Old Starvation and Old Death come skulking down on us, we put up a united front and fight them side by side" (4–5). Even the simple gesture of using "we" unself-consciously to speak for the Creek residents is a sign of how much Rawlings felt accepted as a part of this community after living there for barely a decade.[54] She suggests that their immersion in nature engenders the cooperative spirit possessed by her and her neighbors. Feeling an intimate, personal connection with the lives of the plants and animals with which they coexist daily seems to foster a kinship among the human inhabitants that is somehow lost in the primarily human realm: "I am often lonely. Who is not? But I should be lonelier in the heart of a city" (5). Loneliness is impossible,

Rawlings says, when one conceives of nature not as an always foreign "other," but as a network of relations of which the self is an integral part, as she illustrates in a ruminative passage that closes the introductory section of *Cross Creek:*

> Folk call the road lonely, because there is not human traffic and human stirring. Because I have walked it so many times and seen such a tumult of life there, it seems to me one of the most populous highways of my acquaintance. I have walked it in ecstasy, and in joy it is beloved. Every pine tree, every gallberry bush, every passion vine, every joree rustling in the underbrush, is vibrant. I have walked it in trouble, and the wind in the trees beside me is easing. I have walked it in despair, and the red of the sunset is my own blood dissolving into the night's darkness. For all such things were on earth before us, and will survive after us, and it is given to us to join ourselves with them and to be comforted. (6)

Rawlings apparently feels that the majority of the "civilized" human population has lost this connection and become alienated from nature. Her recipe for reintegration with "the cosmic life" entails lowering the barriers between self and other until one knows "that Life is vital, and one's own minute living a torn fragment of the larger cloth" (39).

An interesting and important consequence of such an interdependent conception of the world is an implicit critique of the commodification of nature and of capitalism in general. Radical geographer David Harvey astutely summarizes the connection in *Justice, Nature and the Geography of Difference:* "[P]ursuit of monetary valuations commits us to a thoroughly Cartesian-Newtonian-Lockeian and in some respects 'anti-ecological' ontology of how the natural world is constituted. If we construe the world, in the manner of deep ecology, as networks or fields of relations in which things participate and from which they cannot be isolated, then the money valuation of things in themselves becomes impossible."[55] Seen in this light, Rawlings's exclusion of virtually any reference in her fiction to life outside the Florida scrub and its surrounding hamlets is perhaps not only the avoidance of the discord of modern society, as she herself claims. Her deliberate isolation is also a tool for portraying a self-sufficient world that is more or less impervious to the rise of capitalism and industrialism and their itinerant boom and bust cycles that dominated the lives of millions of Americans in the 1920s, '30s, and '40s. While the reality is that Cross Creek was not as untouched by the outside world as we might surmise from her writing, Rawlings consciously chooses to portray it as such by depicting traditional and

timeless activities—like hunting, fishing, cooking, and farming—to the exclusion of practically all else.

However, Rawlings's portrait of this community as self-sufficient and in-
sular is at odds with the network model of interdependency promulgated
elsewhere in *Cross Creek, South Moon Under,* and *The Yearling.* It is as if she
wants to have it both ways: an interdependent network within this remote
community but without any ties to the world outside the boundaries of this
pastoral retreat. The "confusion" and "discord" that Rawlings associates with
the "outside" world do, in fact, infiltrate the pages of *Cross Creek* despite her
attempts to suppress them. The residents of the Creek and the scrub cross
the river boundaries all the time to obtain goods and socialize in town. Rawlings wants to use the Creek's isolation as a guarantor of its difference from
the town, but the network model she employs subverts the text's claims of
self-sufficiency in this case. Returning to Martyn Lee's terms, social processes cannot be divorced from human agency and spatial location. The connections are there and, as I will discuss a bit later, they sometimes reveal the
Creek's society to be just as hierarchical as the "artificial," modern world that
Rawlings is fleeing.

The episodes and anecdotes of *Cross Creek* are held together by the strong
sense of place that Rawlings conveys by vividly detailing the life around her,
animal and plant as well as human. For example, a chapter that describes
many of the quirky, eccentric people who live at the Creek is followed by
one that gives equally nuanced and compelling portraits of the wide variety
of animals that populate this environment. Throughout the book, Rawlings
displays an intimate knowledge of the plant life, from detailed descriptions
of individual species to explanations of four different types of Florida hammock, a junglelike terrain distinct from the piney woods scrub country. An
entire chapter on food, "Our Daily Bread," illustrates how the residents of the
Creek, both human and animal, eat and use nearly everything around them,
illustrating a web of interdependencies wherein the deaths of some creatures
sustain the lives of others.

The notions of relative value and cooperation are established by the text
as natural and then applied to human behavior as a way of asserting the superiority of life at the Creek to the rest of American society. Introducing a
discussion of ants and her nagging desire "to exterminate the last one" of
these pests, Rawlings pauses to consider the philosophical implications of
her own longing for ant genocide and of the ants' unyielding pursuit of every available scrap of food: "In a still predatory world, good and evil are not
fixed values, but are relative. 'Good' is what helps us or at least does not hin-
der. 'Evil' is whatever harms us, or interferes with us, according to our own

selfish standards" (151). Rawlings's wish to exterminate the ants that interfere with her is not "evil" nor "antiecological," to use Harvey's term, because the complex fields of relations that constitute the natural world render such absolute values and rigid dichotomies artificial, insofar as they are human constructions not reflective of how nature "actually" works.

A few paragraphs after the ant discussion, Rawlings extends this line of reasoning, explaining the danger of assuming mastery over nature in the pursuit of self-interest. The "old-timers," she says, have learned from extensive experience not to spray the orange groves in order to kill "unfriendly parasites" because the "friendly" ones (those that kill the unfriendly ones) are often wiped out as well. Acting purely out of short-term self-interest, it seems, is as likely to be harmful as helpful to one's own interests, as well as to those of others. This same principle is evident in the custom Rawlings describes of taking only half of the turtle eggs from the nests that the locals raid for these regional delicacies. When Rawlings's aunt comes for a visit, they go quail hunting and Aunt Wilmer is appalled at the killing of the "darling" birds. Rawlings explains that sensible hunting—using what one kills as opposed to wanton slaughtering—can actually benefit the quail population: " 'It's really not so frightful to shoot them,' I told her, 'for if a covey isn't shot into and broken up, it stays together and the quail don't mate that year' " (320). The workings of the natural world allow Rawlings to recognize the subjectivity of categories like good and evil, the same thinking she applies to traditionally fixed conceptions of gender identity in her novels, presenting a changeable, relative view of gender as a more natural alternative.

Cooperation among neighbors is another important manifestation of the network model, and the book is rife with examples of neighbors going to extraordinary lengths to help one another. Rawlings lends her car to those who need to go to town, pays lunch money for children whose families cannot afford to, and arranges for medical care for sick neighbors, driving into town to bring the doctor and paying the bill afterward. She is given extra meat from hunting trips, antique furniture, and other possessions from people with little to call their own, and, most important for a single woman running an orange grove, countless hours of labor. When she is out of town on a hunting trip, one of her neighbors even takes it upon himself to work all night protecting Rawlings's newly planted Valencia trees from an unexpected freeze, saving the entire orchard. Compared to the competition for resources depicted in *Tobacco Road*, this mutual network of support is a healthier and more natural mode of existence, along the lines of Alfred North Whitehead's description of the benefits of a forest to a tree: "A single tree by itself is dependent upon all the adverse chances of shifting circumstances. . . . But in nature the normal way in which trees flourish is by their association in a forest. . . . A forest is the triumph of the organisation of mutually dependent species."[56]

The sharing of resources does not mean the abolishment of private property. The denizens of the Creek still pride themselves on self-reliance, and they maintain private ownership of their possessions; by custom and consent, neighbors freely borrow items for indefinite periods and they repay each other by whatever means and in whatever amount they can, creating a sort of middle ground between communal and private property. Rawlings writes of gasoline disappearing from her truck and tools being taken from her barn, explaining that "this is only because some man needs a shovel and a shovel is available." Although she is often repaid with a gift of frogs' legs or an offer of free labor, Rawlings pointedly describes this borrow and trade system as eminently natural: "This seems no more predatory than the taking of fallen timber from the open woods, the drinking of water from a stranger's well." In this sense, the social network exemplifies Robert McElvaine's definition of cooperative individualism, as opposed to the acquisitive individualism that many people felt was a major cause of the Great Depression. Outside the ruthless capitalist system in the pastoral haven of Cross Creek, the cooperative system is not only better for people, but it also makes people better: "The evil and dishonorable . . . do not stay long at the Creek, for we are too busy to be bothered with neighbors we cannot trust. We leave our houses wide open. I sleep alone in my rambling farmhouse with never the latching of a door, and I am away for weeks at a time, with the place as free of access as a public picnic ground" (123).

Thus, Rawlings uses the Creek's independence from a money economy to emphasize its distance from modern society as well as to critique the competitive acquisitiveness of that world according to more pure and natural standards. However, paying people in scrip or with commissary credits are not cash systems, either. Sharecropping (with labor traded for goods and often no cash changing hands) is a sort of barter system, too, but that does not necessarily mean that these exploitative arrangements are more natural. Of course, one might point out that parasitic relationships are natural ones, too, but that is not the type of natural system Rawlings wants to portray. At a time when farmers were being paid by the Agricultural Adjustment Administration to plow under their crops and food sat rotting in warehouses while millions went hungry, this trading among neighbors in need is presented as a more efficient, but also morally superior, way to utilize resources. The simplicity of the Creek's trade and barter economy, what Rawlings describes as an "elemental exchange of goods" (97), would also seem to imply a less stratified, more egalitarian social structure. As Leo Marx says of the pastoral, "[T]he absence of economic complexities makes credible the absence of their usual concomitant, a class structure."[57] Yet this does not always turn out to be the case, as the class- and race-based hierarchies of the "outside" world occasionally disrupt the idyllic picture that Rawlings paints.

Rawlings, the Brices, and the Glissons, along with a couple of other white families who are peripheral to *Cross Creek,* form the upper echelon of the tiny community. Rawlings interacts mostly with these families and has relatively few dealings with the poor whites of the area. J. T. Glisson writes in his own memoir that, aside from the four families who lived closest to her, "Mrs. Rawlings had little contact with most of the Crackers, having set herself apart from them by displaying an air of intellectual and social superiority."[58] Martha and Will Mickens are the heads of the Creek's extended black family, and Rawlings describes "Aunt Martha" as "a dusky Fate, spinning away at the threads of our Creek existence" (17), a testament to her central role in both the community and Rawlings's book. As Carolyn Jones has shown, one's position in this social hierarchy creates "levels of responsibility and obligation, but in a nuanced way that Rawlings had trouble grasping."[59]

The most telling example is Rawlings's failure in dealing with a poor white couple, Tim and "Tim's wife," who live in her ramshackle tenant house. When Tim's wife complains that the poor condition of the house prevents her from keeping "the antses outen Tim's breakfast" (66), Rawlings is puzzled. She writes that she would learn only later that poor people cook only once or twice a day "and the previous evening's biscuits and greens and fat bacon were set aside for the early breakfast." More important, she fails to recognize the implied responsibilities of a landlord to her tenants in this rural culture: "I did not yet understand that in this way of life one is obliged to share, back and forth, and that as long as I had money for screens and a new floor, I was morally obligated to put out a portion of it to give some comfort to those who worked for me." As in the larger society from which Cross Creek is ostensibly separate and outside, class and race hierarchies are bound together. Rawlings violates this order by asking Tim if his wife will do her washing. "A white woman don't ask another white woman to do her washin' for her, nor to carry her slops" (67), Tim replies, implying that even though they are poor, the couple is at least better than blacks. As Jones says of this incident: "What Tim reminds Rawlings of is that whiteness confirms his and his wife's humanity. . . . Rawlings cannot romanticize them into her vision of unity of person and place."[60]

Building on Jones's analysis, I would point out that the ants invading the house are an odd combination of nature and culture. The holes in the tenant house allow nature to come right in, but the blend is not a harmonious one because of class. While Rawlings perhaps can afford to romanticize bonding with nature as the owner of a seventy-four-acre orange grove, her tenants have a different experience. As people who must work the land for a living, nature is not some alienated concept which, when encountered, inspires rapturous feelings of awe and transcendent communion. In fact, Rawlings's treatment of her tenants is quite conventionally pastoral in the sense that it effaces the role of those whose labor maintains the garden, as was often the case with slave labor in nineteenth-century Southern pastoral works. The difference for Rawlings is that she is aware of her transgression, and she admits using Tim's wife as the basis for characters in two other novels in an effort to assuage her conscience: "The woman came to me in my dreams and tormented me. . . . Now I know that she will haunt me as long as I live, and all the writing in the world will not put away the memory of her face and the sound of her voice" (68).

Race proves to be another disruptive category, one that is not easily assimilated into Rawlings's attempt at a revised pastoral vision. Like class, race stratifies the community that Rawlings wants to portray as more fluid, egalitarian, and natural than its urban counterparts. At times in *Cross Creek* Rawlings asserts that racial differences should be attributed to economic and social factors rather than to essentialist assumptions about the "natural" inferiority of African Americans, similar to her critique of gender in *South Moon Under*. However, her racial views fluctuate (within the book as well as over her lifetime), and there is never a sustained critique of societal racial norms approximating her challenges to gender roles. This is precisely the type of complicated issue that Rawlings refers to in her term "the confusion of our generation" and that she claims to want to avoid in her writing. Accordingly, the first sentence of the somewhat ominously titled chapter "Black Shadows" is a disclaimer to the reader: "I am not of the race of southerners who claim to understand the Negro" (180).

Overall, Rawlings appears genuinely puzzled by questions of race, and she cannot see black equality as a "natural" condition. She claims not "to understand the Negro," then asserts that the stereotypical depictions by whites of "Negroes" as "childish, carefree, religious, untruthful and unreliable" seem to her "reasonably accurate." However, these are only "superficial truths," she says, employed as necessary "defense mechanism[s]" in an unjust system that further obscure "the mystery of the primitive African nature." Continuing this vacillating line of thought, Rawlings claims that the "mental and emotional turmoil" of African Americans is "past the comprehension" of white

Southerners, but almost immediately she concludes that "only in rare instances can a Negro work for long on his own initiative" (181), although this, too, she attributes to economic and social oppression.[61]

Rawlings uses the term "nigger" in several letters written in the 1930s, but the term gradually disappears from even her most private letters. In a 1942 letter, she describes her meeting with Zora Neale Hurston at the hotel owned by Rawlings's second husband, Norton Baskin, and praises her fellow Floridian's "ingratiating personality," "brilliant mind," and "fundamental wisdom that shames most whites." This letter is written, oddly enough, using the persona of Rawlings's dog, Moe, who is writing to Patrie, the dog of her friend Norman Berg. Perhaps seeking some ironic distance from which to criticize her own ambivalent racial attitudes, Rawlings has Moe chastise her lack of conviction, apparently referring to Hurston using the back stairs, rather than the front elevator, of the segregated hotel in St. Augustine: "The Missus has had quite a jolt and feels rather small. By all her principles, she should accept this woman as a human being and a friend—certainly an attractive member of society acceptable anywhere—and she is a coward. If she were on her own, she would do it. She feels that she cannot hurt her husband in a business way. But her pioneer blood is itching."[62] Interestingly, she seems to suggest that in St. Augustine (in the city, that is) racial prejudice is more difficult to fight than it is back in the wilderness, where, presumably, her "pioneer blood" would be free to treat Hurston more naturally/equally, free of the pressures of the city society. However, Idella Parker, one of Rawlings's maids, describes how when Hurston visited Cross Creek, she had to sleep in the maid's cabin, sharing a bed with Parker despite two empty bedrooms in the main house: "As liberal and understanding as Mrs. Rawlings was about the poor treatment of blacks by whites, she couldn't bring herself to let a black woman sleep in her house."[63]

Regardless of her private professions, in *Cross Creek* Rawlings's racial attitudes are more akin to the paternalistic stance of the plantation school of Southern pastoral. She blithely writes of "buying" a young, black girl for $5 and of her difficulties in training blacks to be "servants." She explains that "for all of Lincoln," the white/black relationship is still one of master/slave (181) and that she could never hire a white woman as a maid because she would have to treat her more as an equal than a servant (329). It is Martha Mickens, however, who often seems to be the central character of *Cross Creek*, "a dusky Fate" weaving together its disjointed, episodic structure. Although Rawlings would later claim that she had exaggerated Mickens's role, Carolyn Jones notes the numerous times that Rawlings attributes her own knowledge of the natural environment to Martha.[64] Of course, positioning Martha as an interpreter of nature brings Rawlings perilously close to the stereotype of blacks as somehow closer to nature, a facet of the type of pastoral she is elsewhere at pains to subvert and revise. Rawlings wants to present a "natural" community where differences are erased, but racial and class hierarchies find their way into the text anyway. She winds up showing inadvertently in *Cross Creek* what was explicit and intentional in *The Yearling:* the pastoral desire for a sanctuary isolated from the rest of the world is a naïve and futile one.

In the book's final two chapters, Rawlings is able to elide the divisions of class and race through images of ego effacement in nature and by employing a cosmic perspective that asserts a generalized unity of all life. For example, she summarizes her contention that simple binary oppositions fail to account for the dynamism and fluidity she witnesses in nature: "All life is a balance, when it is not a battle, between the forces of creation and the forces of destruction, between love and hate, between life and death. Perhaps it is impossible ever to say where one ends and the other begins, for even creation and destruction are relative" (364). There are other instances in the book where Rawlings asserts the relativity of the boundaries of selfhood. When the connections she feels to the vitality in nature around her are particularly strong, it becomes difficult to say where she ends and the world begins. Rather than feeling frightened at the prospect of the negation of her individual identity, Rawlings feels comforted by the almost tangible connection she experiences with an eternal natural world. It is useful to quote a rather lengthy passage from early in the book, prompted by Rawlings's encounter with a wild pig and her newborn litter, which exemplifies these sentiments:

> The jungle hammock breathed. Life went through the moss-hung forest, the swamp, the cypresses, through the wild sow and her young, through me, in its continuous chain. We were all one with the silent pulsing. This was the thing that was important, the cycle of life, with birth and death merging one into the other in an imperceptible twilight and an insubstantial dawn. The universe breathed, and the world inside it breathed the same breath. This was the cosmic life, with suns and moons to make it lovely. It was important only to keep close enough to the pulse to feel its rhythm, to be comforted by its steadiness, to know that Life is vital, and one's own minute living a torn fragment of the larger cloth. (39)

This sublime moment does not result from the traditional awe-inspiring mountain or castle of Burkean aesthetics, but from the sight of helpless, infant pigs discovering their mother's teats for the first time. This rather domestic, even mundane, image is the catalyst for a more general, transcendent knowledge about the oneness of the world. For Rawlings, the temporary loss of her subjective self in the cosmic unity of her natural environment allows a stronger self to emerge with a clearer understanding of the permeable boundary between life and death, imperceptible twilight and insubstantial dawn, self and other.

In the penultimate chapter of *Cross Creek,* the well-known "Hyacinth Drift," Rawlings again demonstrates the necessity of loss, echoing the theme of life coming from death in *The Yearling.* The chapter begins with Rawlings confessing, "Once I lost touch with the Creek. . . . I loved the Creek, I loved the grove, I loved the shabby farmhouse. Suddenly they were nothing" (342). Immersed in depression, Rawlings agrees to go with her friend Dessie Smith on a several-hundred-mile river trip in her small boat. At one point, the pair becomes lost in a labyrinth of false channels, the water obscured by countless floating hyacinths. Unable to navigate with the map and compass, they rest for the night and in the morning simultaneously realize that, by turning off the motor, they can follow the drift of the hyacinths along the channel they had lost. Rawlings must abandon her map, compass, and motor in the same way that Ike McCaslin relinquishes his gun, watch, and compass in order to find Old Ben the bear in *Go Down, Moses.* In both instances, an intuitive natural knowledge reveals what the implements of culture and technology cannot. Rawlings comments that, when they floated away on the current, "we gave ourselves over to it. . . . The strangeness of flowing water was gone, for it was all there was of living." Reflecting on her complete immersion in nature, where the difficulties of life that spurred the trip have completely disappeared, Rawlings is able to recognize transcendent truth: "Like all simple facts, it was necessary to discover it for oneself" (347).[65]

Returning home, Rawlings rediscovers her affinity with the place of Cross Creek that she had felt was lost. The chapter's opening sentiments that "the Creek was torture" and "life was a nightmare" (343) are transfigured in the closing paragraph to "[t]he Creek was home" and "the only nightmare is the masochistic human mind." The encounter with the sow and her young allows Rawlings to merge her identity with the life around her so that she might find a stronger self. Similarly, in "Hyacinth Drift," Rawlings loses her deep attachment to the Creek and her conception of that place as "home" only to rediscover those feelings with more intensity upon her return: "[W]hen the dry ground was under us, the world no longer fluid, I found a forgotten loveliness in all the things that have nothing to do with men. . . . Oleanders were sweet past bearing, and my own shabby fields, weed-tangled, were newly dear" (358).

The "Hyacinth Drift" episode represents a mini pastoral retreat in itself: a withdrawal into nature that permits a clearer vision upon return. Implicitly at least, Rawlings acknowledges that the "outside" world is always present in the pastoral locale. The pastoral mode has always been a means of criticizing and reforming the society from which one retreats: "In the best of pastoral literature, the writer will have taken the reader on a journey to be changed and charged upon return for more informed action in the present."[66] In the structure of *Cross Creek,* Rawlings returns from the "Hyacinth Drift" journey with insights to challenge readers' perceptions and assumptions in the book's final chapter. Her cosmic perspective challenges the centrality of humans in the world and encourages readers to view the natural world, and hence the entire world, differently.

Rawlings employs the pastoral pattern of retreat and return but with an important revision. Rather than returning from nature better equipped to directly critique and reform the culture of the city, Rawlings keeps the focus on nature:

> Who owns Cross Creek? The red-birds I think, more than I. . . . And after I am dead . . . a long line of red-birds and whippoorwills and blue-jays and ground doves will descend from the present owners of nests in the orange trees, and their claim will be less subject to dispute than that of any human heirs. . . . It seems to me that the earth may be borrowed but not bought. It may be used, but not owned. It gives itself in response to love and tending, offers its seasonal flowering and fruiting. But we are tenants and not possessors, lovers and not masters. Cross Creek belongs to the wind and the rain, to the sun and the seasons, to the cosmic secrecy of seed, and beyond all, to time. (368)

The natural is given primacy in the book's conclusion, swallowing up the cultural in an almost complete reversal of Caldwell's vision. *The Yearling* uses a similar strategy in its reversal of the pastoral retreat and return. Jody leaves his wilderness home and ventures into the outside world of the city and modern society, only to return with a more chastened and wiser view of both the natural and cultural realms. Indeed, for Rawlings nature and culture are nearly always intertwined, each informing the other. Of course, the blending of nature and culture is a staple of the pastoral tradition, but Rawlings revises the pastoral mode in important ways to suit her own purposes.

Shifting the pastoral site to the wilderness is central to Rawlings's reformulation of traditional pastoral gender roles. Whereas Caldwell maintained continuity with the pastoral tradition of gendering nature as female, Rawlings refuses to do so. She also rejects passive versions of nature and women in favor of active ones, constructing a dynamic natural environment that makes fluid definitions of gender a natural alternative to the artificially limited designations she associates with the "outside" world. Thus, identification with nature becomes an empowering association for women, an important revision to the male-dominated pastoral tradition of the South. Rawlings's revision of masculinity is equally compelling for its inclusion of tolerance, humility, nurturing, and respect in an environmentally conscious portrait of manhood.

Rivers play an important role in Rawlings's work as fluid and permeable boundaries where rigid distinctions melt away. The fluidity and freedom of the river are extended to all of the natural world, and Rawlings associates those qualities with an alternative vision of society wherein an individual's status is relative and fluid, rather than absolute and fixed, and wherein values of cooperation, nurturing, and sharing supplement the principles of domination, independence, and progress, traditionally coded as masculine. Life at the Creek exhibits these values because of its isolation from mainstream society and its proximity to unspoiled nature. All three of the works examined in this chapter present numerous instances of residents uniting temporarily for a common cause: protecting orange groves from frost, caring for sick neighbors, building fences, hunting wolves or bears preying on livestock, and even enforcing their own brand of justice on one of their own who has done wrong.

What emerges is a portrait of an organic community, aligned with nature and loosely knit enough to incorporate aspects of the larger, external society without losing its core of individualism. A prime example of McElvaine's notion of the "cooperative individualism" that the American middle class was attracted to during the Depression, this banding together to survive in a natural setting also suggests that a harsh environment need not be seen as hostile. In this case, the challenges of nature produce and foster the cooperative spirit of this community of individuals. Rawlings implies that the external, larger culture can learn from this type of community, in the same ways that the community of her wilderness pastoral learns from the natural world itself. In times of crisis, Rawlings shows people pulling together rather than turning on one another in violent competition for limited resources. Nature, then, is both a model of a network of mutual interdependencies and a force that necessitates such cooperation in the first place (through storms, droughts, freezes, wolves, etc.).

Nature is complex in Rawlings's wilderness pastoral, a radical departure from the pastoral of Simms and Page, for whom the simple, primitive countryside was an antidote to the complexity of the city. Glen Love writes about a shift in the pastoral experience and in popular conceptions of nature in the 1970s and 1980s in response to increased environmental concern: "If the key terms for relatively untrammeled nature in the past were *simplicity* and *permanence,* those terms have shifted in an ecologically-concerned present to *complexity* and *change.* Instead of seeing wilderness as an appealing but ultimately impossible alternative, it is now increasingly studied and interpreted as the model of a complex diversity and a new pattern for survival."[67] Rawlings's ecopastorals represent an early forerunner to the conceptual shifts that Love discusses. Indeed, the 1930s and 1940s were a period of growing environmental awareness for many writers, including Aldo Leopold, whose posthumously published *Sand County Almanac* is often considered the bible of the ecology movement of the late twentieth and early twenty-first centuries. Leopold and Rawlings contribute to a general shift in cultural thinking that has resulted in the concept of wilderness replacing that of the garden as the pastoral ideal of a "natural" state, and therefore becoming the privileged position from which to judge a corrupt, fallen society (a premise Faulkner challenges in *Go Down, Moses*).

Rawlings's wilderness-infused ecopastorals illustrate what Lawrence Buell refers to as "pastoral's multiple frames" in claiming that "American pastoral has simultaneously been counterinstitutional and institutionally sponsored."[68] Even as Rawlings's work challenges readers to rethink their relationships to nature and envisions the natural environment as having value for its own sake, more than simply *terra nullius,* it may also contribute to a romantic conception of wilderness that, as Cronon warns, "embodies a dualistic vision in which the human is entirely outside the natural." Rawlings's reverential portraits of a vanishing Eden may encourage more people to seek out such places before they are gone, ironically hastening their demise. As J. T. Glisson said of his former neighbor, "No one could have known that [she] would bring about more change in Cross Creek than all of the roads and Crackers combined."[69]

3
Connecting Inner and Outer Nature

Zora Neale Hurston's Personal Pastoral

Like Rawlings, Zora Neale Hurston uses a revised version of the pastoral to write about changing characters in a changing Florida landscape. Clashes of nature/culture, rural/urban, and wilderness/civilization are perhaps more pronounced in Florida than in any other Southern state during the early twentieth century, principally due to an astronomical increase in the state's urban populace. In fact, by 1930 Florida was the first Southern state with a population over 50 percent urban, a benchmark not reached by Georgia (30.8 percent in 1930), South Carolina (21.3 percent), Alabama (28.1 percent), and Mississippi (16.9 percent) until the 1960s or even the 1970s. During the 1920s, Florida's urban population increased 114.9 percent and the rural population only 15.2 percent,[1] so that even with the population booming in the cities, there remained many sparsely populated, relatively wild natural places. While Hurston's fiction does not focus on the specifics of roads, fences, and property rights in the way that Rawlings's does, both *Their Eyes Were Watching God* (1937) and *Seraph on the Suwanee* (1948) examine the general cultural anxiety that inherently valuable and underappreciated rural communities are quickly vanishing forever. As in the works of Caldwell, Rawlings, and Faulkner, the physical terrain of the author's homeland becomes a contested space in which these conflicts are played out and, occasionally, resolved.

Hurston's versions of ecopastoral examine how people live and work in specific regions and ecosystems in Florida, while also using more dense natural symbolism than Rawlings's variations. Her two female protagonists, Janie Starks in *Their Eyes* and Arvay Meserve in *Seraph,* undertake pastoral retreats into the wilds of their inner natures (which often correspond to actual journeys) only to return and reform the self, which has been made less authentic by a male-dominated culture. In this chapter, I discuss how Hurston creates more of a "personal pastoral" in these two novels, in which the pastoral ideal of harmonic balance is sought as much internally (in the person) as it is externally (in the landscape). Like Rawlings, Hurston does not categorically reject the association of women and nature; instead, she critically investigates the implications of that connection. For Janie, this bond becomes an active and empowering one, while for Arvay the link retains much of its traditional connotation of passive subjugation. The goal of Hurston's personal pastoral is to reform not culture or the city but the self. Janie, for example, seeks to balance her desires for individualism and a loving relationship, while Arvay struggles to maintain equilibrium between her past and present. Wilderness for Hurston, like Rawlings, is a more authentic, more natural place in many ways, but it is not somewhere to seek total immersion. Rather, the ideal is a more traditional pastoral middle state, and trips to (relatively) wild nature help to restore that balance.

In *Their Eyes,* one important way that Hurston counters the traditional pastoral notion of a passive natural world is by incorporating elements of Afro-Caribbean Vodou,[2] a religion that posits nature as living, dynamic, and sacred. This animistic vision of nature allows Hurston to shift Janie's symbolic connections to nature over the course of the novel, from beast of burden to raging hurricane. Hurston does not replace the polarized categories of culture/nature, male/female, and subject/object so much as she reverses them. In typical pastoral fashion, she seeks ways of combining these extremes, but the hierarchies become reversed as she exposes the shortcomings of white authority and male dominance. Hurston suggests in both of these novels that the acquisitive values of white-dominated society foster an alienating conception of nature as something distinctly "other," estranging people from a natural world regarded as little more than an amalgamation of commodities.

In *Seraph on the Suwanee,* Hurston's focus on white characters allows her to concentrate more fully on the connections of the natural world to issues of gender and class. Thus, in addition to the personal pastoral of Arvay Meserve, Hurston creates what might be termed a "working-class pastoral" defined by Jim Meserve's ability to profit from Florida's abundant natural resources. Nature itself facilitates an improvement of social standing via avenues that are accessible to lower- or working-class people in ways that formal education and white-collar jobs often are not. However, the largely financial benefits to humans can easily change a mutually rewarding balance into a one-sided, exploitative relationship. As Jim's ventures become more and more profitable and he moves his family into the middle class, the working-class pastoral becomes more consumerist or bourgeois. The symbolic links between the natural world and Arvay's inner nature further complicate attempts to interpret decisively Jim's relationships to his wife and the environment. This

extremely complex novel, which has often been overlooked or oversimplified
in Hurston scholarship, presents a complicated picture of land-use issues in a
rapidly developing Florida alongside a personal pastoral narrative of Arvay's
quest for identity that mirrors Janie's similar journey in surprising ways. In a
sense, Hurston attempts to blend a female-oriented personal pastoral with a
more male-centered class pastoral, a project perhaps not entirely successful.

Although Hurston's knowledge of Vodou has little bearing on *Seraph*, it
surely influenced the composition of *Their Eyes*, especially its representations of nature. Hurston studied anthropology under Franz Boas and Ruth
Benedict before collecting folklore in Florida, Louisiana, South Carolina,
Alabama, Honduras, Jamaica, the Bahamas, and Haiti.[3] From April of 1936
until March of 1937 Hurston traveled extensively in Jamaica and Haiti on
a Guggenheim Fellowship to study Afro-Caribbean Vodou. *Tell My Horse*
(1938) is the compelling account of her observations and firsthand experiences with this still widely misunderstood religion. Although this account of
her travels was written after her return to the United States, Hurston composed *Their Eyes Were Watching God* in seven weeks while living in Haiti.

Of course, Vodou is only one of many strands of Hurston's "complexly woven religious sensibility," and her works reveal her interests in Christianity;
Norse, Greek, and Roman mythology; and Egyptian and other African religions.[4] Much of her other work, including *Seraph on the Suwanee*, confirms
that Hurston's own brand of "Deism" has much in common with Vodou's
conception of nature.[5] It is, therefore, perhaps more accurate to say that Hurston found the syncretism of religious beliefs that characterizes Vodou to be
compatible with her own eclectic spiritual views rather than that she adopted
its tenets after her indoctrination. In this chapter, I will suggest the importance of recognizing a general Vodou aesthetic at work in *Their Eyes*, but also
include Vodou as one of several modes Hurston employs as she grapples with
the material and cultural effects of human relationships with nature.[6]

Hurston's stay in Haiti while composing *Their Eyes* is an interesting variety
of pastoral retreat itself, providing her with a certain critical distance from
her home and subject matter. One effect of this distance is a focus on values
such as equality in personal relationships rather than a direct engagement
with the problems of the Depression-era United States.[7] Of course, larger social issues are addressed in the novel, and this, in one key way, is what makes
it pastoral: a mask of simplicity is used in order to comment on contemporary social issues. As discussed in earlier chapters, Jan Bakker says that even
antebellum Southern pastoral (usually considered the most sentimental and
simple variety) "deals with the complexities of life against a background
of apparent simplicity," echoing William Empson's classic definition of the

pastoral as the "process of putting the complex into the simple."[8] What I am calling Hurston's personal pastoral emerges as the principal focus of multiple pastoral frames in my reading, with social and political critiques as subsidiary concerns. This complex use of the pastoral helps to explain the diverse and often conflicting range of interpretations of the novel. As Rosemary Hathaway says, critics who focus on "the notion of Janie as a questing hero" or "the issue of Janie's voice in the text" are destined to overlook its more political dimensions.[9]

Hurston's Vodou-influenced conception of nature in *Their Eyes* contributes to her revision of the male-dominated pastoral tradition in Southern literature by identifying her female protagonist with an active natural world and empowering her to protect herself. Particularly in the Reconstruction-era pastoral of a writer like Page, males were the protectors of both the improved garden and the women of the plantation, and this notion of women as property extended to African Americans as well. For example, in the story "Meh Lady," Page employs a former slave narrator who longs for the "good old days" before the Civil War and who fondly recalls the Union army colonel who saves the estate and its defenseless residents by marrying the former plantation mistress. The white Southern woman is explicitly associated with the plantation land in the story, and thus both she and the ex-slave narrator remain property, debased objects used to reaffirm the dominant position of the white, male subject.

In *Their Eyes,* Hurston shows that the traditional pastoral elevation of some people (whites, males) over others (blacks, females) denies the humanity of those below. Although this attitude is a product of the predominantly white power structure in the South, Hurston depicts her black characters as equally susceptible to the lure of self-aggrandizement at the expense of others. Robert Hemenway summarizes the appeal of authority to someone like Janie's second husband, Joe (Jody) Starks: "Whites had institutionalized such thinking, and black people were vulnerable to the philosophy because being on high like white folks seemed to represent security and power."[10] Janie's grandmother, Nanny, is a former slave who wants this security and power for Janie and sees only two possibilities for her granddaughter's life: high or low. Nanny was forced to hide in the swamps at the end of the Civil War with her daughter, Leafy, the child of her former master, who conceives Janie years later after she is raped in the forest by her teacher. Nanny therefore understandably accepts the Manichean division of plantation and wilderness into high and low categories, and she aspires to "throw up a highway through the wilderness" so that Janie might "take a stand on high ground lak Ah dreamed."[11] Janie discovers, however, that the high ground, as symbolized by Logan Killicks's sixty acres and Joe Starks's "big house," can be more threatening than wild nature and that the low ground of the Everglades is potentially liberating and empowering.[12]

The portrait of Vodou that emerges from Hurston's *Tell My Horse* is of a transformative, creative, and dynamic religion that challenges institutionalized binary hierarchies by embracing the intermingling or interpenetration of polarities (a version of the pastoral middle ground). Through rituals "that locate the sacred within nature and within female sexuality,"[13] Vodou reverses the hierarchies that situate women alongside nature (and therefore below men and culture). Hurston seeks a blend of opposite extremes (true to the pastoral form), but like Rawlings, she revises the association of the female with nature: from a tamed, passive, orderly natural world to a wild, active, powerful, and even sacred one. Using *Tell My Horse* as a guide to Hurston's understanding of Afro-Caribbean Vodou, I suggest there are two important themes from that work that are also central to *Their Eyes:* the natural world can embody resistance to a dominant group while offering liberation (if only temporarily) to oppressed people, and black women's sexuality can be a source of pride and power.

The animistic conception of nature inherent in Vodou counters the mechanistic, Newtonian view endorsed by Christianity and its reductive opposition of human as active subject to nature as passive object, of humans as stewards of God's garden. Certainly there is not a monolithic "Christian" viewpoint of nature, but I want to emphasize a general and important difference in Vodou and Christian understandings of the location of the sacred and divine. Gordon Kaufman summarizes the Western theological separation of nature and humanity: "The great religious struggle between Israel and Canaan was over the relative metaphysical importance of natural power and process on the one hand and personal moral will on the other. When Yahweh won that struggle it meant that the object of ultimate loyalty and devotion for humans in the West would be conceived increasingly in terms of models rooted in our moral and personal experience, not in our sense of dependence upon and unity with the orders and processes of nature."[14] Since Vodouisants locate the divine spirit in all parts of nature, they have a different relationship to the natural environment than do Christians, who conceive of nature as divinely given to humans to control, but not divine in and of itself. This ideological clash is actually quite tangible in Haiti, where the Catholic Church is, for many reasons, often openly hostile toward Vodou and its mostly lower-class practitioners, although many people actively participate in both religions. Accordingly, Vodouisants often mask their beliefs, creating a religion that operates largely behind the scenes and subverts the authority of Haiti's ruling-class minority, as Annette Trefzer explains: "As a religion that developed in the context of slavery and colonialism, voodoo marks a fluid boundary between domination and resistance and defines a zone of struggle between public and private discourses of dominant and subordinate groups."[15] Hurston's portrait of nature in *Their Eyes* works in a similar manner, subtly subverting the dominant white male culture of the South from the background of a story about a black woman's search for a voice.

Numerous important Vodou ceremonies are held at sacred trees, rocks, and springs, and some stones are kept in families for generations because they are believed to literally contain a *lwa* (or *loa*), one of many lesser Vodou gods. In *Tell My Horse,* Hurston describes one particularly festive ceremony that celebrates the spirits and gods who inhabit the heads of streams and the cascades and grottoes below them. The ceremony *Tete l'eau,* or head of the water, which venerates the source of a stream or spring, was witnessed firsthand by Hurston. She describes seeing hundreds of people disrobing and climbing through the "eternal mists" of the waterfall: "[I]t was a moving sight to see these people turning from sordid things once each year to go into an ecstasy of worship of the beautiful in water-forms."[16] The nearby Catholic church seeks to prevent the ceremony, but Hurston sides with the masses and celebrates their transformation from "sordid things" to ecstatic worshipers, from colonial objects to full-fledged participants in a divine natural world.

In addition to this kind of sacralization of nature, Vodou also offers an alternative to the degradation of black women (which Hurston finds in Jamaica, Haiti, and the United States) through its acceptance, and even worship, of black women's sexuality. Hurston witnesses another ceremony in which the Mambo, or priestess, is asked, "What is truth?" She answers, Hurston writes, "by throwing back her veil and revealing her sex organs. The ceremony means that this is the infinite, the ultimate truth. There is no mystery beyond the mysterious source of life. . . . It is considered the highest honor for all males participating to kiss her organ of creation, for Damballah, the god of gods, has permitted them to come face to face with the truth" (113–14). The sexuality that is denigrated as base, bestial, or natural in a negative sense, both by colonial Caribbean society and the patriarchal culture of the American South, is reconfigured here as a site of worship for males, and Hurston embodies this idea in Janie, whose sexuality is a source of attraction and envy for nearly every male character in the novel.[17]

Another interesting Vodou ritual with a more obvious connection to *Their Eyes* is performed at the site where a sacred palm tree once grew. Hurston relates the legend in *Tell My Horse* of a "beautiful, luminous virgin" who ap-

pears in the tree, sings a song, and disappears. People begin worshiping the
tree in droves after reports of miraculous cures spread throughout Haiti.
When the Catholic priest of the parish tries to chop down this rival shrine,
the machete bounces off the tree, hits the priest in the head, and fatally
wounds him. The tree is later removed and replaced with a Catholic church.
However, several churches burn to the ground on the site, including one destroyed by lightning, signifying nature's role as active subject. Trees, in general, are important symbols in Vodou, often as emblems of "the sexual and
spiritual union of the primary male and female deities,"[18] and Hurston employs this idea of the union or merging of opposites in the pear tree in *Their
Eyes*, which represents Janie's resistance to the limiting racial and gender roles
imposed upon her.

    In the well-known pear tree scene of chapter 2, Janie experiences a vision
of communion in nature, and the blending of sexual and spiritual imagery
recalls the Vodou ceremonies of Haiti: "She was stretched out on her back beneath the pear tree soaking in the alto chant of the visiting bees, the gold of
the sun and the panting breath of the breeze when the inaudible voice of it
all came to her. She saw a dust-bearing bee sink into the sanctum of a bloom,
the thousand sister-calyxes arch to meet the love embrace and the ecstatic
shiver of the tree from root to tiniest branch creaming in every blossom and
frothing with delight. So this was marriage! She had been summoned to be-
hold a revelation. Then Janie felt a pain remorseless sweet that left her limp
and languid" (10–11). Again, black, female sexuality is celebrated, even ven-
erated in the religious imagery, and some fundamental binary divisions are
challenged. The distinctions between subject and object, observer and participant, human and nature are blurred, if not erased, in the language of
Hurston's description. The "marriage" is not only between bee and bloom,
but also between Janie and the tree. Both unions efface the gender oppositions normally associated with marriage, thereby offering the possibility of
a truly egalitarian partnership, in contrast to Janie's grandmother's conception of marriage as a means to provide Janie with the security of property.
As Nanny explains to her granddaughter, "'Tain't Logan Killicks Ah wants
you to have, baby, it's protection" (14). Janie's internal response is that "[t]he
vision of Logan Killicks was desecrating the pear tree" (13).

    While the pear tree is a metaphor for Janie's inner nature, it also metonymi-
cally represents the entirety of the natural world, encompassing and con-
joining seemingly contradictory terms: "Janie saw her life like a great tree
in leaf with the things suffered, things enjoyed, things done and undone.
Dawn and doom was in the branches" (8). Hurston's syntax here suggests
nature's ability to interpolate binary constructions, moving from the iden-

tical noun/opposite verb structure of "things suffered, things enjoyed" to the single noun with a compound verb in "things done and undone" to the oddly appropriate compound subject/singular verb structure of "Dawn and doom *was* in the branches." Indeed, before the end of chapter 2 Hurston shows nature as a site both of refuge (during Nanny's flight to the swamp with Leafy) and of threat (when the teenage Leafy is raped in the forest by her teacher). This antithetical pairing is transferred to Janie's body in the novel's opening sequence, where Hurston describes her grapefruitlike buttocks and "pugnacious breasts trying to bore a hole in her shirt" (2). The imagery reemphasizes the reading of body as landscape (and vice versa) and again contains the potential of both sustenance and destruction. Thus, Hurston retains the association of the female body with landscape, but empowers both with an active, threatening aspect that counteracts more circumscribed versions of femininity.[19]

Janie forges an identity by moving freely between poles that are usually defined by the dominant culture as mutually exclusive, and much of the scholarship on this novel has concentrated on Janie's dual character. Melvin Dixon, for example, argues that "Hurston replaces Nanny's idea of social class conferring high or low status with Janie's preferable and dynamic act of travel between the two." Susan Edwards Meisenhelder similarly claims that Janie struggles with two identities, one drawn from the white world and "a more vigorous model of black womanhood she tries to forge for herself." John Lowe notes Hurston's childhood fascination with Roman mythology and makes an extensive comparison of Janie and the two-faced Janus.[20] Although Janie's navigation and mediation of opposing forces has been amply described by various critics, it is important to emphasize Hurston's knowledge of Vodou in order to recognize that she locates these principles of mediation, reconciliation, and transcendence in nature itself. Thus Janie's quest is pastoral because she seeks a middle ground between unpalatable extremes. It is a personal pastoral in that she is searching for her own identity in her travels. Similar to Rawlings's version of the pastoral, landscapes that are closer to wilderness offer greater opportunity for liberation. However, Hurston's personal pastoral creates natural environments that are more richly symbolic than Rawlings's. In Janie's journeys through farm and town, she is therefore not rejecting particular land-use patterns so much as the personal affronts that they symbolize.

Janie's resistance to Nanny's mutually exclusive options for an African American woman's life—either the high seat or "de mule uh de world" (14)—is inspired by the pear tree vision that serves as the paradigm by which she judges herself and her relationships. However, Vodou is but one of Hurston's influences, and she was well aware that natural imagery also can be used to reinforce hierarchies and denigrate people. Nanny's reference to black women as the mules of the world alludes to a historical association of blacks and mules.[21] Hurston titled her collection of African American Southern folklore *Mules and Men* (1935), and Hemenway cogently rebuts the opinion that this title is derogatory and servile: "The protest impulse was not subordinated, but stylized so that it could survive.... The phrase meant not only that black people were treated as mules, but also that they were defiantly human—mules *and* men. The identification itself demonstrated how a negative relationship (slave : mule : beast of burden) could be transformed into a positive identity (beast of burden : mule : slave : man), with the content of the positive identification concealed from outside understanding."[22] Hemenway's language recalls both the subversive nature of Haitian Vodou and the enabling process of Harrison's female pastoral that changes women's interaction with the land from "passive association" to "active cultivation." Janie's first husband, however, exhibits the negative side of this process, making her his mule even as he places her on the high seat.

Although Logan Killicks's "often-mentioned sixty acres" constitute "protection" in Nanny's eyes, they seem to Janie "like a stump in the middle of the woods where nobody had ever been" (20). This stunted, lifeless image of her marriage is an obvious counterpoint to Janie's earlier vibrant bee-and-blossom image of marriage. Logan Killicks, she feels, "was desecrating the pear tree" (13), and although she waits "a bloom time, and a green time and an orange time" (23), the relationship fails to improve. Janie's seasonal conception of time suggests her harmony with nature's cadences, as does her apparent ability to understand the language of an animistic universe: "She knew things that nobody had ever told her. For instance, the words of the trees and the wind. She often spoke to falling seeds and said, 'Ah hope you fall on soft ground,' because she had heard seeds saying that to each other as they passed" (23–24). Janie's hope for the seeds is also a hope for herself that foreshadows her eventual landing on the "soft ground" of the muck. Logan's purchase of a mule that "even uh woman kin handle" (26) is the final straw for her first marriage.

Although mules are obviously part of nature, Hurston represents Janie's figuration as a mule as unnatural because it places her below her husband. Logan plans to have Janie plow his potato fields, giving the lie to Nanny's claim that her granddaughter can either sit on the high seat or toil as a mule of the world. With Logan she does both. His desire to elevate himself at his wife's expense is brought home by his snide comment that Janie should respect him more because of his higher standing in society: "Youse powerful independent around here sometime considerin' . . . youse born in a carriage 'thout no top to it, and yo' mama and you bein' born and raised in de white folks back-yard" (29). The particular combination of culture and nature that Janie finds here, in the traditional pastoral farm setting, fails to meet the "natural" standards of the pear tree vision. Likewise, her marriage is killing, not nurturing, her inner nature, sending her hurrying off with Jody Starks. She thinks he could be a "bee for her bloom," but "the seat beside him" on his hired rig ominously portends their future: "With him on it, it sat like some high ruling chair" (31).

In her characterization of Jody, Hurston pointedly aligns him with white society and its emphasis on commodity, pitting him against the natural symbolism associated with Janie. Working for whites his entire life, Jody "had always wanted to be a big voice, but de white folks had all de sayso where he come from and everywhere else, exceptin' dis place dat colored folks was buildin' theirselves" (27). Eatonville appeals to Jody not as a place to escape the inequities and stratification of white society, but as a place where he can finally occupy the top rung of the hierarchy himself. He swoops into town, and within six weeks he has purchased five hundred acres of adjoining land to sell in parcels, organized the men to "chop out two roads" in the forest, had himself proclaimed mayor, and built a store in the middle of town. This store—which bears more than a passing resemblance to a plantation commissary—is the "heart" of the town, according to Jody, and one of its first commodities is Janie, on display at the grand opening: "Jody told her to dress up and stand in the store all that evening. . . . She must look upon herself as the bell-cow, the other women were the gang" (39). This debased natural image divisively separates a silenced Janie, placing her above the other women in town with Jody over the entire herd.

Hurston emphasizes Janie's separation and silence in Tony Taylor's ceremonial welcoming speech and its linguistic juxtaposition of Jody's property: "Brother Starks, we welcomes you and all dat you have seen fit tuh bring amongst us—yo' belov-ed wife, yo' store, yo' land" (39). Significantly, when Janie is asked by the townsfolk to say a few words after her husband speaks, Jody silences her voice: "[M]ah wife don't know nothin' 'bout no speech-makin.' Ah never married her for nothin' lak dat. She's uh woman and her place is in de home." Hurston immediately adds that Jody's action "took the bloom off of things" in Janie's mind (40–41). Although Jody would never allow Janie to plow in the fields, as this would signal a lack of affluence to others, he is content to have her toil wordlessly inside the store. Her enforced silence links Janie with mules in a different sense, one that Hurston introduces in the novel's opening pages: "It was the time to hear things and talk. These sitters had been tongueless, earless, eyeless conveniences all day long. Mules and other brutes had occupied their skins. But now, the sun and the boss-man were gone, so the skins felt powerful and human. They became lords of sounds and lesser things. They passed nations through their mouths" (1–2). Connecting silence and mules in this passage, Hurston suggests a return to humanity at the end of the workday. On the store porch in Eatonville, the townspeople are transformed from mules back into speaking subjects who feel "powerful and human," recalling Hurston's description of Haitian wor-shippers shedding their identities as "sordid things" in the ceremony Tete l'eau. Janie's exclusion from the conversations on the porch keeps her in the passive, objectified realm of "sordid things" and mules.

Jody's class ambitions demand that he accumulate property and display his possessions. He buys a large desk similar to those of white businessmen in nearby Maitland and a gold spittoon "just like his bossman used to have in his bank up there in Atlanta." The most prominent symbol of difference, one that "cowed the town," is a huge house, painted "a gloaty, sparkly white," that makes the rest of the town look "like servants' quarters surrounding the 'big house'" (44). Even Jody's physical appearance is described by Hurston as "[k]ind of portly like rich white folks" (32), a characteristic she also uses as a sign of unhealthy emulation of whites with the "puzzle-gutted" Otis Slem-mons in "The Gilded Six-Bits" (1933). Jody's elevation in status comes at the cost of positioning others as slaves and animals.

The incident with Matt Bonner's mule illustrates how the same thinking that locates humans above merely corporeal nature can justify the subjuga-tion of some humans, especially blacks and women, as natural. Jody pur-chases and then frees the underfed mule in an apparent act of magnanimity that Janie compares to Lincoln freeing the slaves. Hurston's wry commentary on the continuing inferiority of African Americans following their emanci-pation also applies to Janie's position in her marriage. Jody acquires Janie and frees her from working as Logan's plow mule, only to recast her as a "free" mule by "building a high chair for her to sit in" (58). When the mule dies, Jody delivers a speech while standing on its carcass, elevating himself by standing on an animal that Hurston uses as a symbol for black women in the novel, as well as for all blacks in the title of *Mules and Men*.[23] Janie seeks a less restric-tive environment, which entails for Hurston, as it did for Rawlings, a move-ment toward wilderness.

After seven years of marriage, Janie "wasn't petal-open anymore" (67) with her husband, reflecting her alienation from the empowering aspects of nature and from her own inner nature. Hurston, in fact, cleverly unblends the connotations of human nature (as in an individual's fundamental character) and Nature (as in flora and fauna) that she had joined in Janie's original pear tree vision: "She had no more blossomy openings dusting pollen over her man, neither any glistening young fruit where petals used to be. She found that she had a host of thoughts she had never expressed to him, and numerous emotions she had never let Jody know about. Things packed up and put away in parts of her heart where he could never find them. She was saving up feelings for some man she had never seen. She had an inside and an outside now and suddenly she knew how not to mix them" (68). The inside/outside divergence parallels the high/low imagery and demonstrates how feminine nature can be reconstructed as an empowering identification. For Janie, it is only "the shadow of herself" that is managing the store and "prostrating itself before Jody," while in her mind "she herself sat under a shady tree with the wind blowing through her hair and her clothes" (73). She protects the internal pear tree from being subsumed by her external bell-cow/mule identity through this act of separation. Recalling Trefzer's description of Vodou as "a fluid boundary between domination and resistance," Janie's defense mechanism wards off Jody's potentially indoctrinating view that "[s]omebody got to think for women and chillun and chickens and cows" (67) by countering with the positive associations of the pear tree: "She got so she received all things with the stolidness of the earth which soaks up urine and perfume with the same indifference" (73). This balancing strategy permits Janie to hold opposing forces in abeyance until a more egalitarian love allows her to fuse them again and "re-pear" the split.

After Janie's famous verbal undressing of Jody in public hastens his impending death, she reclaims her voice and rediscovers the inner self she had hidden so long from her husband. When she later meets Vergible "Tea Cake" Woods, Janie also rediscovers her inner visions of the pear tree and egalitarian marriage. After years of oppression from Logan Killicks and Jody Starks, she literally becomes Janie Woods when she marries Tea Cake, who "could be a bee for her blossom—a pear tree blossom in the spring" (101). Although much has been made by critics of Tea Cake's name (especially his obviously appropriate surname),[24] the study of the influences of Vodou suggests other possible meanings. In the Haitian patois (as in other French-based dialects), the term 'ti is commonly used as an appellation meaning little. Short for petite, the word is often attached to the front of a name, to designate, for example, a son with the same given name as his father. Given that Hurston composed the novel while immersed in Haitian folklife, we might read Tea Cake as 'Ti Cake, which would be an appropriate partner for LilBit, Logan's nickname for Janie (and Hurston's own nickname). The name also approximates the Haitian 'ti cay, literally, "little house," an image that fittingly contrasts with the "big house" and the sixty-acre homestead that symbolize Janie's unfulfilling marriages. Just as Caldwell and Rawlings reject the farm and the town as sites for genuine pastoral harmony, Hurston has Janie spurn these places and find a personal equilibrium in a community on the edge of the wilderness. When Janie and Tea Cake travel to "de muck" in the Everglades, the houses are small, but nature is big and wild, and Janie's soul "crawl[s] out from its hiding place" (122).

The community of the muck replaces the limitations of the dominant society with a looser, more dynamic system of relations in which men and women dress alike, work together, and equally participate in the singing, dancing, fighting, and storytelling that characterize the playful, less restrictive atmosphere enjoyed by the transient population. Money is spent as quickly as it is earned, and Jody's acquisitiveness seems almost quaintly artificial. The relative lack of stratification of this frontier community in comparison to Eatonville is encapsulated in the transformation of the male-dominated store porch into the more inclusive doorstep of Tea Cake and Janie: "The men held big arguments here like they used to on the store porch. Only here, she could listen and laugh and even talk some herself if she wanted to. She got so she could tell big stories herself" (127–28). The denim overalls that Janie wears to the fields are not only the uniform of the labor class, but also an androgynous garment that signifies the abatement of culturally imposed gender roles on the muck as, for instance, when Tea Cake helps to cook after Janie begins working alongside him in the fields. Thus, the home that might easily symbolize gender-imposed confinement is reclaimed by Janie and becomes a symbol of equality and shared responsibilities for men and women: both earn money outside of it, both help complete domestic chores inside of it, and both participate in the playfulness of the porch. Everything seems more vibrant and dynamic to Janie on the muck, and the poor people who flock to the small town of Belle Glade are able to trap, hunt, and fish as well as earn high wages in the fields.

Immersion in the "soft ground" of the muck seemingly alleviates the class, gender, and racial hierarchies of society, but Hurston reveals that this pastoral paradise (like Tea Cake) is more problematic than it appears. The muck needs to be viewed as a pastoral place in every sense. It is not going far enough to say that "[l]ife on 'de muck' is presented by Hurston in idyllic terms reminiscent of Ovid's description of the Golden Age of the world" in order to call "attention to the imperfections and corruptions of the present time."[25] As I have been arguing, the ecopastorals of this era also self-reflexively critique the pastoral mode itself. Hurston is not presenting a simple, unproblematic pastoral refuge in order to criticize the outside world. She is also turning a critical gaze on the pastoral place, revealing that the muck is not actually separate from the "outside world" at all.

Class, gender, and racial divisions may be tempered and masked in natural surroundings, but they are not eliminated. The white owners of the fields are barely mentioned in the text, but they do still exist, profiting from the droves of people who show up needing work and charging rent even to those who must sleep with no shelter. While class stratification is perhaps flattened within the community of bean pickers, this picture of harmony masks the iniquities that persist. Hurston does not emphasize cooperative values, as Caldwell and Rawlings do for Scottsville and Cross Creek, but instead presents the muck as more of a personal pastoral site, a place where Janie finds an inner psychic balance and a fulfilling partnership with Tea Cake. But he, too, it turns out, hides aspects of his personality that are revealed in his responses to the racism of Mrs. Turner, a self-loathing, light-skinned African American woman who "can't stand black niggers" (135). Her desire to "class off" from those with darker skin imitates the hierarchy of the white world, and her view of society is like "the pecking order in a chicken yard" (138), with skin pigmentation the sole criterion of rank. Hurston pokes fun at Mrs. Turner's adoration of Janie's light complexion and mocks her belief that "somehow she and others through worship could attain her paradise— a heaven of straight-haired, thin-lipped, high-nose boned white seraphs."[26] Even though Tea Cake leads an effort to boycott and vandalize the Turners' restaurant, Hurston's narrative suggests that he does not forget her "altar" to "Caucasian characteristics" so easily as it may seem (139).

Tea Cake's character seems to change gradually after the arrival of Mrs. Turner's brother, a straight-haired unemployed carpenter, whom she desperately wants to fix up with Janie. Jealous of this imagined rival for his wife, Tea Cake beats Janie "to show he was boss," and because "[b]eing able to whip her reassured him in possession" (140). This incident represents a significant and quite sudden shift in the language Hurston uses to describe Janie's seemingly perfect mate. The "bee for her blossom" now seems more like Jody Starks in his desire for ownership of Janie, and, as the hurricane nears, Tea Cake also begins to resemble Jody in his imitation of the white power structure. The true threats to pastoral harmony, Hurston suggests, come not from outside forces but from within the "natural" community and within one's own inner nature. Janie's retreat to the muck allows her the clarity to critique her earlier marriages upon returning to Eatonville, where the novel's frame story begins and ends. Again, Hurston is employing conventions of the pastoral but signifying on them, as the seemingly idyllic muck community turns out to be only a temporary or false paradise. This shift perhaps indicates Hurston's contention that a pastoral Eden does not exist for blacks in the South: they are always at the bottom of hierarchies. Thus, the vision of "mule-heaven" in chapter 6, where "mule-angels would have people to ride on" (61), is the only place where such hierarchies are reversed, except for inside Janie at the novel's end—a personal pastoral.

Interestingly, Hurston has to efface the actual history of the muck region in order to present it in the manner she does. Lake Okeechobee (Hurston spells it with only one 'e' in the second syllable) is the source for much of the water that fills the Everglades. The Everglades is, in fact, a river that runs about a hundred miles from just south of the lake to the Gulf of Mexico. Marjory Stoneman Douglas called it a "river of grass" in the title of her famous book, *The Everglades: River of Grass* (1947), which called attention to the environmental damage the river was enduring. What is striking, though, is how much of the history of the Lake Okeechobee region Hurston leaves out. The extreme constructedness of the landscape, the resulting environmental damage, and even the character of towns such as Belle Glade are neglected or altered in Hurston's portrayal. Construction of a series of canals that would lower the level of the lake and drain water from the Everglades continued throughout the first half of the twentieth century: "Officials and most residents firmly believed the Everglades of use and benefit only if drained and converted to farmland."[27]

The "reclaimed" farmland created through the immense drainage projects spawned three major problems: soil subsidence, saltwater intrusion, and fires. The loss of water allowed the proliferation of bacteria "able to reverse the process of soil formation."[28] According to Mark Derr, by 1940 "the farmlands around Lake Okeechobee had lost at least half of their initial 14 feet of soil."[29] Drainage also permitted saltwater to flow up into the new farmlands and into over a thousand wells in south Florida. Fires ravaged the newly exposed land, often burning for weeks, with the smoke from these "muck fires" enveloping entire towns for days at a time.[30] Additionally, towns that relied on migrant labor, like Belle Glade, where Tea Cake and Janie go, are described by Derr as "models of oppression" that kept workers in thrall as much as sharecropping and tenant farming: "[T]hey came to represent the worst of the company town—poor, dirty, crime- and alcohol-ridden places where people often lived without hope. . . . Lake Okeechobee had become the land of the corporate farm."[31]

So why would Hurston leave so much of this detail out of her portrayal of the muck? The answer, in my reading, is that her primary concern is Janie's personal development. The habitus of the muck is certainly beneficial for Janie. Its playful, unstructured lifestyle is liberating, and "her soul crawl[s] out from its hiding place" (122). Janie and Tea Cake's bee-and-blossom relationship can flourish there until his need to possess her forces Janie to see the reality behind the idyllic façade. For readers, knowledge of the Lake Okeechobee region can do much the same thing, for recognizing the artificiality of this "natural" environment reveals that it is not the perfect place for a protagonist aligned with nature imagery throughout the novel. Through the hurricane scenes, Hurston has nature reclaim this land and vanquish the man who threatens Janie's identity.

Hurston's description of the climactic hurricane is both factual and symbolic. Destructive and creative powers are conjoined in the storm, and its effects transform Janie into an independent woman. As part of the Everglades drainage project, a levee five to nine feet high and forty feet wide was built around the southern rim of Lake Okeechobee, but it was no match for the hurricanes that hit the state in 1926 and 1928, on which Hurston based the storm in *Their Eyes*.[32] The 1926 storm killed 370 people, while in 1928 the lake was driven over and through the dikes on the south shore, washing away the town of Belle Glade. About 2,000 people died throughout Florida in that storm (quick burials of decaying bodies made an exact death toll impossible), and, as Derr relates in his history of the state: "The tragic irony is that Indians had foretold that Lake Okeechobee would spill over its rim once again to feed the Everglades."[33] Of course, Hurston also shows the Indians as adept at reading nature, as they leave the area while Tea Cake and Janie stay behind.

As the storm approaches, Tea Cake refuses to leave "because de money's too good on the muck." He invests too much authority in the white bosses who remain behind and dismisses the notion that the scores of animals and groups of Seminoles fleeing the area is a signal to evacuate: "Dey don't always know. Indians don't know much uh nothin' tuh tell de truth. Else dey'd own dis country still. De white folks ain't gone nowhere. Dey oughta know if it's dangerous" (148). But the hurricane reveals the limitations of white authority and the inability of Tea Cake to read nature's signs properly. For Tea Cake, knowledge is falsely equated with ownership and status.

The huge Lake Okeechobee resembles an anthropomorphized God in Hurston's description, sitting in judgment and enacting its vengeance as it rolls over everything in its path: "The monstropolous beast had left its bed. The two hundred miles an hour wind had loosed its chains. He seized hold of his dikes and ran forward until he met the quarters; uprooted them like grass and rushed on after his supposed-to-be conquerors" (153). Anthropomorphizing the lake locates power, agency, and divinity in nature as it reclaims this constructed pastoral site. As the lake bursts free, it converts the seemingly stable wall of man-made dikes into a fluid boundary, similarly re-

versing distinctions between life and death and collapsing distinctions between humans and animals: "[T]he wind and water had given life to lots of
things that folks think of as dead and given death to so much that had been
living. . . . They passed a dead man in a sitting position on a hummock, entirely surrounded by wild animals and snakes. Common danger made common friends. Nothing sought conquest over the other" (153, 156). Racial differences, too, are blurred when Tea Cake and other men try unsuccessfully
to distinguish white and black decomposing corpses for burial in segregated
graves, as mandated by the attempts of white authorities to maintain the societal divisions that nature has undone.

The personification of the lake suggests the scenes must be read symbolically as well. Thomas Cassidy's reading of the storm as "an embodiment of
the rage which [Janie] is not even aware of feeling" makes sense in this context. As he explains, Janie has suppressed her own voice out of a desire to be
"one self-identical person" with Tea Cake "to the extent that her identity is
simplified into being Tea Cake's wife."[34] I agree with Cassidy that Janie's lack
of protests about Tea Cake's jealousy and violence threatens the identity she
has forged in spite of the oppressive behaviors of her other husbands. However, the storm and lake also resemble the Vodou deities who inhabit the
natural world, and they rise up to defend the suddenly silent Janie, one who
has always been able to understand "the words of the trees and the wind"
(23). In *Mules and Men*, Hurston describes a hoodoo initiation ceremony that
she undergoes in New Orleans in which she is given the spirit name "Rain-
Bringer." A lightning bolt is painted across her back, and this is her hoodoo
sign: "The Great One was to speak to me in storms" (191). So Hurston, as the
author/goddess of her fictional world, swoops in to save Janie with her own
version of a deus ex machina.

Before the storm is over, Tea Cake is bitten by a rabid dog while saving
Janie, and the disease that infects him is again an example of the natural
world striking back at Tea Cake. His desire for possession of Janie aligns him
with Logan and Jody. Janie, on the other hand, is cleansed in the floodwaters,
recalling the Tete l'eau ceremony of *Tell My Horse* (Lake Okeechobee is the
"head water" for the Everglades) in which Hurston describes the worship-
pers escaping their status as "sordid things." Hurston describes "this strange
thing in Tea Cake's body" (173) in a manner reminiscent of Vodou possession
rituals that confound the fundamental dualism of self and other. The title
of *Tell My Horse* comes from a familiar expression used in Haiti by an individual temporarily possessed by a lwa. The lwa is said to mount the person,
who is then the deity's horse (*cheval*), and the lwa speaks through the individual, who later has no recollection of what he or she has said or done while

mounted.[35] The phrase "Tell my horse" (*Parlay cheval ou*, in Hurston's trans-
lation) is uttered before the lwa publicly describes the recent, often embar-
rassing, sins and/or misdeeds of the cheval.

The odd scene where Tea Cake is bitten by the rabid dog that is riding a
cow through the floodwaters suggests a slightly distorted, metaphorical version of these possession rituals. Janie, who has been both a "bell-cow" and a
mule, seems clearly figured by the swimming cow,[36] but what are we to make
of the ferocious dog that attacks as Janie clings to the cow's tail? The image
of a "massive built dog . . . sitting on her [the cow's] shoulders and shivering
and growling" (157) seems so intentionally striking and strange that Hurston
must have been thinking of the horse and rider metaphor of Vodou possession, especially considering that possession is often foreshadowed by discomfort in the nape of the neck.[37] The mad dog, then, may represent the type of
fiercely possessive love that has repeatedly assailed Janie's identity and from
which even Tea Cake has shown he is not immune.

Tea Cake has already shown his capacity for jealousy, possessiveness, and
violence toward Janie, and the bite from the rabid dog transfers completely
this malevolent spirit to him. Cassidy's reading accurately notes the resemblance of Tea Cake in his final days to Logan and Jody, and he recognizes that
"Tea Cake's transformation after the dog bite does not seem to be the result
of a totally foreign element invading his psyche as much as an acceleration
of forces already evident in his personality before the storm."[38] When Janie
says that "Tea Cake was gone" and that "[s]omething else was looking out of
his face" (172), she seems to be justifying the absence of the Tea Cake she fell
in love with. In fact, she makes much the same complaint to Jody just before
he dies: "[Y]ou ain't de Jody ah run off down de road wid. You'se whut's left
after he died." In both cases, when the men begin to threaten Janie's inner nature, she must move on in order to serve herself. Her final words to Jody are
an assertion of her own authority and a rejection of "[a]ll dis bowin' down,
all dis obedience under yo' voice" (82).

On a more literal level, rabies as a disease transmitted from animal to
human blurs the boundary of self/other in a threatening way. Rawlings's
work embraces a fusion with nature, describing it in the positive terms of
reintegration, "a torn fragment of the larger cloth." Here, however, Tea Cake
becomes sick and is eventually killed because of his synthesis with nature.
Janie's identity is similarly threatened by Tea Cake's possessiveness and even
by the "self-crushing love" she feels for him (128). As a black woman, she
must repeatedly stave off others' attempts to control, possess, and define her
by choosing personal integrity and autonomy.

Thus, Hurston's personal pastoral emphasizes the importance of the individual much more than Rawlings's wilderness pastoral. Upon completing the traditional pastoral pattern of retreat and return, Janie suggests that her experiences and memories are all that she needs to be content: "So Ah'm back home agin and Ah'm satisfied tuh be heah. Ah done been tuh de horizon and back and now Ah kin set heah in mah house and live by comparisons" (182). Whereas Rawlings emphasizes the need to expand the self outward and join the larger web of life in nature, Hurston describes almost an opposite process: an internalization of an existing connection with the natural world. The difference is at least partially attributable to race. As a fairly progressive white woman, Rawlings imagines herself and her characters reaching out to the otherness around them, and the otherness of nature has always been related to the otherness of race and gender. Hurston, as a doubly "otherized" black woman, seeks to use the black woman's association with nature in a way that empowers her.

This speculative formula becomes much more complicated, however, when Hurston writes about white characters, with a white woman as the heroine of a personal pastoral. *Seraph on the Suwanee*, Hurston's much-maligned "white novel," explores many of the same themes as *Their Eyes*, only from the perspective of white characters Jim and Arvay Meserve. This novel has been dismissed and disparaged by critics as a betrayal of her African American roots and/or as a blatant, flawed attempt to cash in by appealing to a wider audience and even to Hollywood.[39] Hemenway, for example, says that in writing this novel "Hurston largely turned her back on the source of her creativity . . . the celebration of black folklife," resulting in "an unsuccessful work of art." This assessment is echoed by the majority of criticism that has followed, exemplified by Mary Helen Washington's judgment of the book as an "awkward and contrived novel, as vacuous as a soap opera." More recently, some critics have countered the prevailing view of *Seraph on the Suwanee* as a misguided, flawed effort of a writer in the decline of a brilliant career. Janet St. Clair, for one, feels that Hurston does not capitulate "to the antifeminist sentiment of the conservative postwar forties," and she rightly chides those who ignore or condemn the rags-to-riches tale of Jim and Arvay Meserve: "Critics of Hurston should know her principles, processes, and publications well enough to avoid a facile dismissal of this novel."[40]

Indeed, as Susan Edwards Meisenhelder points out, the many striking similarities between *Seraph* and *Their Eyes* should alert readers to the "subversive attack on the values of what she [Hurston] called 'Anglo-Saxon' civilization" masked as a traditional fairy tale of a poor white girl rescued by an upwardly mobile young suitor.[41] Given the similar veiled criticism of white authority in *Their Eyes*, it is somewhat surprising that *Seraph* has so often been read as an unironic capitulation to the tastes of white publishers and a wider/whiter reading public. My own reading of the novel builds upon the work of those critics who have pointed out its subversive aspects, but also rejects the notion that the story is strictly a critique and satire of the dominant white culture. Specifically, I argue that the nature imagery and the attitudes of Jim and Arvay toward the natural world reveal Hurston's complex and ambiguous feelings about race, gender, class, and the destruction of nature, and that this ambiguity stems from pastoral's multiple frames. A class frame and a gender frame provide different interpretive windows on the same scenes in the novel. Their constant overlapping and juxtaposition helps to account for the often conflicting critical interpretations of a complicated text.

In many ways, *Seraph on the Suwanee* contains the most conventional pastoral elements of any of the works examined in this study. It is the story of one man's effort to extract value from nature and to transform the landscape from wilderness to profitable garden. The past is not romanticized as a golden age, but the novel does dramatize the problems of trying to create a pastoral paradise in the present. Arvay is linked to the passive natural world that Jim controls, and she seems to accept servitude (or at least inferiority) as wife and mother. Yet, as Bakker says of the pastoral of the Old South, "[P]astoral imagery can trick cursory readers by lulling them into accepting its picturesque bucolic nostalgia on face value alone." St. Clair makes much the same point about *Seraph* in her reading of "a subversive feminist substory" that lurks "just beneath the vapid and saccharine surface" of the narrative: "Every character and incident is rent by dualities; every narrative assertion self-destructs. Nothing is as it seems; nothing retains its shape." By emphasizing the various uses of the pastoral, my reading emphasizes the novel's "subversive undertow" and its more conventional surface current, as I keep in mind what Buell says of American pastoral in general: "More often than not, accommodationism and reformism are interfused."[42]

The vast majority of critical responses to *Seraph* have conformed to an either/or pattern: either the novel is a vacuous capitulation to white culture or it is a veiled critique that has been misinterpreted as selling out. However, this is a complex novel that continues the gender-based personal pastoral of *Their Eyes* but also deals with class and land-use issues. Thus, while at first glance the active, empowering natural world of *Their Eyes* appears to have been replaced by a mechanistic, passive environment exploited by Jim Meserve, closer examination reveals a more ambivalent portrait of the conversion of the Florida wilderness for human subsistence and profit. As is the case in Rawlings's *South Moon Under,* there is a precarious balance between humans and nature in *Seraph on the Suwanee,* and the line between exploitation and husbandry is not easily demarcated. Hurston ultimately presents Jim's relationship with nature in positive terms, creating a "working-class pastoral" that affirms the value of knowing nature through labor.

In the novel's class frame, there seems to be a conventional attitude toward nature: unimproved land gains purpose and value when transformed by active, masculine power into useful commodity. Within the gender frame, Arvay is struggling to find a vibrant identity of her own while the overbearing Jim threatens to tame her as he does the swampy terrain. While these frames are working at cross-purposes, there are also conflicting currents within each frame. Arvay seems to find and assert herself, but the book's ending suggests a willful capitulation to Jim's authority. Hurston's narrative voice endorses Jim's ability to work Florida's diverse environment for profit, even though his destruction of swampland is symbolically tied to his repressive control of his wife. Moreover, the working-class pastoral that condones Jim's work with nature becomes more bourgeois and upper class as he becomes increasingly wealthy. His actions go from using nature as a leveling force, an arena in which a clever, hardworking, poor person can make a living, to working nature solely for profit, the type of acquisitive individualism decried by Caldwell and Rawlings. Leo Marx notes that a defining feature of the American version of the pastoral shepherd, the "noble husbandman," is that he is not in it for the money: "The goal is sufficiency, not economic growth—a virtual stasis that is a counterpart of the desired psychic balance."[43] For Jim, this applies as both husband and husbandman. He wants to help his wife drain the psychic morass that plagues her and to bring her to a level of understanding with him, but he goes beyond balance to "profit" in his insistence at always being above her. Hurston is not, however, clearly critical of her characters' acquisitive individualism in the ways that Caldwell and Rawlings are, which forces the reader to question what type of work in nature is responsible and what is excessively destructive.

Hurston undoubtedly was thinking of Rawlings's "cracker" fiction while writing this novel, which she hoped would provide the popular success her fellow Floridian had attained. She switched for this novel to Scribner's, Rawlings's publisher, in her quest for a wider audience, and the novel is dedicated: "To Marjorie Kinnan Rawlings and Mrs. Spessard L. Holland With Loving Admiration." Rawlings had already proven the commercial viability of the subject matter of poor, rural Southern whites, both in print and on film with the success of the movie version of *The Yearling* (1946). The opening paragraph of *Seraph*, in fact, provides an intriguing response to the opening of *Cross Creek*, published six years before Hurston's novel. Rawlings indicates the location of her home by emphasizing its distance from human landmarks and its proximity to natural ones: "Cross Creek is a bend in a country road, by land, and the flowing of Lochloosa Lake into Orange Lake, by water. We are four miles west of the small village of Island Grove, nine miles east of a turpentine still, and on the other sides we do not count distance at all, for the two lakes and the broad marshes create an infinite space between us and the horizon" (1). Rawlings goes on in these opening pages to extol the remoteness of the Creek "from urban confusion," implying a virtuousness of both the place and its people, whom she rather generously describes as "all individualists" (2).

Hurston's opening offers a similar physical description of her fictional town's location, but depicts the environment as vitiated by human activity:

> Sawley, the town, is in west Florida, on the famous Suwanee River. It is flanked on the south by the curving course of the river . . . running swift and deep through the primitive forests, and reddened by the chemicals leeched out of drinking roots. On the north, the town is flanked by cultivated fields planted to corn, cane potatoes, tobacco and small patches of cotton. . . . For the most part they were scratchy plantings, the people being mostly occupied in the production of turpentine and lumber. The life of Sawley streamed out from the sawmill and the "teppentime 'still." Then too, there was ignorance and poverty, and the ever-present hookworm.[44]

The emphasis here is on the commercial value of nature, and the ignorance and poverty of the citizens signify a mutually debasing relationship with the environment. The "life of Sawley" comes from the sawmill and turpentine still, the mechanical instruments that convert nature into commodity, whereas for Rawlings, life emanates from the biota itself: "Every pine tree, every gallberry bush, every passion vine, every joree rustling in the underbrush, is vibrant" (6).

Both writers assert a bond between humanity and nature, but while Rawlings reverently proclaims, "There is of course an affinity between people and places" (2), Hurston offers a decidedly less rosy view: "The farms and the scanty flowers in front yards and in tin cans and buckets looked like the people. Trees and plants always look like the people they live with, somehow" (1). The absence of the animistic natural world portrayed in *Their Eyes* is indicative of a traditional pastoral linking of female and passive nature. It is not clear in this early passage whether this mechanistic environment is a tool for a veiled critique of white culture and its treatment of nature or rather a sign of female submissiveness and evidence of Hurston's growing conservatism in the postwar 1940s. By employing a stereotypical poor-girl-marries-rich-boy story that she claimed was "the favorite white theme," Hurston introduces the indeterminacy and ambivalence that has led Meisenhelder to conclude that Hurston is criticizing white culture "from behind the trickster's mask of praise," while Alice Walker describes the same novel as "reactionary, static, shockingly misguided and timid."[45]

The relationship of humans with nature dominates the book, and nature must be read both symbolically and as a presence for its own sake. As a personal pastoral, Arvay's story is surprisingly similar to Janie's in many ways. In this frame, Jim's use of nature for profit can be equated with his domination of his wife. In the frame of the working-class pastoral, the same work with nature can appear responsible and beneficial to black (and white) laborers. The ambiguity created by the multiple pastoral frames can be seen, for instance, in the opening description of Sawley quoted above. It can be read as showing an exploited, diseased environment that mirrors the degeneracy of the "Anglo-Saxon" culture that controls the town. At the same time, it might be noted that the people of Sawley are not alienated from their environment but actually immersed in the natural world and dependent on the resources of the land for both profit and survival. The mere existence of the turpentine and timber industries does not necessarily mean that Sawley's white male power structure is subjugating and exploiting the environment and, by extension, women and African Americans. Hurston's tale is more complex than that, and as the novel is a story of the growth and transformation of both nature and people, its ambiguity and its resistance to being read in terms of either/or, black/white categories grow through the course of the narrative.

The controlling symbol of *Their Eyes* is the pear tree, and in the opening chapter of *Seraph on the Suwanee* the narrator offhandedly notes the existence of pear trees at the Henson household, trees that "bore pears that were only good for preserving" (9). While this description seems to make a rather unfavorable comparison of Arvay to Janie, it emphasizes chiefly that the twenty-one-year-old Arvay is simply not yet ready to begin the journey of self-discovery that Janie initiates at age sixteen under the bursting buds and creamy blossoms of her pear tree. Arvay's "temple" and "sacred place" is instead a mulberry tree still on the verge of blossoming, with its "new green leaves, punctuated by tiny fuzzy things that looked like green, stubby worms" (37). Under these boughs of nascent mulberries, Jim culminates his curious courtship of Arvay in an ambiguously described rape scene.

Just prior to the rape, Hurston includes a brief section detailing Jim's work as an overseer in the turpentine camp. His job is to run the commissary (shades of Joe Starks) and total the accounts of the workers' paychecks based on the number of trees pierced with a phallic "streaking iron" and drained of their valuable resource. While such imagery creates a symbolic connection between women and nature, Hurston also includes detailed accounts of turpentine work as work, not just as a symbol for masculine/feminine power structures: "It was his job to 'ride the woods' before the semi-monthly payday and evaluate the work of the chippers and dippers. . . . The limit of a 'drift,' a territory of one chipper, is known as the 'butting-line or block,' so as Jim rode his horse from drift to drift, he could enjoy both the beauty and the solitude of the pine woods. Free from the press of details around the camp Jim came alive and stretched out his soul." The understanding of the land and trees that Jim displays throughout the novel comes from knowing nature through labor. His reprimands of workers for improperly piercing trees because it will kill them unnecessarily combined with his appreciation of "the beauty and the solitude of the pine woods" (42) make it difficult to see Jim only as a crass exploiter of nature. Within the working-class pastoral frame, he works with nature in order to make a better life for himself and his intended bride. Although his "ancestors had held plantations on the Alabama River," their land and money were wiped out by the Civil War, and Jim arrives in Sawley "with only a small bundle, containing his changing clothes" (7). The Southern turpentine industry offered notoriously low-paying and undesirable work (often preformed by prisoners), but for Jim the job is the first step to prosperity through working with nature.

Undoubtedly, in the context of the personal pastoral, the act of piercing trees is explicitly tied to the rape that follows this chapter by the advice Jim receives from his employee and "pet Negro" Joe Kelsey about how to ensure possession of Arvay: "Most women folks will love you plenty if you take and see to it that they do. . . . From the very first jump, get the bridle in they mouth and ride 'em hard and stop 'em short. They's all alike, Boss. Take 'em and break 'em" (46). The equivocation of women, horses, and trees provides Jim with justification for his act, but Hurston's depiction of the scene under the mulberry tree complicates any attempt to neatly categorize Arvay as passive victim.

Arvay's initial response to the rape is to hold Jim tightly, hoping that he never leaves her, and this reaction has been troubling to many readers and critics. Meisenhelder, for example, suggests that Hurston is critiquing "the white world's model of male sexuality" by portraying Arvay as an emblem of the debased woman produced by "Anglo-Saxon" culture. By "richly contrasting" this scene with the pear tree of *Their Eyes*, Meisenhelder says, "Hurston underscores the fact that, although Arvay may seem a Cinderella figure, she in fact becomes a glorified 'spit cup' in her marriage."[46] However, this reading glosses over important similarities with the pear tree scene and cannot fully account for Arvay's puzzling perception of her rape as cleansing and cathartic.

As noted earlier, the "tiny fuzzy things" on the green leaves of the mulberry tree are not so much different in kind from the "sister-calyxes" of the pear tree as in degree: they are "young mulberries coming on" (37) and are not yet fully developed, like Arvay herself. Although Meisenhelder points out several word-for-word parallels between *Seraph* and *Their Eyes,* she omits an important instance that establishes a continuity, rather than a contrast, between the women in these texts. At the masturbatory climax of the pear tree scene, "Janie felt a pain remorseless sweet" (11), while at the end of her forced encounter under the mulberry tree, "Arvay knew a pain remorseless sweet" (51). Surely this repetition is not accidental, and it implies an affinity between the two female protagonists that is (understandably) easy to miss or ignore. There is, no doubt, some irony in Hurston's portrait of her often-annoying white heroine, but the echo of the phrase "pain remorseless sweet" suggests what Andrew Ettin calls pastoral's double voice, "carrying on two discussions simultaneously on different levels of significance."[47] Thus, Jim's actions constitute both a rape and a catharsis, at least in Arvay's twisted psyche. Much the same process is at work later in the novel when Jim drains the swampland that represents Arvay's psychological problems. Those actions illustrate and strengthen Jim's control of his wife, but they also represent a purging of Arvay's psyche, which contributes to her gradual awakening into self-awareness.

While the rape may be detestable to modern readers, Hurston's presentation of the events reveals that her characters do not view this assault in that way: there are two levels of significance. Arvay, after fixing her clothes, hugs and kisses Jim until the two wind up off their feet again: "It seemed a great act of mercy when she found herself stretched on the ground again with Jim's body weighing down upon her" (53). Jim also confuses the matter by whisking her straight to the courthouse to get married and offering an explanation of what has happened that muddles the meaning of the word rape in this particular context: "Sure you was raped, and that ain't all. You're going to keep on getting raped . . . every day for the rest of your life." Jim's euphemism for marriage, in fact, is "rape in the first degree," and Arvay couldn't be happier to learn that they are to be married immediately. She even conceives of her rape as cathartic, the "cleansing of her sacred place" needed to expiate her guilt over her former secret attraction to her sister's husband, the Reverend Carl Middleton: "Her secret sin was forgiven and her soul set free! . . . She had paid under that mulberry tree" (57). These sorts of confounding passages are precisely what have led critics either to dismiss this novel as an anomaly in Hurston's oeuvre or to conclude that every sentence is an ironic, subversive indictment of the book's characters and culture.

Although the latter may seem more appealing to Hurston fans and scholars, I am arguing that either reaction oversimplifies the complexity of the multiple pastoral frames at work in the text. It seems unwarranted, for instance, to assert that female sexuality in the novel is characterized only by "passivity, receptivity, and loss of self"[48] when, following the rape, Hurston writes that an "unknown power" takes hold of Arvay as she pulls Jim close to her: "She must eat him up, and absorb him within herself. Then he could never leave her again" (53–54). There is a complicated overlapping of gender and class in these passages. The mulberry tree symbolizes Arvay's girlhood self, like Janie's pear tree, and so the rape scene signifies the end of her childhood and the (troubling) beginning of her married life. Her reactions of relief, gratitude, and fear of abandonment stem from her feelings of class inferiority, as becomes clear later. Her shame over her cracker ancestry prevents her from having a strong identity as a woman, so she imagines herself enveloping Jim in the way the tree has swallowed her in its boughs, protecting her in a green, pastoral haven: "It was like a green cave under there, or like being inside a big green tent" (49). Arvay's journey to wisdom and self-empowerment is more protracted than Janie's, but the characters' similarities suggest that Hurston ultimately sees their trajectories as quite similar. Arvay is pleased to leave behind the poverty and insecurity of her past, and Hurston's language recalls Janie's association of Jody with change and the horizon: "Where this man was hurrying her off to, she had no idea, but she was going, and leaving her old life behind her" (54).

Jim's view of both nature and women mirrors that of Jody Starks, and, curiously, so do his words.[49] Jody, as seen earlier, dehumanizes women with statements like, "Somebody got to think for women and chillun and chickens and cows. I god, they sho don't think none themselves" (67). Jim offers his version of this idea, adding the stereotype of women as naturally subservient and emotional: "[W]omen folks were not given to thinking nohow. It was not in their makeup to do much thinking. That was what men were made for. Women were made to hover and to feel" (105). Hurston even has Jim tell Arvay, "I see one thing and can understand ten. You see ten things and can't even understand one" (261); this is surely an intentional reprise of Jody's assessment of Janie in chapter 6 of *Their Eyes:* "When Ah see one thing Ah understands ten. You see ten things and don't understand one" (67). Jim's resemblance to Jody is unmistakable, and the actions of both men betray their words by revealing that they have very little understanding of their wives.

Yet Hurston's narrative voice is conspicuous by its absence at such misogynistic moments in *Seraph*. Janie's plight is presented sympathetically, but Arvay is consistently portrayed as responsible for Jim's dissatisfaction with their
marriage.

The text's apparent endorsement of Jim's point of view may indeed be an
element of subterfuge, but Hurston seems genuinely to have identified per-
sonally with Jim. In a letter to Burroughs Mitchell, her editor at Scribner's,
Hurston discusses her planned final revisions of the novel: "I shall bring Arvay along her road to find herself a great deal faster. I get sick of her at times
myself. Have you ever been tied in close contact with a person who had a
strong sense of inferiority? I have, and it is hell." She goes on to mention a
"man that I cared for" whose feelings of inferiority confounded and annoyed
her, relating her experience to Jim's frustration with Arvay:

> You know how many marriages in the literary and art world have bro-
> ken up up [*sic*] such rocks, to say nothing of other paths of life. A busi-
> ness man is out scuffling for dear life to get things for the woman he
> loves, and she is off pouting and accusing him of neglecting her. She
> feels that way because she does not feel herself able to keep up with
> the pace that he is setting, and just be confident that she is wanted no
> matter how far he goes. Millions of women do not want their husbands
> to succeed for fear of losing him. It is a very common ailment. That
> is why I decided to write about it. The sufferers do not seem to realize
> that all that is needed is a change of point of view from fear into self-
> confidence and then there is no problem.[50]

Although she also identifies with Arvay's insecurities, Hurston's sympathy for
Jim's position in this relationship helps to account for the differences in her
presentation of Arvay and Janie. Arvay has no positive self-image for much
of the novel, and she therefore accepts Jim's characterization of himself as
a victim and of herself as an ignorant ingrate, "a hog under a acorn tree . . .
never even looking up to see where the acorns are coming from" (262).

Arvay's constant self-doubt stems from two main sources: her guilt over
having secretly loved her sister's husband and her intransigent embarrass-
ment about her poor cracker roots. The Meserves' deformed first child, Earl,
is a manifestation of this guilt and shame: "the physical projection of her own
repressed 'Other,'" according to Lowe, and "punishment for the way I used
to be" (69) according to Arvay herself.[51] His birth intensifies Arvay's desire
to move away from Sawley but also allows her to assert her own agency. Her
hours of work massaging Earl's "feeble hands and feet" (76) aid the child's de-

velopment and represent the tentative beginnings of her efforts to form a vigorous identity of her own. Described as an almost feral child, Earl makes clear
the connection between inner and outer nature. He hides out in the swamp
that borders their house in Citrabelle after attacking the daughter of a Portuguese laborer who works for Jim, perhaps acting out Arvay's resentment of
"those Gees" (130) as she disparagingly calls them. Earl is then killed in the
swamp after he attempts to shoot his father, an expression of rage that again
seems linked to Arvay's unconscious desires to lash out at her husband.

The swamp is terrifying to Arvay, as it represents her own tangled psychic
wilderness, which she tried to leave behind in Sawley: "I don't want no parts
of that awful place. It's dark and haunted-looking and too big and strong to
overcome. It's frightening! Like some big old varmint or something to eat you
up" (80). Jim, on the other hand, views this "finest stretch of muck outside the
Everglades" (77) as a feminine space where old-growth forest and sandy soil
promise economic gain for someone industrious enough to take advantage
of its seemingly wasted fertility. *Seraph* actually shows what *Their Eyes* ignores: the transformation of swamp to farmland. This is the pastoral impulse
in action, turning unimproved nature into the garden, with implications in
both the personal and working-class pastoral frames. The reclaimed farmland, like the muck in *Their Eyes,* represents a false paradise for the woman
protagonist. The place seems promising at first, especially when Arvay has a
healthy, beautiful baby girl just after the swamp is cleared. The draining of
the swamp is symbolically cleansing for Arvay, but she begins "to feel jealous
of her own child" (88) because of the attention Jim lavishes upon the baby.

A change in physical location does not mend the underlying problems of
their relationship because the habitus of the place she inhabits remains essentially unchanged. As discussed earlier, a particular place "exercises a certain determinacy upon both the population and the social processes located
upon its terrain." The habitus of place is a "conceptual lens through which
particular understandings or interpretations of the social world are generated and as such invite particular forms of response or action to the social
world."[52] Throughout much of *Seraph,* the habitus of place keeps Arvay complacent. Her household amenities increase along with her income, and Jim
sees it as a husband's responsibility "to work and fetch in every dad-blamed
thing that his wife thinks she would like to have" (25). Transforming the potentially wild swamp into an orderly pastoral grove is not just symbolic of
Jim's control of his wife; it actually helps him achieve and maintain it to
some degree by shaping the "conceptual lens" through which Arvay understands the world and her place in it. However, the changing nature of place
means that Jim's conversion of the landscape also helps to set in motion pro-

cesses that tend in another direction, toward self-awareness as well as self-abnegation.

Within the personal pastoral frame, then, the clearing of the swamp signifies a small step on Arvay's "road to find herself," as Hurston calls it, even as new problems are brought to the surface. Within the class frame, clearing the swamp to plant fruit trees enables Jim to continue his economic rise, one that is facilitated by Florida's natural environment every step of the way. In this sense, Hurston's portrayal of nature is different from that of the other authors in this study. For Caldwell, Rawlings, and Faulkner, reaping profits by exploiting natural resources tends to be equated with destroying and abusing nature. Their focus is generally on large industries (e.g., cotton farming, textile mills, and timber) that abuse the environment to the detriment of individuals struggling to live off the land. Hurston, however, in this novel, presents the natural world as a relatively egalitarian arena in which an individual like Jim Meserve can improve his family's economic standing.

Jim's various enterprises provide the reader with something of a tour of Florida's wonderfully diverse environment, creating the impression that Hurston is proudly displaying her home's natural abundance and the economic possibilities it affords its citizens. In fact, Hurston began working for the Federal Writers' Project in Florida in 1938 while in dire financial straits, earning a relief salary of $67.50 per month for her work on Florida's folk cultures.[53] As part of her work, Hurston researched and wrote about the turpentine and citrus industries for a Works Progress Administration guidebook to the state. This work aligns her with Jim in yet another way: both adeptly use Florida's natural resources and its people to pull themselves out of poverty.

Within the class frame of the novel, Jim appears industrious, forthright, and even admirable as he uses his earnings as a turpentine boss and a citrus picker to purchase a home for his family: "I never did like the idea of no child of mine being born on borrowed land" (78). In this sense he resembles Lant, Rawlings's model of ecological responsibility, but the line between responsible use and exploitation of nature for profit is tricky to demarcate, and it may shift depending on one's perspective. Marx's distinction between sufficiency and economic growth helps to highlight a key difference between Lant, who barely manages to eke out a living, and Jim, whose profits steadily rise. However, Hurston's working-class pastoral revises the traditional "critique of avarice" that Terry Gifford discusses as a convention of much pastoral literature: "The retreat from the urban world of court and commerce, where riches are valued, not only provides an opportunity for criticising material values, but implies that others should not aspire to them."[54] Hurston does quite the opposite in this novel, presenting Jim's economic climb in largely positive terms, perhaps owing to the affinities she felt with him: her poverty, her somewhat conservative political views, and even her rabid anti-Communism.[55]

The best argument that Hurston is actually being subversively critical of her white characters throughout *Seraph* is that Jim's treatment of blacks and women mirrors his crass exploitation of nature. Hurston does, at times, equate Jim's misogyny toward Arvay with a rapacious attitude toward nature. These are the places where the personal and working-class pastoral frames clash and Jim proves to be a chauvinist lout even as he is a resourceful hustler and provider. It is more difficult, however, to categorize his interactions with black characters. Realizing that "since the colored men did all of the manual work, they were the ones who actually knew how things were done," Jim frequents the "the jooks and gathering places in Colored Town," hanging out, swapping stories, and buying "treats" when he first moves to Citrabelle (74). He shrewdly utilizes the "underground system in Colored Town that the whites did not know about" (82) in order to complete the clearing of the swamp with cheap labor by providing a place and the supplies for a barbecue and party after the land is cleared. In just one weekend, the entire five-acre plot is slashed and burned and transformed into an orderly, pastoral grove of neat rows of "the very finest and the most money-making" citrus trees (83).

This endeavor is another instance in which Jim's behavior could be read as exploitative and oppressive: his success at subduing wild nature parallels his control of both his wife and his African American workforce. To be sure, Jim profits from the deal, but so do the laborers, pickers whom Jim works beside in other groves, as do the black carpenters he hires to build his house. The men assure Jim that they are "only too glad to oblige him," and only Arvay objects that they have stolen all the scrap wood after building the house. Jim explains to his wife that the wood is part of the deal that allows him to build their house for less than market value: "If I act like I don't notice it, I got a lot of willing friends. . . . All of 'em would feel hard towards me if I went around asking about those scraps of wood" (82). Hurston does not describe the exchange as one in which one party is the exploiter and the other the victim; rather, both parties are somewhere in between. Jim cultivates a mutually beneficial relationship with the black workers, and this reciprocity is mirrored in his decision to plant black-eyed peas throughout the grove to benefit humans, animals, and plants: "That crop served a three-fold purpose. It provided an enormous amount of additional food. . . . The cows could eat pea-vines for hay. It was a cover crop that added nitrate to the soil" (95). Unlike Caldwell's monocrop farmers, Jim displays an understanding of nature that facilitates his rise from orange picker to grove owner, which makes it problematic to castigate his relationships with nature, blacks, and women as one-sided and exploitative.[56]

It is nearly twenty years later when Jim is ready to undertake the project of clearing a large tract of the Big Swamp (the novel frequently skips years at a time between chapters). Describing the swamp as having "held the town from growing west long enough" (193), Jim now appears to be an agent of a culture that views nature antagonistically, as a challenge or obstacle to human progress. The reward for meeting this challenge and conquering nature is primarily financial, as Jim explains to his son-in-law, Hatton Howland, while persuading him to purchase the land, sell its timber, and fill in the swamp for future development. The bulk of the profit, however, is reserved for the white, male owners of the land, Jim and Hatton, rather than for those who work it. In the scenes on the muck in *Their Eyes,* Hurston is careful to point out the profits being turned by the black laborers, while the white bosses are virtually absent from the text itself. In *Seraph,* we see things from the other side, and the focus is on the profit from negotiating deeds, timber contracts, and development deals.

Although the emphasis may not be on the profits of the manual laborers, Hurston provides subtle indications that Jim and Hatton are not simply exploiting the black workers. As discussed above, Jim's bargaining to clear his land and build his house is one example that he need not be reductively categorized as simply an abuser of nature and minorities, and another occurs when Joe Kelsey and his family move into a house on the Meserve grove. The incident is briefly mentioned and easy to overlook; Jim forms a moonshining partnership with Joe that benefits both of them: "Jim, eager to accumulate and prosper as well as to help Joe out, had set Joe up in a whiskey still. . . . Joe could pay back the money that Jim had put out as he went along. All over a certain profit was to go to Jim after that. Both men considered that fair as Jim was to furnish the customers while Joe ran the still" (96). Hurston later notes that Joe uses his profits to buy land and build a house for his family, which hardly seems to support a unilateral reading of "Jim's effect on the black characters in the novel [as] . . . pernicious and insidious."[57] In fact, Arvay is the one who more often comes across as intolerant and racist. She accuses Jim of thinking that "[e]ven niggers is better" than her family of "piney-woods Crackers" (126), and her opinion of the Portuguese Corregio family is that "no foreigners were ever quite white" (120).

Jim certainly has his share of negative qualities as well. Perhaps the most notable and disturbing are his disparaging opinion of women's intellectual abilities and his profit-driven willingness to destroy nature. These attitudes indicate that Hurston's ecopastoral retains some of the more conservative aspects of the traditional pastoral mode even as it modifies others. Accordingly, the men who actually clear the Big Swamp are obscured and even dehumanized through a seemingly odd association with both machines and nature: "As Jim had predicted, modern machinery and methods had cleared that swamp in an amazingly short time. Arvay, from her seat on the front porch, had watched the gangs of husky black roustabouts rumbling past in truck loads.... the horde of black men sang and chanted and swarmed and hacked, machinery rumbled and rattled, huge trucks grumbled and rolled until one day Arvay saw the sun setting behind the horizon of the world" (195). Here again we see the pastoral impulse at work, but with some subtle but significant changes from earlier scenes.

The swamp is being cleared not for an orange grove and a home for Jim's struggling, working-class family, but for a modern subdivision and golf course. Jim's goals are more profit oriented, although he does want to provide for his daughter, Angeline, and her new husband, who become rich as the swamp is filled with sand, "[r]aw, dark gashes made by the bulldozers" become streets, and sewer, water, and electric lines are quickly installed (196). Instead of working with the black workers, Jim is now only an overseer, and the workers are consigned to the anonymity of the background with both the machinery used to clear the land and nature itself. Arvay's role as passive observer recalls the "high seat" of Nanny's restrictive ideal of womanhood from *Their Eyes* and aligns Arvay with a more passive version of the natural world than the Vodou-influenced environment of Hurston's earlier novel. Gone are the hurricanes, lightning strikes, and other signs of nature's resistance, replaced with a thoroughly dominated nature that reflects the oppression of women: "Arvay was surprised at finding herself feeling a sympathy with the swamp" (195).

The entire development actually seems like an early version of a suburb, a category of place designed to achieve a utopian or pastoral middle state through meticulous environmental planning.[58] The centerpiece of the development is a new golf course, perhaps the ultimate symbol of exclusivity and of nature carefully contrived for the purpose of profit. Hurston's description of the young Howlands' activities seems straight out of a John Cheever story: "Angie and Hatton played tennis and golf, went in swimming, canoed and motor-boated with the rest, and talked about getting sun-tanned." However rosy this bucolic, bourgeois scene may appear, the subtext of exploitation and stratification along class and racial lines is always present: "The Howland Development exerted a tremendous effect on Citrabelle and the surrounding country. It came along and stratified the town. The original line of the swamp gave accent like a railroad track. Those who belonged moved west"

(197). Such passages seem to undermine Jim's notions of value and progress that are elsewhere condoned by the text. One or the other of these contradictory impulses need not be given priority, however. They may be reconciled by crediting Hurston with a more nuanced approach that acknowledges that one group's material advances may very well reinforce the class stratification that its new wealth helps it transcend. It is also important to remember that the text's references to Colored Town and the white merchant class that profits from its residents imply that Citrabelle is not exactly a bastion of integration and financial equity before the construction of the Howland Development.

Within the personal pastoral frame, there are similar conflicting implications. Arvay's sense that the Howland Development is "infinitely more threatening to her than the dark gloom of the swamp had been" (197) reflects her fears that her son-in-law will domesticate and shape her daughter just as he has the swamp—and just as Jim has done to her—making Angeline, in effect, little more than another showpiece of the Howland Development. Indeed, Angeline is equated with the land by Jim's gift of both to Hatton. He basically gives the land to his son-in-law instead of purchasing it himself, and simultaneously he secretly facilitates the couple's elopement, recalling his spiriting away of Arvay after the rape scene. Angeline's marriage to a Yankee echoes a common motif of Reconstruction-era Southern pastoral, the marriage of the Southern woman and Northern man that saves the plantation and symbolizes national unity. Although the context is updated, Hatton converts his bride into a neopastoral Southern garden, a suburban neighborhood complete with golf course.

At the same time, the swamp also represents the morass of Arvay's psyche and her deep-seated feelings of guilt and shame from her past. Arvay "hated and feared the swamp," we are told, but she also "hated to see it go" (195). When Jim clears the small swamp earlier in the novel, Arvay's feelings are dredged up and confronted, with the birth of a healthy Angeline immediately following. The draining of the "Big Swamp" for the Howland Development again represents a confrontation with her buried fears of inferiority and exclusion: "Jim was a Meserve. Angeline was a Meserve. Kenny was a Meserve, but so far as they were concerned, she was still a Henson. Sort of a handmaiden around the house. She had married a Meserve and borned Meserves, but she was not one of them" (199).

Despite the implications of masculine control over feminine nature, this is a healthy process for Arvay psychologically: Hurston explicitly ties Arvay's gradual self-discovery to the family's economic rise. The quasi-pastoral image of the golf course implicitly contains an ideal of balance between opposing forces, and it is really no more or less of a managed landscape than a manicured garden. Less natural than an undisturbed swamp yet less artificial than the buildings and paved streets of the town, the golf course has the potential both to alienate and to connect people and nature. For Arvay, a new sleeping porch that Jim adds to the house has the same potential. Throughout the novel, Arvay is associated principally with the house, and her lack of an outside identity fosters her constant assumption that she is not worthy of her husband. Hurston implies that Arvay must go out into the world, into nature, in order to discover her inherent worth. The lack of solid walls on the sleeping porch both buffers her from and joins her to the outside world, permitting Arvay to venture outward safely and to begin sensing her intrinsic value: "As she went [into the house], the perfume from the flowers surged around her. The moon was rising, and some mocking-birds in a tangerine tree began to trill sleepily. The whip-poor-will was still sending out his lonesome call. Arvay paused in the door and looked back on the softly lighted porch. It was to her the most beautiful and perfect scene in all the world. She was as near to complete happiness as she had ever been in her life. The porch told her that she belonged" (237). The sleeping porch confirms that the rewards of the working-class pastoral ethos are largely items of bourgeois leisure, but Hurston does not, as might be expected, associate the rise to a middle-class lifestyle with an increase in modernist alienation.

Although there is a current of antimaterialism associated with Janie's natural imagery in *Their Eyes,* Arvay's new possessions actually have a liberating effect. The difference is that Janie has a strong self-image from nearly the beginning of the novel, and her pear tree vision of herself is threatened by men's attempts to make her into a possession. Jim, on the other hand, works to accumulate wealth and property in order to demonstrate his love for his family. The novel's narrative voice seems to confirm his motives by frequently suggesting that his desire to communicate his affection is the driving force behind all of his labors: "Jim felt that he would stand on the mount of transfiguration when Arvay showed some appreciation of his love as expressed by what he was striving to do for her" (77). Her rise to material prosperity—symbolized by the addition of the sleeping porch—gradually begins to convince Arvay that she has value as an individual: "She had seen that kind of porches [*sic*] attached to houses of people, but of a class of folks whom she thought of as too high-toned for her to compare with. . . . She felt highly privileged to have it under her care, but she could not feel that she had any right to be there" (233–34).

This is an odd convergence of the gender and class pastoral frames. The destruction of the swamp removes an obstacle to Arvay's burgeoning self-awareness, yet her continued identification with passive nature makes this development another sign of her subordination to her husband. Jim's destruction of wild nature makes him the money to buy things like a sleeping porch, and the material rewards are what bolster Arvay's self-image and help her to assert herself. The traditional pastoral critique of greed discussed by Gifford is altered by Hurston. The working-class pastoral becomes more consumerist and bourgeois as the Meserves clearly rise above their working-class roots and their possessions actually enable Arvay's growth.

Eventually, she begins to feel that the porch belongs to her: "It built Arvay up. . . . It was a kind of a throne room." In short, the permeable boundaries of the screened porch gently coax her outside and buttress the self-confidence she needs to fully confront the past that continues to stunt her development: "Just looking around her gave her courage. Out there, Arvay had the courage to visit the graveyard of years and dig up dates and examine them cheerfully. It was a long, long way from the turpentine woods to her sleeping porch" (234). Significantly, Arvay associates herself with natural imagery just after this encouraging episode, finally able to clarify the vague affinity she had earlier experienced with the swamp: "She felt like a dammed-up creek. Green scum was covering her over" (253). Although this stagnant and confined organic image reflects the current state of her own inner nature, it represents the tentative beginnings of self-awareness necessary to counter Jim's most damning accusation, delivered in a fit of rage: "You're my damn property" (216).

While Jim's categorization of his wife leaves much to be desired from a feminist standpoint, Arvay's failure to demonstrate that she is anything other than a passive object is perhaps equally disappointing. Hurston seems to go out of her way to create an infuriatingly docile heroine, including having Arvay repeatedly resolve in her mind to leave Jim and, on one occasion, to commit suicide, only to change her mind before actually doing anything. As Jim recognizes, she has considerable difficulty thinking for herself: "She would follow her pride and go back home to her mother. No, Jim was her husband and she would stay right where he put her. Back and forth . . . always wondering what Jim wanted her to do" (270–71). This weakened version of femininity accounts for the fact that Hurston does not associate Arvay with any powerful natural symbols for the vast majority of the novel.

As a number of critics have noted, the name Meserve implies that Jim demands that others serve him. A more ambiguous reading, however, adds the possibility that the name means that Jim serves himself. Angeline and Kenny, like their father, possess a certain brashness and self-assuredness that ensures they will take care of their own needs and desires—serve themselves—before worrying about those of others. In this sense, Arvay is surely not a Meserve, but, as she says, a servant to the other members of her family. Her discovery of how to serve herself as well is signaled by her reidentification with the mulberry tree and coincides with a more visibly active natural world.

Arvay's separation from her husband and brief return to Sawley are precipitated by Jim's nearly fatal encounter with a rattlesnake, the first instance in which nature threatens to overwhelm him in the novel. In his typically childlike way, Jim calls Arvay to come and see him holding an eight-foot rattler, "like a little boy turning cartwheels in front of the house where his girl lived" (254). When the snake begins to wriggle free and constrict itself around Jim's midsection, Arvay is paralyzed with fear and does nothing to help her husband, who is saved by Joe's son Jeff an instant before the snake frees its head. Hemenway notes that this scene "is almost topheavy with phallic and Christian symbolism,"[59] and Jim feels that Arvay's failure to understand things from his point of view is the proverbial snake in the garden: "I'm just as hungry as a dog for a knowing and a doing love. You love like a coward. . . . Unthankful and unknowing like a hog under a acorn tree. Eating and grunting with your ears hanging over your eyes, and never even looking up to see where the acorns are coming from. What satisfaction can I get out of that kind of a love, Arvay?" (262) Jim fails to see (and the text fails to condemn) his own selfishness and foolishness in this episode: he knows his wife has a fear of snakes, and he surely understands the imprudence of grabbing an eight-foot rattler. For Arvay, the snake signifies an unconscious desire to see Jim die, replacing the passive natural symbol of the swamp. Although she still does not act herself, the new natural imagery foreshadows the changes that will accompany Arvay's journey back to her cracker roots in Sawley.

After Jim leaves her and heads for his shrimp boats on the coast, Arvay learns that her mother is on her deathbed and heads for home, and the change of physical location is an important element in her impending transformation. Upon arriving in her hometown, Arvay learns from her taxi driver that the sawmills and turpentine camps have been replaced by peanut farms, tourist camps, grocery stores, and a modern hotel. Carrying designer Mark Cross luggage that costs "more than a turpentine worker ever handled in a year" (an apt symbol for her psychological baggage), Arvay nostalgically elevates her previously shameful cracker roots, commenting that "in the good old days, the folks in Sawley was good and kind and neighborly [and] I'd hate to see all that done away with" (273–74). The driver's incredulous reply hints that Arvay's return to her past will indeed be revelatory: "Lady! You must not know this town too good. I moved here fifteen years ago and . . . I ain't seen no more goodness and kindheartedness here than nowhere else. Such another back-biting and carrying on you never seen. They hate like sin to take a forward step" (274).

What shocks Arvay most, however, is the deplorable state of her sister's family and her childhood home, practically Caldwellian in their squalor: Larraine is dipping snuff on the crumbling front porch; Carl, whose face is "marred" and body "shaped by making too many humble motions," is working under the hood of "an unbelievably battered old Model T"; the couple's "mule-faced" daughters are mutely peeping around corners; and mother Maria is wasting away inside a house "with the strong odor of rat-urine over everything" (276). Surveying the town and her former home, Arvay sees what her own fate would have been had she married Rev. Middleton, and she realizes that Jim has made the difference between her life and Larraine's. This reappraisal of her position gives her new appreciation for her marriage, but, more important, it bolsters Arvay's image of herself: "Maybe she was not as bad off as she had thought she was. It made her feel to hold up her head and to look upon herself" (298).

After Maria's funeral, Arvay rebuffs an attempted extortion by Carl and Larraine, who loot the house that Arvay now owns in response and pile trash around the pear trees in order to burn them. Displaying a newfound ability to see and understand herself and the world, Arvay recognizes a symbolic significance in the landscape. The mulberry tree, her "sacred symbol," effects a vision of rebirth and vitality that recalls the creaming, frothing blossoms of Janie's pear tree: "[S]oon now . . . tender green leaves would push out of those tight little brown bumps; badges that the tree put on every spring to show that it was in the service of the sun. Fuzzy little green knots would appear. These would turn out to be juicy, sweet, purple berries before the first of May. But most of all, this tree would become a great, graceful green canopy rolling its majesty against the summer sky. Here had been her dreams since early girlhood. Here, in violent ecstasy, had begun her real life" (305). The tree is in virtually the same state as it was at the beginning of the novel: not quite ready to bloom, which indicates Arvay's lack of growth over the course of the narrative. Now, however, she does begin to bloom and to view the world and her life differently because of her elevated confidence, which comes from her prominent class status.

She sees the decrepit house as the "monstropolous accumulation" of the sources of her long-festering feelings of guilt and shame. Confronting and naming them releases their hold on her, and she symbolically burns her former home with the trash meant to torch the trees: "Seeing it from the meaning of the tree it was no house at all. . . . It had soaked in so much of doing-without, of soul-starvation, of brutish vacancy of aim, of absent dreams, envy of trifles, ambitions for littleness, smothered cries and trampled love, that it was a sanctuary of tiny and sanctioned vices. . . . The physical sign of her disturbance was consuming down in flames, and she was under her tree of life" (306–7). In her determined destruction of the house Arvay simultaneously reclaims the mulberry tree as her personal symbol, replaces her former passivity with decisive action, and refines her introspective vision, becoming conscious "for the first time in her life" of a feeling of "exultation . . . followed by a peaceful calm" (307).[60] She becomes a white trash phoenix rising from the ashes of poverty with designer luggage in hand. Although there is an element of mockery in this image, Hurston presents the moment of burning the house as a true awakening and an empowering act.

Linking Arvay's "tree of life" with Janie's empowering pear tree suggests that Hurston intends both characters to be read similarly. Indeed, her description of Arvay under the mulberry tree could easily be applied to either heroine: "[T]he woman had triumphed, and with nothing more than her humble self, had won a vivid way of life with love" (306). Additionally, Arvay decides to turn her childhood home into a public park, with the stipulation that her mulberry tree be preserved, similar to Janie's bringing a pack of seeds home to plant and figuratively planting a seed in Pheoby with her story. What becomes especially troubling in the novel's conclusion is the way that Jim and Arvay's marriage is reconstituted. According to Jim, "[T]wo people ain't never married until they come to the same point of view" (266), yet when Arvay becomes "no longer divided in her mind" (307), it is only because her new viewpoint is identical to Jim's.

The park, with its pastoral implications of nature improved and made orderly, is a fitting legacy for Arvay. It is an imitation of Jim's clearing of the swamp for a golf course, in the sense that both house and swamp represent her guilt and fears and in the pastoral implication of nature tamed and ordered. Her donation of her inherited land for the park also exemplifies how the working-class pastoral develops into more of a bourgeois pastoral. Certainly, Arvay would never have been financially secure enough to give away her family's only property were it not for Jim's successes at working the environment for profit. The upwardly mobile Meserves' wealth thus allows the rat-infested house to permanently become a park rather than another grocery store, tourist camp, or highway in rapidly expanding Sawley.

The recognition that she is above others (especially her sister) because of her class standing gives Arvay confidence and power to act. She becomes a freshly empowered woman who feels confident in her newfound knowledge of herself without knowing whether she and Jim will ever reconcile: "It could be that she had stumbled and fumbled around until it was too late to take in the slack. If that was the case, she would never be really happy in her lifetime. But even so, she knew her way now and could see things as they were. That was some consolation" (308). Although she is identified only with passive pastoral landscapes, this seems preferable to the shack of poverty or "a dammed-up creek" covered with scum (253).

Arvay exercises her freedom of choice by reaffirming the value of her roles of wife and mother, vigorously pursuing a reunion with the husband she loves. Hurston makes a point to show her as more decisive, more considerate, and simply more aware of the world and people around her. Arvay's changed attitude surprises Jim, and when she asks to go out on the boats, he outfits her in the kind of "blue jeans that the fishermen wore, two blue shirts, and the tall rubber sea-boots." This androgynous clothing, like the overalls Tea Cake gives Janie on the muck, is meant to signify a new equality between husband and wife in a frontierlike setting. The racial egalitarianism of the shrimping community even surpasses that of the muck, where white bosses supervise work, intraracial prejudice abounds, and the neighboring Seminoles are mocked. The Portuguese Alfredo Corregio, the Meserve's former tenant, reappears as the captain of one of Jim's boats, and "a husky Negro" commands another: "There were as many if not more colored captains than white. It was who could go out there and come back with the shrimp. And nobody thought anything about it. White and Negro captains were friendly together and compared notes. Some boats had mixed crews" (323). These lines are another illustration of the key difference between Hurston's working-class pastoral and the nineteenth-century Southern pastoral of writers like Page and Simms: those who actually perform the labor profit from their skill and hard work, as the natural environment in *Seraph* is a leveling force.[61]

However, the same egalitarian spirit is not so obvious when it comes to gender. Arvay determines to accept Jim, despite his faults, because she knows that she is incomplete without him. Again, this sentiment closely resembles Janie's devotion to Tea Cake even though he flirts with other women, gambles with her money, and physically assaults her. Hurston effects the reunion of Arvay and Jim on the vastness of the ocean, with Jim piloting the *Arvay Henson* toward the open sea. Jim decides to challenge the elements and "cross the bar" out of the haven of the harbor before the water has risen to a safe level. In this obviously symbolic scene, Hurston provides a momentary glimpse of the powerful and destructive capabilities of nature that are absent from the novel until the snake incident that precipitates Arvay's transformation: "Perhaps ten boat lengths ahead was a colossal boiling and tumbling, grumbling and rumbling of the sea that sent a white spray mounting. . . . Havoc was there with her mouth wide open" (328). As Jim struggles to maintain control of the vessel, the mate wraps himself around his captain's leg, pleading Jim to turn around. This moment clearly is meant as a counterpoint to Jim's battle with the rattler, and this time "Arvay saw and acted almost instinctively" (329), pulling the mate away and allowing Jim to pilot the boat through the rough sea and into the calm waters of the Atlantic. Although Arvay does finally become an active participant in this scene, nature is overcome and rendered harmless by Jim. Indeed, after she pulls the sailor from Jim's leg, Arvay's position hardly signifies equality with her husband: "She stood just back of him and looked fearfully over his shoulder" (330).

Again, though, it proves difficult to read such scenes in only one way. Just as Jim's clearing of the swamps signifies not only his control over a passive natural world but also the removal of Arvay's morass of psychological problems, his apparent power over the ocean cuts both ways. Jim subdues the roiling sea, and the crew kills and discards a feminine array of "soft-looking queer shaped things" while shrimping: "Few soft-bodied things had a chance. Arvay watched the slaughter with pity" (335–36). Surely it is not wrong to see this as "the fate of the feminine in Jim's world," as Meisenhelder does,[62] but the raising and killing of these "strange unimaginable-shaped things from the bottom of the sea" (335) reprises the symbolism of the swamp and also represents mining the depths of Arvay's unconscious, coming as it does just before the couple's final reconciliation.

The ocean becomes Arvay's symbol at the end of the novel, and Hurston portrays it as encompassing opposing forces. Alternately placid and menacing, the sea appears dominated when the sailors are extracting shrimp or killing a shark, but it can also kill these men in an instant, as the fishermen constantly remind themselves with barroom tales of their departed comrades. As Jim says when Arvay mentions the beauty of the water's constantly changing colors, "It's pretty like you say, and then it can be ugly. It's good and it's bad. It's something of everything on earth" (330). Arvay, too, is described in similar terms: "All that had happened to her, good or bad, was a part of her own self and had come out of her" (349–50). Thus, the ocean appears as a decidedly feminine force in Hurston's depiction, and it has a power that the pastoral garden does not. As Jim rests on Arvay's bosom like a child returning "to the comfort of his mother," the boat carrying them is similarly cradled by the maternal and eternal sea: "The *Arvay Henson* rode gently on the bosom of the Atlantic. It lifted and bowed in harmony with the wind and the sea. It was acting in submission to the infinite, and Arvay felt its peace. For the first time in her life, she acknowledged that that was the only way" (349).

Despite the potential of the ocean to be an active natural force like the hurricane in *Their Eyes*, it seems, like Arvay, to be nonthreatening and passive in the end. Arvay's personal awakening and triumph in Sawley seems to pave the way for an assertion of independence that never comes. The book's ending undercuts Hurston's intention to dramatize Arvay's personal growth, which Meisenhelder validly views as Arvay's "internalization of [Jim's] values."[63] However, there is an important distinction between Jim's misogynistic values and his economic ones, the gender- and class-based pastoral frames at work in the novel. Arvay's gradual journey to self-awareness and self-confidence is due in large part to her internalization of Jim's economic values. The superiority she feels to the crackers back in Sawley allows her to feel her own self-worth. Tellingly, she is suddenly accepting of black and Portuguese people after her trip home. She has moved from a race-based conception of "otherness" to a class-based one, a point emphasized by Cynthia Ward in her analysis of class in the novel: "[T]o maintain the economic status and identities of the middle classes, a white subclass—often unabashedly denominated trash—may replace the ethnic or racial other."[64] Now that she has poor crackers against whom to favorably measure herself, Arvay no longer needs to harbor racist sentiments.

Arvay does not, in my view, internalize Jim's chauvinist values in the same manner, or at least to the same degree. Throughout the novel, he attempts to create a traditional pastoral paradise, a replacement for the plantation his family was dispossessed of in the Civil War, so he tends to view his property, including his wife, as raw material to be improved. Janie successfully resists attempts to turn her into property, but Arvay becomes equated with a passive and controlled nature. Quite improbably, Hurston turns this identification with property into an empowering one. Somewhat similar to Harrison's female pastoral, in which a woman's "interaction with the land changes from passive association to active cultivation,"[65] Arvay becomes empowered by her association with material prosperity, and she is not ultimately a Southern belle in need of male protection. Neither, however, does she turn the tables on Jim and become master/owner of him. Rather, the metaphor of possession is rejected altogether in favor of the natural symbol of the ocean and the nurturing power of a mother.

At the novel's end, she sees Jim in rather condescending terms, as "a little boy who had fled in out of the dark to the comfort of his mother" (349). Arvay's decision to embrace the role of mother is, of course, her own choice, but her maternal impulse and her conviction that "[s]he was serving and meant to serve" (352) is a source of consternation for some critics. Hurston, however, defines her mothering metaphorically and metaphysically, in addition to literally, effecting a sense of a powerful, oceanic maternity: "Her father and Larraine had taken from her because they felt that she had something to take from and to give out of her fullness. Her mother had looked to her for dependence. Her children, and Jim and all. Her job was mothering. What more could any woman want and need? . . . Holy Mary, who had been blessed to mother Jesus, had been no better off than she was" (351). This passage describes a creative and nurturing power that Arvay has recognized in herself, and this kind of service should not be confused with subservience. The revelation that Arvay arrives at independently is that she needs to be self-serving—a true Meserve—and then she can freely choose to offer service to others, a willful commitment to serve rather than a proscribed servitude.

Hurston also includes service in her description of Janie, a character who, unlike Arvay, is very rarely considered a mindless servant. After killing Tea Cake, "Janie held his head tightly to her breast and wept and thanked him wordlessly for giving her the chance for loving service" (175). Perhaps because Janie is a strong, independent woman throughout her story and because her husband dies, it is easier to see in her case that service need not imply subjugation, but rather a mutually beneficial service to self and others. Despite their differences, both of Hurston's heroines appear remarkably similar at the ends of their respective stories: both have overcome damaging treatment from their families and husbands, are financially well-off, at peace with themselves, and content with their choices of commitment. Both are even identified with the working-class and somewhat masculine image of a fishnet: Janie pulls in the horizon "like a great fish-net" and drapes it over her shoulder (184), and Arvay is "going overboard with the drag and sweep the very bottom" (343).

It is, in fact, the natural imagery of both novels that is the key to understanding the similarities of their female protagonists. For both women, the outside, the natural world, represents the inside, their own inner natures. The most affirming visions of their inner natures are the pear and mulberry trees, and when these symbols are embraced and internalized, they foster a deeply rooted strength that is then projected back out to the world. That is, when Janie and Arvay learn to serve themselves, their trees blossom and provide nourishment for those they love. There is a neat symmetry in the internalization of outer nature and the externalization of inner nature, and this network is reflected in the legacies of Tea Cake's seeds that Janie plants, the public park that Arvay creates, and the metaphorical seeds they both plant in the people closest to them. Janie forsakes her childhood vision of a bee-and-blossom marriage after finding it impossible to sustain such a relationship of egalitarian reciprocity, and Arvay discovers a similar truth. This is not to suggest that the novels or their heroines are therefore equals. *Their*

Eyes ends with Janie's triumphant completion of the pastoral retreat and return as wiser, stronger, and more unconditionally free than Arvay ever is. The
type of ecopastoral presented in *Seraph* is all about compromise, for better
and for worse, and this often makes the novel's middle ground feel more like
tedium than medium. In a state where the environment was under constant
assault from a population that was doubling every two decades, Jim and Arvay's marriage is, in fact, the uneasy marriage of the pastoral itself: city and
country, culture and nature, masculine and feminine wedded together in a
union that, despite the ideal, is never truly one of balance.

4

The Postpastoral of William Faulkner's
Go Down, Moses

William Faulkner once said that the South is "the only really authentic region in the United States, because a deep indestructible bond still exists between man and his environment."[1] Despite the differences in the ways that Caldwell, Rawlings, and Hurston interrogate this connection, they all create ecopastorals that retain such traditional features as the contrast between city and country and a desire for a harmonic middle ground, while paying special attention to the reciprocal relationships of humans and nature. Certainly, many of Faulkner's Depression-era works could be considered ecopastorals, each quite distinct from the others in pastoral perspective. *As I Lay Dying* (1930), a novel Faulkner began writing October 25, 1929, the day after panic broke out on Wall Street,[2] undermines the notion of the independent yeoman farmer in similar fashion to Caldwell's *Tobacco Road*. Jeeter Lester and Anse Bundren bear more than a passing resemblance, and both families are being torn apart by crisis. However, Faulkner's novel is not the straightforward antipastoral that Caldwell's is. The journey of the family gives *As I Lay Dying* mythic, epic qualities, and the Bundrens are not as desperate and destitute as the Lesters because of the communal network that supports them. Despite important formal and thematic differences, both novels reject sentimental pastoral notions of hardworking farmers living in harmony with nature.

Absalom, Absalom! (1936) is similar in that the violence and ruthlessness that Thomas Sutpen uses to fulfill his plantation fantasy reveal the hidden costs of the pastoral ideal. Indeed, the first mention of Sutpen in the novel suggests the violation of a naïvely idyllic pastoral picture: "Out of quiet thunderclap he would abrupt (man-horse-demon) upon a scene peaceful and decorous as a schoolprize watercolor."[3] *Go Down, Moses* (1942) is the novel that most directly confronts the issues of stewardship, wilderness, and the pastoral ideal that Caldwell, Rawlings, and Hurston also explore to varying degrees, and I will concentrate on that novel in this chapter since I cannot adequately cover all of Faulkner's works that are related to the pastoral.

While the plot(s) and narrative structure of *Go Down, Moses* are not conventionally pastoral, the novel confronts issues that are vital to the ecopastorals of this era: ownership of land, human responsibility for nature, imagined Edens, associations of women and blacks with nature, and the idea of wilderness as the antithesis of civilization. Faulkner's version of ecopastoral in this novel, though, is significantly different from the others considered in this study, especially in its critical evaluation of the pastoral mindset itself. I read *Go Down, Moses* as an early example of what Terry Gifford calls postpastoral, a work of literature that "has gone beyond the closed circuit of pastoral and anti-pastoral to achieve a vision of an integrated natural world that includes the human."[4] Gifford's postpastoral can be thought of as a particular type of ecopastoral, especially applicable to works that self-consciously examine the pressing environmental concerns of the twentieth and twenty-first centuries. Although the ecopastorals of Caldwell, Rawlings, and Hurston possess some postpastoral elements, none of their works exemplify them to the degree that *Go Down, Moses* does. Gifford chiefly considers poetry and the work of British authors in his discussion of postpastoral, but I want to extend his idea to an American novel in order to suggest future possibilities for exploring the relevance of this category to a variety of authors and works.

The issues of land ownership and destruction of wilderness in *Go Down, Moses* makes this work one of the most significant American novels to tackle environmental themes. Leonard Lutwack calls it "the most eloquent statement on behalf of the wilderness" in twentieth-century American literature, and John Elder describes it as a profound book that "depicts the shifting balance between man and nature in American history." Annette Kolodny sees it as a critique of the American pastoral impulse that has traditionally feminized the land in order to justify its possession, and Judith Bryant Wittenberg remarks that Faulkner's treatment of humans' relationship with nature connects *Go Down, Moses* with "a significant aspect of the cultural context, the growing discussion of environmentalism and ecology that was taking place during the 1930s and the 1940s." She notes several works that appeared or reappeared in these decades as particularly important contributions to public environmental awareness, including Aldo Leopold's *Sand County Almanac,* widely regarded as "the bible of the ecology movement of the latter twentieth century." Buell also makes an explicit comparison of the connections between Faulkner and Leopold as voices of an emerging environmentalism, concluding that both writers "set in motion complex processes of ethical reconsideration whereby, in Faulkner, familiar hierarchies of gentry/subaltern and human/nonhuman were subjected to question in ways that intertwined them."[5] In short, the decades leading up to the composition and publication of *Go Down, Moses* were a time of growing awareness of environmental concerns on a national scale, and Faulkner's novel grapples with these issues as they affected his own ecologically traumatized "postage stamp of native soil."[6]

In the 1930s the cut-and-get-out phase of lumbering in the South was nearing the end of an ecologically devastating fifty-year boom. Trees provide a material connection among the seven sections that make up *Go Down, Moses,* from the Big Woods sold for their lumber to the sawmill where Rider works in "Pantaloon in Black" to Isaac (Ike) McCaslin's chosen profession of carpentry and even to the paper sheets of the commissary ledgers containing the details of the McCaslin family history. A sentence about trees may, in fact, be about actual trees, even as it simultaneously functions as a metaphor for, say, the realm of the subconscious or a prelapsarian ideal of communal brotherhood. Faulkner suggests that the way we treat nature matters profoundly, for the environment we create determines to no small degree who we are. In *Go Down, Moses,* the natural world is active not in the way of anthropomorphic storms or symbolic floods, but more in the sense of habitus, pervading people's daily lives so much that it affects, as well as is affected by, human behavior. Faulkner emphasizes the unintended, long-term, and far-reaching consequences of actions in the human community that correlate to those in the biotic community, providing a metaphorical link between culture and nature.

In 1940 Mississippi still had over 80 percent of its population living in rural areas,[7] and its vitiated landscapes suggest a parallel between the wanton destruction of the environment and the harmful exploitation of African Americans. The Mississippi of Faulkner's lifetime was a state where most people's lives were concretely and significantly affected by natural processes, primarily through the agricultural and timber industries. The activities of these industries also permanently altered the landscape, often with disastrous results for those who depended on Mississippi's air, land, and water for their livelihood, as Faulkner would have witnessed.[8] As Don H. Doyle remarks in *Faulkner's County: The Historical Roots of Yoknapatawpha,* "By the time Faulkner began writing about his native land in the 1920s, the evidence of destruction was everywhere to be seen. He grew up in a land torn apart by gullies that ran down the hillsides, with creeks and rivers clogged by quicksand sludge, a landscape also of denuded fields pocked with stumps left by the lumbermen who had cut their way through the woods like locusts."[9]

In *The Hamlet* (1940), Faulkner provides his own description of the dese-
crated landscape that echoes Doyle's:

> [A]fter the Indians it had been cleared where possible for cultivation,
> and after the Civil War, forgotten save by small peripatetic sawmills
> which had vanished too now, their sites marked only by the mounds of
> rotting sawdust which were not only their gravestones but the monu-
> ments of people's heedless greed. Now it was a region of scrubby
> second-growth pine and oak among which dogwood bloomed until it
> too was cut to make cotton spindles, and old fields . . . gutted and gul-
> lied by forty years of rain and frost and heat into plateaus choked with
> rank sedge . . . and crumbling ravines striated red and white with al-
> ternate sand and clay.[10]

The gullies and ravines referred to in this passage (also called "Mississippi
canyons") are created when fields that are left bare form a hard surface that
sloughs off water in torrents that carry away huge amounts of topsoil, leaving gullies ten- to twenty-feet deep resembling "bleeding sores" that drain
"the lifeblood of the land."[11] Even as far back as the 1870s, state geologist and
University of Mississippi professor Eugene Hilgard found "a wasteland of
eroded fields, deep gullies, and silt-filled creeks" in the north central region
of the state that includes Lafayette County, and he blamed the "rapacious,
short-sighted strategy of its migratory inhabitants" who stripped the land of
vegetation, wore out the soil, and exposed it to erosion by planting only cotton and corn year after year, before moving on to the next frontier.[12]

Similar to Caldwell's Georgia, there is ample blame to go around for the
harmful effects of tenant farming. Often with half their crop pledged to the
landlord in advance, the tenants, who habitually moved yearly, had more immediate worries than the long-term productivity of the soil they worked,
while the landowners simply wanted the most cotton possible to recoup their
yearly investments in the volatile cotton markets and to repay bank loans.
Even more dramatic and startling were the changes to the landscape and
the environment produced by a virtual explosion in the lumber industry of
Mississippi between 1880 and 1920. The state's ever-increasing taxes on forest land led to rapid clear-cutting and immediate selling of cut-over land.
Moreover, the timber was often used as security for the debts of lumbermen,
while mills constantly operated near maximum capacity so that payments
could be met.[13]

From 1881 to 1888 over 5 million acres of federal land were sold in "the five
southern public land states," 68 percent of those going to Northern lumber-

men and dealers. The vast numbers of trees that were cut, as well as the manner of their removal, had rippling effects throughout interdependent ecosystems, as Cowdrey explains: "[F]rom any point of view except that of immediate personal profit for a few, the South's treatment of its forests in the Gilded Age was fundamentally in error. . . . Not only were the best trees cut, the worst were left to reproduce. Destruction did not stop with the forest. The relationship between forests and soil, rivers, and wildlife amplified the losses, implying disruption of the linked systems which constituted the natural regimen of the landscape."[14]

While northern Mississippi was a bit slower to jump on the deforestation bandwagon, the economies of some coastal counties were dominated by lumbering as early as 1860. An 1876 bill legalizing private sales of public lands with no limits on purchase size opened the door for lumbermen and speculators who, for the next twelve years, bought over 2.6 million acres of federal pineland in Mississippi at bargain rates as low as $1.25 per acre.[15]

Such developments were merely a precursor to the large-scale lumber production that spread throughout the state in the time of Faulkner's childhood, a time described by Nollie Hickman as the end of "the pioneer phase of the lumber industry in Mississippi" and by Doyle as the "final desecration of the land . . . when lumber companies came into the hills of Lafayette County and cut huge swaths through the hardwood forests."[16] In 1880 there were 295 sawmills statewide with a total capital investment of $1 million, growing to 338 mills with $3 million invested in 1890. By 1899 the figures had leaped to 608 sawmills and $10.8 million, and in 1909 the mushrooming totals were 1,647 mills and almost $40 million of investment capital.[17] Combined with increasing saw speeds and the construction of "tramroads," usually standard-gauge rail lines, into previously inaccessible areas, the vast number of mills and their workers (many of whom were displaced tenant farmers eager for the steady wages) led to the near-total destruction of the state's virgin pine forests.

A more dramatic example of the consequences of this profit-driven approach is the wide use of "skidders" after 1900 in order to decrease costs. These steam-powered skidders used steel-wire cables a thousand feet or more in length, which were unwound from drums on the tramroads and attached to logs in the woods. As the revolving drums reeled in the cables, five to fifteen logs were dragged to the track on each pull-in, but these devices also destroyed everything in their path as they dragged trees across the ground. Hickman describes the devastating results: "No trees or vegetation of any kind except coarse wire grass remained on the skidder-logged hill and ridges. For miles and miles the landscape presented a picture of bare open land that graphically illustrated the work of destruction wrought by the economic activities of man. . . . Nor was the work of destruction a temporary condition, for twenty-five years later the boundaries between skidder-logged areas and those where other methods prevailed were apparent even to the untutored eye."[18]

This barren wasteland is precisely the type of scenery that Ike would have viewed during trips from Jefferson to the hunting grounds: "the land across which there came now no scream of panther but instead the long hooting of locomotives."[19] Indeed, James E. Fickle's *Mississippi Forests and Forestry* shows "the symbiotic relationship between Mississippi's lumber industry and railroads." The devastation of the landscape by the skidders, "which virtually destroyed any prospects for natural reseeding of the cutover lands," leads Fickle to conclude that "[t]here has never been a more short-sighted or destructive method of logging."[20]

It is within this context of wanton environmental destruction that Faulkner composed *Go Down, Moses* and in which the novel's action takes place. The mournful descriptions of the Big Woods that are sold to the lumber company recall Caldwell's lamentations for the lost family farm and the neglected farmer in *Tobacco Road*. Like Caldwell, Faulkner shows humans dominating their natural environment to such a degree that interdependent natural and cultural systems are degraded. The traditional pastoral desire for balance is overwhelmed by the lure of profit, an especially resonant motive during the Depression. However, Faulkner's novel goes beyond Caldwell's antipastoral text into the realm of the postpastoral.

Gifford's useful description of postpastoral, which I want to appropriate and extend to Southern literature, has six aspects: awe of and respect for the natural world; "recognition of a creative-destructive universe equally in balance in a continuous momentum of birth and death, death and rebirth, growth and decay, ecstasy and dissolution"; "the recognition that the inner is also the workings of the outer, that our inner human nature can be understood in relation to external nature"; "awareness of both nature as culture and of culture as nature"; an acknowledgment that "with consciousness comes conscience"; and, finally, the understanding that "the exploitation of the planet is of the same mindset as the exploitation of women and minorities." These criteria are by no means conclusive, as Gifford himself notes: "[T]he six elements suggested here are probably capable of further elaboration, or elision, so that readers might want to expand my definition to twelve elements or reduce it to three." I will emphasize two particular ideas that I feel should be included more explicitly in a characterization of postpastoral: a sense of nature as active agent rather than passive background and a critical consideration of the pastoral mode itself. Adding these to Gifford's categories, I hope to further the discussion about a progressive, contemporary version of pastoral, or, as Buell says, "an ecocentric repossession of pastoral."[21]

Explaining the sense of awe of the natural world that he makes the first aspect of the postpastoral, Gifford cites Gerard Manley Hopkins's poem "God's Grandeur" (1918) as exemplifying "the way this positioning of the self towards nature leads inevitably to a humbling that is a necessary requirement of the shift from the anthropocentric position of the pastoral to the ecocentric view of the post-pastoral."[22] Faulkner gives voice to similar sentiments through the novel's central consciousness, Ike McCaslin, who has learned to revere and comprehend nature under the tutelage of his part-Indian, part-black mentor, Sam Fathers. Ike's expressions of awe are often fused with lamentations for humans' exploitative destruction of their natural environment, "that doomed wilderness whose edges were being constantly and punily gnawed at by men with plows and axes who feared it because it was wilderness" (185). Ike's reverence stems in no small part from his intuition of nature's agency and power, which he learns from his very first hunting trip with Sam: "an unforgettable sense of the big woods . . . profound, sentient, gigantic and brooding, amid which he had been permitted to go to and fro at will, unscathed, why he knew not, but dwarfed and, until he had drawn honorably blood worthy of being drawn, alien" (169). Faulkner shows that this awareness of being "dwarfed" by the wilderness, which is "almost inattentive" to the hunters "because they were too small" (170), fosters a sense of humility, the opposite of the attitude of humans as masters of nature.

Ike's sense of himself as part of the natural world means that he is attuned to its destruction and conscious of his own responsibility for it. The deaths of Sam Fathers and Old Ben the bear are symbolically tied to the destruction of the woods, and when Ike returns to Sam's grave on the logging train in part 5 of "The Bear," he recognizes that "the same train, engine cars and caboose" that had been "harmless once" now resemble the proverbial snake in the garden: "[T]his time it was as though the train (and not only the train but himself . . .) had brought with it into the doomed wilderness even before the actual axe the shadow and portent of the new mill not even finished yet and the rails and ties which were not even laid" (306). Faulkner also shows that, even with this knowledge, the pastoral retreat to nature can be either what Marx calls the complex or the sentimental version of pastoral. While the complex pastoral uses this retreat to nature to explore the problems of the society left behind, the sentimental variety allows Ike to evade conflict by withdrawing into an aestheticized landscape that hides the train's very existence: "Then it was gone. It had not been. He could no longer hear it. The wilderness soared musing, inattentive, myriad, eternal, green; older than any mill-shed, longer than any spur-line" (307). Ike wants to reject the pastoral land of the family farm, but by imagining the woods as separate and distinct from the town and plantation, he is replicating the dualistic thinking that artificially opposes wilderness and civilization in the first place. Their interdependence is brought home when the woods are soon sold for their lumber and cultivated like so much farmland, and Ike's conception of the wilderness as beyond time is revealed as a sentimental fantasy.

The second postpastoral element, the recognition of a balance of creative and destructive powers in the world, is another facet of nature's agency, its transcendent ability to cycle death into life and life into death. Humans are inextricably part of the network of nature from this perspective, an empowering conception that even suggests immortality: "[T]here was no death, not Lion and not Sam: not held fast in earth but free in earth and not in earth but of earth, myriad yet undiffused of every myriad part, leaf and twig and particle, air and sun and rain and dew and night, acorn oak and leaf and acorn again, dark and dawn and dark and dawn again in their immutable progression and, being myriad, one" (313). Faulkner's language in this passage emphasizes both the opposition between sun and rain, dark and dawn, or life and death and their continuity, their fluid boundaries, and their cyclical patterns. This sense of the unity of "every myriad part" as well as Ike's sense of losing himself in the wilderness recall Rawlings's epiphany in *Cross Creek*: "We were all one with the silent pulsing . . . the cycle of life, with birth and death merging one into the other in an imperceptible twilight and an insubstantial dawn . . . one's own minute living a torn fragment of the larger cloth" (39). For both Rawlings and Faulkner, this type of awareness necessarily leads to an ecological sensibility, what Buell calls "environmental consciousness" and Cronon refers to as "an ethical, sustainable, *honorable* human place in nature."[23]

In *Go Down, Moses*, it is important that the joining of the human and natural is not achieved solely through interment in the earth, since that would imply an inherent fatalism to environmental ethics. After killing his first deer, Ike sees what is apparently the buck's spirit, which Sam salutes as the spirit of his ancestor: "'Oleh, Chief,' Sam said. 'Grandfather'" (177). Ike discusses the incident with McCaslin (Cass) Edmonds, who admits that he, too, was shown a similar vision by Sam after killing his first deer. Cass's explanation of the vision to Ike recalls Lant's reclaiming of the trees left by the lumber company in *South Moon Under* as it emphasizes an active, natural network that includes humans: "Think of all that has happened here, on this earth. All the blood hot and strong for living, pleasuring, that has soaked back into it. . . . And all that must be somewhere; all that could not have been invented and created just to be thrown away. And the earth don't want to just keep things, hoard them; it wants to use them again. Look at the seed, the acorns, at what happens even to carrion when you try to bury it: it refuses too, seethes and struggles too until it reaches light and air again, hunting the sun still" (179). This regenerative power of a cyclical, natural network suggests the possibility of revision through repetition, which counterbalances the fatalism the elder Ike of "Delta Autumn" attaches to Roth's repetition of old Carothers's incestuous miscegenation.

Faulkner's epic time scale and shifting chronology in the seven sections of *Go Down, Moses* help to reinforce the importance of the past in the living present. "Delta Autumn," for example, and its revelation that Roth has had a child with the granddaughter of Tennie's Jim, immediately follows "The Bear," which takes place some fifty-five years earlier and details Ike's act of relinquishment that she blames for the continuing pattern of philandering, incest, and miscegenation in the McCaslin family: "You spoiled him . . . [w]hen you gave to his grandfather that land which didn't belong to him" (343). To use a more natural idiom, the novel's disjointed form demonstrates that the seeds of both a ruined land and a vitiated family had been planted many decades before by men blind to the long-term consequences of their actions. Through the McCaslin family history, Faulkner illustrates both materially and metaphorically the third element of postpastoral, the comprehension "that our inner human nature can be understood in relation to external nature."

L. Q. C. McCaslin would have been among the first wave of white settlers in Mississippi, since he purchases Eunice in 1807 and fathers Tomey in 1810, while the official sale of most Chickasaw lands and that tribe's mass exodus do not occur until 1837, the same year as the McCaslin patriarch's death.[24] The cotton farmers in this formative period of Mississippi agriculture closely resemble the lumbermen who would appear at the end of the century in their widespread and long-lasting environmental destruction in quest of immediate profits. John Hebron Moore describes the state's agriculture in the first three decades of the nineteenth century as "extensive and exploitive rather than intensive in nature," causing land erosion and soil exhaustion on small farms and large plantations alike. The lack of grass in cotton and corn fields that were kept in continuous cultivation, for example, denied the land protection from heavy rains, and, consequently, "top soil began to wash away almost as soon as newly cleared fields were put to use." After just a few years of use, large ravines would form, the productivity of the soil would abate, and new land would be cleared to begin the cycle anew: "In retrospect, this unending process of clearing, cultivating, and destroying the fertility of the soil—a process which was one of the principal characteristics of agriculture of the Old South—resembled nothing so much as a cancerous growth spreading death and desolation across the face of the earth." Moore's assessment of planters, like the fictional Carothers McCaslin, who damaged the land for future generations of farmers is even harsher: "All too frequently, they regarded their soil as a cheap and expendable raw material which, when worked by slaves, could be converted easily into marketable produce. Furthermore, the relatively high price of labor caused farmers and planters to conserve labor and waste land—the cheaper item. Thus early Mississippians were almost unique in history: they were farmers largely devoid of that deep and abiding love for the land characteristic of agricultural peoples everywhere."[25] The degraded environment is directly tied to the instincts and values, the human nature, of the people who inhabit and work it. A century later "old Carothers" is still a domineering and influential force in the lives of Ike, Lucas, Roth, and McCaslin Edmonds (and, by extension, all of their families as well) in much the same way that the rapacious treatment of the land by early settlers continues to impact Mississippi's inhabitants well into the twentieth century, and even to the present day. In both cases, the effects of irresponsible actions cannot be fully known for many years. Suggesting an interdependency both among humans and between nature and humanity, Faulkner does not condemn certain actions as bad or evil, but eschews an authoritative center of value by portraying the rippling consequences of those actions through interconnected networks.

The convoluted McCaslin family tree is just such a system, where individual identities are chiefly derived from one's relationships to others within the network as in an ecosystem. Lucas, for instance, who is considered black and therefore inferior by some standards of Southern society, can nonetheless be considered superior by other standards in relation to Zach Edmonds because Zach is "woman-made" and four generations removed from "old Carothers," while Lucas is a direct male descendant. Additionally, the extended family metaphorically mirrors the particularities of the ravaged natural environment in which Faulkner was raised, reflected in the McCaslin tree's dying branches and "polluted" bloodlines (polluted, that is, insofar as they violate cultural taboos against incest and miscegenation). Amodeus "Buddy" McCaslin has no children, nor does his nephew Ike, ending the legitimate male line of descent. The other branch of the family begins with Carothers's affair with his slave Eunice, continues with his subsequent incestuous union with their daughter Tomey, and ends with the execution of Samuel Worsham "Butch" Beauchamp, although the child expected by Nat

Beauchamp and George Wilkins does offer a hint of hope for the future. On the "woman-made" Edmonds side, the only descendant left at the end of the novel is the son born from the intrafamilial, interracial coupling of Roth and his unnamed cousin (the granddaughter of Tennie's Jim).

The network of the McCaslin-Beauchamp-Edmonds family is contained within the larger systems of Southern society and, moving out concentrically, a natural world that includes humanity. Collapsing the division of nature and culture in this way posits a material, rather than only a metaphorical, connection between humans and their environment. Ike seems to assert the importance of both links when he rails that "[t]his whole land, the whole South, is cursed, and all of us who derive from it, whom it ever suckled, white and black both, lie under the curse" (266). In Ike's mind, the people who occupy the land cannot be separated from the curse that lies on the land itself, and the reason for this is his conflation of the sins of owning people and owning private property. Yet there is also a more literal explanation of this curse from an ecological perspective.

The South's dependency on slave labor largely arises from its fiscally expedient, but ecologically devastating, reliance on cotton. As Cowdrey explains in *This Land, This South,* in order to "fuel an expansion of the character and speed that occurred between 1790 and 1837, the South needed some commercial crop adapted to the climate, demanded by the overseas market, and suitable for production in circumstances ranging from the frontier farm to the great plantation." Moreover, the costs of raising cotton favored wealthy planters who could afford to own large numbers of slaves, plant vast amounts of cotton, and fertilize their crops heavily. As illustrated in *Tobacco Road,* the inordinate amounts of fertilizer used in the South helped deplete the soil's fertility, and Cowdrey also notes that the hot climate breaks down soil nutrients faster than in other regions of the country. The combination of this highly erosive, mediocre-quality soil and the short-sighted, destructive agricultural habits of the monocrop South reveals that, in one sense, there was indeed a curse on the land, and humans' treatment of their environment served only to exacerbate its effects: "[O]ver time the South's natural dower of soil . . . can only have imposed a constant, tenacious drag upon the growth and wealth of human societies so long as they drew the basis of their livelihood from the land."[26]

If humans and the land are seen as part of the same natural network, it becomes evident that Ike's figurative curse covering both is, in fact, a very real "constant, tenacious drag" on the entire system. Faulkner, too, seems to accept this premise that the human, plant, animal, and mineral realms are part of an encompassing network when he parenthetically interjects (parentheses themselves being a tool to join disparate strands of the same sentence) that the incoming and outgoing accounts in the commissary ledgers function as "two threads frail as truth and impalpable as equators yet cable-strong to bind for life them who made the cotton to the land their sweat fell on" (245). Having seen in his own time the deleterious results of humans' assault on the Mississippi landscape, Faulkner juxtaposes the legacy of the South's defeat in the Civil War that Ike inherits "as Noah's grandchildren had inherited the Flood although they had not been there to see the deluge" (276) to the "dark and ravaged fatherland still prone and panting from its etherless operation" (284) that is the legacy of the South's abuse of its natural resources.

An important consequence of Faulkner's portrayal of humans as enmeshed in natural networks is that nature itself becomes an active participant, recalling Faulkner's description of *Absalom, Absalom!* as a novel about "a man who outraged the land, and the land then turned and destroyed the man's family."[27] There are no violent storms, floods, or earthquakes that punish humans and thereby reveal a hidden spiritual agency of an animistic natural world in *Go Down, Moses*. Rather nature's agency is felt as a material factor in the lives of those who live on the land, underscoring the symbiotic relationship of humans and their environment. The irresponsible use of forests and fields by earlier generations (along with wholly natural forces like climate and weather patterns) deteriorates the condition of the land, which, in turn, impacts the lives of later generations in numerous ways. Rupert Vance, in *Human Geography of the South*, perhaps captures the process most succinctly in language that prefigures Bourdieu's notion of habitus: "[P]lace conditions work, work conditions the family organization, and the family is the social unit which makes up society."[28]

The differences in the inner natures of first cousins Ike and Lucas Beauchamp are to some degree attributable to their experiences of the habitus of location. To reiterate, habitus is best understood as "a conceptual lens through which particular understandings or interpretations of the social world are generated and as such invite particular forms of response or action to the social world." These actions or outcomes are not, however, predetermined, but "are most appropriately characterized as dispositions: that is, a propensity or inclination, rather than a compulsion, towards certain types of action." The final important point is that habitus is not static: "[W]hilst the habitus is the product of a history, that history is always in the process of being made . . . [and] the habitus is always in a state of becoming and never one of simply being."[29]

Thus, the specific location of the McCaslin plantation generates a very particular "conceptual lens" for its inhabitants. That does not mean, however,

that individuals will behave in identical ways, since human agency and social processes play equally significant roles. Ike and Lucas, for example, both
seem to understand the world as broken into two groups of people: exploiters and exploited. Ike wants to dissociate himself from the exploiters, so he
renounces his claim to the family farm built through ownership of humans.
Lucas, however, identifies himself with the exploited, and his actions are designed to ensure he is no longer taken advantage of, even at the risk of becoming an exploiter himself. On his twenty-first birthday, Lucas forcefully
claims from Ike the inheritance bequeathed by their grandfather: "The rest
of that money. I wants it." Ike feels compelled to leave the physical prem-
ises of the farm and assumes Lucas will do the same: "'You're going too,' he
said. 'You're leaving too'" (105). But Lucas's decision to stay on the land may
change the habitus and history of the place, while Ike's relinquishment, as
most critics agree, seems an ineffectual, if well-intentioned, response.

While both cousins have strong bonds with nature, those connections are
also tellingly different. Ike feels a spiritual attachment with the wilderness,
but has only contempt for the "tamed land" of the family plantation. His attitude recalls the novels of both Caldwell and Rawlings, as he rejects the traditional pastoral location in favor of wilderness, which seems to promise a
more honorable blend of the human and the natural. Lucas, on the other
hand, develops his own intimate relationship with nature, but one that derives from his labor and physical contact with the land: "But it was his own
field, though he neither owned it nor wanted to nor even needed to. He had
been cultivating it for forty-five years . . . plowing and planting and working
it when and how he saw fit. . . . He had been born on this land, twenty-five
years before the Edmonds who now owned it. He had worked on it ever since
he got big enough to hold a plow straight; he had hunted over every foot of
it during his childhood and youth and his manhood too" (35–36). Lucas has
an intimate knowledge of nature through labor, and Faulkner suggests that
this gives him a truer type of ownership than a legal deed. Ike knows nature
chiefly through recreation, annual hunting trips of the privileged and wealthy
that are more about sport than survival, and he rejects the very idea of owning land, saying that the family farm "was never mine to repudiate" (245).

Faulkner shows with his portrayals of Ike and Lucas an idea similar to
Caldwell's in *God's Little Acre*: those who are alienated from nature are also
alienated from their fellow humans. When Lucas begins to neglect his farming in order to search for gold with a metal detector, his changed relationship with the land is mirrored by his estrangement from his wife. Molly pur-
sues a divorce, threatening to extinguish the powerful symbol of the fire on
the hearth. Once again, it is clear that the concept of knowing nature through

labor does not apply to all types of labor. Farming tends to be portrayed in these Southern ecopastorals as a mutually enriching activity for humans and nature. Even in *Tobacco Road*, Caldwell's problem is with the social systems that govern farming, and he elegiacally describes Jeeter's lost connection to his land. One-sided, exploitative encounters with nature, where the sole interest is personal enrichment, are consistently presented more negatively. Lucas's obsession with the divining machine, like Ty Ty Walden's compulsive digging for gold, alienates him from a feminine natural world and the actual feminine "life force" in his home, illustrating, in a different sense than habitus, Faulkner's recognition of the third postpastoral element, "that the inner is also the workings of the outer."

The fourth postpastoral element, "the awareness of both nature as culture and of culture as nature," is seen most clearly in the hunting episodes of the novel. Faulkner utilizes the motif of the hunt to demonstrate that the supposedly pure wilderness and corrupt civilization are not inimical sites but similarly constructed cultural categories. Although hunting has long been portrayed by American writers as a vehicle for personal and spiritual communion with nature, in *Go Down, Moses* hunting seems to occur as much in town and on the plantations as it does in the wilderness of the forests. In the novel's opening story "Was," Faulkner links the hunt for Tomey's Turl and the chase of the fox, dehumanizing Buck and Buddy's half brother by equating him with the quarry and by showing his affinity with the dogs sent to chase him. The dogs that Buck and Buddy release to chase Turl treat the runaway slave more as one of their own than as an object of pursuit, allowing him to lock them in a cabin and continue his flight to Warwick: "[H]e and the dogs all went into the woods together, walking, like they were going home from a rabbit hunt" (14). Although this scene seems to align African Americans and nature, it also subverts that equation. His white masters may view Turl as the quarry, but Faulkner suggests the slave is in control of this hunt as he manipulates his would-be pursuers to the Beauchamp estate where Buck is now pursued by Sophonsiba and from which Turl returns home with his future wife, Tennie.

This entire hunt is more cultural ritual than actual pursuit, with the participants even dressing up for the game, Tomey's Turl in "his Sunday shirt . . . that he put on every time he ran away just as Uncle Buck put on the necktie each time he went to bring him back" (28). When Buck mistakenly climbs into bed with Sophonsiba, however, he enters the den of his quarry and becomes the hunted instead of the hunter, a reversal Faulkner employs throughout the novel in different guises. Hubert Beauchamp, desperate to have his sister catch her Buck, reiterates the rules of the game: "You come into bear-country of your own free will and accord. . . . You had to crawl into the den and lay down by the bear. And whether you did or didn't know the bear was in it don't make any difference" (21–22). The ensuing card game also mimics the hunt with first one player, then the other taking the lead through constant bluffing, raising, and calling, while Turl ultimately controls the game as dealer. Each time that Faulkner repeats and revises the hunting scenario he reinforces its cultural and performative aspects rather than its naturalness.[30]

Lucas Beauchamp, for example, is involved in several of these hunting episodes, and each helps to undermine the opposition of hunter and quarry. He manages to survive when he marches into the "bear den" of Cass Edmonds's bedroom, intending to kill him, but two more comical incidents better illustrate how easily the roles of pursuer and pursued can be reversed. Seeking to have George Wilkins arrested for moonshining, Lucas hides his own still and alerts the sheriff to George's illegal enterprise. George turns the tables, however, putting his still in Lucas's backyard for the sheriff to find on his arrival. Similarly, the metal detector salesman thinks Lucas an easy mark, but is duped into renting his own machine from his intended target in pursuit of nonexistent treasure.

In "Pantaloon in Black," Rider's actions following Mannie's death mimic those of the hunters in "The Old People" and "The Bear" and further solidify hunting as a cultural production that occasionally (and perhaps only incidentally) occurs in the wilderness. Rider encounters the ghost of his dead wife, who quickly fades away, just as Ike sees the spirit of a buck that Walter Ewell has just killed "as if it were walking out of the very sound of the horn which related its death" (177). Rider next goes to buy a jug of whiskey before continuing on to the sawmill, echoing Ike and Boon's comical trip to Memphis to buy alcohol for the hunting party. Finally, Rider purposely enters the lair of his prey, the watchman Birdsong who runs the crooked dice game, and challenges him there by exposing his cheating and slitting his throat as Birdsong reaches for a concealed pistol. Ike also enters the bear's den of his "own free will and accord," but the bear allows him, even helps him, to leave unscathed.

Rider's death even mirrors those of Old Ben and Sam Fathers, as all three effect a type of willed suicide. After killing Birdsong, Rider does not flee from the lynch mob; rather, the mob unexpectedly finds him sleeping on his porch. Even when he rips the jail cell door off the wall, Rider yells, "It's awright. Ah aint trying to git away" (153), as if he is trying to speed along his own execution in order to join his wife in death. Similarly, when Sam finds Lion's tracks for the first time, there is "foreknowledge in Sam's face" that this dog will be the instrument of his and Old Ben's death: "*And he was glad,* he told himself. *He was old. He had no children, no people, none of his blood anywhere above earth that he would ever meet again. . . . It was almost over now and he was glad"* (206). Faulkner tells us three times that Ike "should have hated and feared Lion" (201, 204, 216), but Ike realizes that the bear's death is inevitable, "like the last act on a set stage" (216), and that Old Ben himself will want the chase to end: "That's why it must be one of us. So it won't be until the last day. When even he don't want it to last any longer" (204). Lion, who is "like some natural force" (209), is a product of the same wilderness symbolized by Old Ben, yet is also the agent of its destruction. This irony, like the repeated reversal of hunter and hunted, subverts the fixed oppositions of the text without uniting them. Instead, Faulkner constantly collapses the juxtapositions that he sets up, but does not offer a clear alternative position.[31]

Major de Spain's pretext for going after Old Ben upon finding his colt slaughtered reveals that the wilderness is not, in fact, a place free from the strictures and ills of society, but rather a different setting where the same cultural rules apply: "It was Old Ben . . . he has come into my house and destroyed my property, out of season too. He broke the rules" (205). This anthropocentric view of nature extends human notions of property lines and proper behavior to animals in search of food in order to justify slaying the bear. Thus culture and nature are yoked together but held apart in this idea of wilderness, in which social norms of private property are imposed on land and unwitting wild animals.

Ike performs essentially the same move in reverse, applying the natural to the cultural. Making the common assumption that the natural equals God's will, Ike argues that man is meant "not to hold for himself and his descendents inviolable title forever, generation after generation, to the oblongs and squares of the earth, but to hold the earth mutual and intact in the communal anonymity of brotherhood" (246). Describing the family land as "accursed" and "tainted" by the unnatural sin of possession, Ike sees himself as divinely ordained to right this wrong, and his explanation links ownership of the land to ownership of slaves: "Maybe He knew that Grandfather himself would not serve His purpose because Grandfather was born too soon, but . . . maybe He saw already in Grandfather the seed progenitive of the three generations He saw it would take to set at least some of His lowly people free" (249). The Southern and American relationships with nature are based on the *wrong kind* of possession, Ike claims, betraying the original promise of "a new world where a nation of people could be founded in humility and pity and sufferance and pride of one to another" (247). This thinking exemplifies the traditional pastoral urge to critique contemporary society by a supposedly purer set of standards with an important difference. Where once the country served as a location from which to critique the city, now that the plantation (once the pastoral middle state) has become as hopelessly corrupted as the city, Ike sees hope in a further shift toward nature, toward the wilderness. The rejection of his tainted inheritance applies Ike's understanding of the natural to the cultural; the wilderness is "bigger and older than any recorded deed" (244), so he repudiates ownership of both land and people.

This use of the wilderness as "the natural, unfallen antithesis of an un-natural civilization that has lost its soul," as Cronon says, would seem to place humans completely outside the natural. Making wilderness the yardstick for judging civilization, Cronon argues, reproduces the cultural values it supposedly rejects by leaving no place for humans to exist in wilderness: "The flight from history that is very nearly the core of wilderness represents the false hope of an escape from responsibility, the illusion that we can somehow wipe clean the slate of our past and return to the tabula rasa that supposedly existed before we began to leave our marks on the world."[32] This would leave no place for humans in the landscape or, in other words, no possibility of a true postpastoral middle ground where humans work in harmony with the environment. However, for Ike humans are always part of the wilderness. Sam and Jobaker embody an honorable and ethical interaction with nature, but Ike knows that most people cannot live up to this ideal. Ike feels that "man was dispossessed of Eden," that the pastoral paradise has been lost forever, tainted by private ownership of nature, and he thinks longingly of a time when the pastoral ideal was still a reality, before private ownership of land, recalling the cooperative language of Caldwell and Rawlings in the phrase "communal anonymity of brotherhood" (246). While Caldwell and Rawlings are clearly sympathetic to popular Depression-era communal and collective sentiments, Faulkner, by making Ike the mouthpiece for this idea, suggests a certain naïveté in such notions.

In *Faulkner and the Great Depression,* Ted Atkinson discusses the "ambivalent agrarianism" evident in several of Faulkner's works. The ambivalence, he argues, produces tensions between competing ideological positions, expressing sympathy for the poor and dispossessed on the one hand, but identifying with the dominant class on the other by registering anxiety over the potential social changes that popular revolt might engender.[33] In *Go Down, Moses,* I would argue, there is a similar ambivalent environmentalism at work. The polyphonic text provides a variety of viewpoints but no clear sense of Faulkner's position.

What is clear is that the combination of different perspectives leads not to any ethical human engagement with the land and its inhabitants, but to destruction of the wilderness, fractured families, racial divisions, brutal vio-

lence, diminishing family prestige, and repetitions of incestuous, miscegena-
tional sex in defiance of cultural norms. Sam's reverence for nature and deep
connection with it are presented in lyrical, wistful passages, but they seem
mystical, surreal, like a vestige of some extinct religion. The Edmonds who
continue farming the McCaslin land after Ike's repudiation appear worn out
and seem to be regressing, judging by Roth's actions. Ike's act of repudiation is shown as ineffectual, if noble, doing nothing to prevent the destruction of the woods he and Sam loved. Lucas is closest to the yeoman farmer
type and he scoffs tellingly at Ike's rejection of the farm; but he seems increasingly comical as he, like Ty Ty Walden, thinks he's better off searching
for gold in the land than farming it. Rider works in the sawmill processing
the trees from the surrounding forests but finds there the same thralldom as
tenant farming. Butch Beauchamp leaves the agrarian South altogether, but
his revolt against the white establishment leads to his death, and he returns
to the Southern soil in a wooden box.

Faulkner does not clearly endorse reverence for the environment nor sanc-
tion its use in the pursuit of profit. The potential social disruption inherent
in Ike's gesture (rejecting private property, patriarchal descent, profit through
slavery, etc.) is contained and negated as the solitary act of an eccentric old
man. In the end, his act does not threaten private property, does not affect
racial subordination, and does not slow the clear-cutting of the wilderness.
The novel is not a blueprint for an alternative to the pastoral ideal, but it does
utilize the various aspects of Gifford's postpastoral in a way that articulates
the necessity of a new paradigm for natural/cultural relations in the South.

The fifth and sixth postpastoral elements are closely related in *Go Down,
Moses,* and I will therefore discuss them together. The fifth aspect, "with consciousness comes conscience," is most evident in Ike's relinquishment of the
plantation. Having learned to value and respect all life from Sam Fathers in
the wilderness that "was his college" (201), Ike's conscience compels him to
reject slavery and the plantation it helped produce. His association of ownership of land and people is the basis of the sixth postpastoral aspect: "the exploitation of the planet is of the same mindset as the exploitation of women
and minorities." Although Faulkner questions Ike's actions, he more posi-
tively portrays the conscience Ike develops. In an interview, Faulkner characterized Ike's thoughts about his inheritance and legacy as, "This is rotten,
I don't like it, I can't do anything about it, but at least I will not participate
in it myself."[34]

Ike's actions do nothing to stop either the destruction of the woods or
the repetition of incestuous miscegenation that he finds so offensive. Never-
theless, he does achieve a clarity of conscience that allows him to see and re-

nounce possession. His ecocentric denial of humans' right to own nature echoes Rawlings's sentiments in "Who Owns Cross Creek?" Just as Rawlings says in the final chapter of her memoir that "the earth may be borrowed but not bought . . . used, but not owned" (368), Ike claims that the family farm has never truly been possessed:

> It was never mine to repudiate. It was never Father's and Uncle Buddy's to bequeath me to repudiate because it was never Grandfather's to bequeath them to bequeath me to repudiate because it was never old Ikkemotubbe's to sell to Grandfather for bequeathment and repudiation. Because it was never Ikkemotubbe's fathers' fathers' to bequeath Ikkemotubbe to sell to Grandfather or any man because on the instant when Ikkemotubbe discovered, realised, that he could sell it for money, on that instant it ceased ever to have been his forever, father to father to father, and the man who bought it bought nothing. (245–46)

This viewpoint is one that Rawlings clearly espouses, but Faulkner presents it as one competing position in Ike's debate with Cass. While Ike's position in this context may appear honorable and principled, the Ike of "Delta Autumn" seems backwards, racist, and contemptible, which forces a reassessment of his earlier statements, like the one above, in a different framework. Again, the novel exposes problems with traditional pastoral ideals but does not espouse alternatives. Faulkner shows that attitudes about race and gender are bound up with how one relates to nature, but the text's ambivalence makes it unclear what Faulkner thinks should be done about it.

While nature is often feminized in *Go Down, Moses*—for Ike the woods are "his wife and his mistress" (311) and even "the old male bear itself . . . his alma mater" (202)—it is not a passive version of femininity as it is for Caldwell. The women of *God's Little Acre* follow Will devotedly, and they willingly yield to his desire for sexual control. The women of *Go Down, Moses* lurk in the margins of the text but frequently exert control through their actions. Molly's pursuit of divorce compels Lucas to give up his quest for gold. Eunice's suicide haunts Ike's mind and is the catalyst for his renunciation of his inheritance. Roth's mistress exposes Roth's cowardice and Ike's prejudices, while she and her son embody what hope for the future there is in the novel.

Ike remembers his last visit to the Big Woods, before "the lumber company moved in and began to cut the timber" (301), in a flashback that comes just after the scene in which his wife offers her body in exchange for the McCaslin farm. Louise Westling argues that this "anachronistic juxtaposition" suggests that "feminine sexuality seems to lead to destruction of the Delta Eden" and disguises the blame of Major de Spain, who actually sells the land to the lumber company. This same formula, where "men are the agents of sin . . . but women . . . are to blame," in Westling's words, applies to the story of Sam Fathers, who was sold into slavery by his father, yet, we are told by Cass, was "betrayed through the black blood which his mother gave him . . . not will-fully betrayed by his mother, but betrayed by her all the same" (162). Westling identifies this pattern as a "cultural habit of gendering the landscape as fe-male," which she traces through a long line of male American writers who "disguise and evade the responsibility of white men for the displacement of another people on the land and the ravishing of an existing ecosystem for their own gain." However, she feels—and I agree—that Faulkner breaks with this tradition as he "writes his way towards an understanding of this process in *Go Down, Moses,* and he comes very close to exposing it totally."[35]

Seen as a postpastoral text, then, *Go Down, Moses* reveals how the femi-nizing of nature helps to justify its exploitation. Ike nostalgically remembers the beginning of his marriage as a time of unity and mutual understanding with his unnamed wife: "[T]hey were married and it was the new country, his heritage too as it was the heritage of all . . . and in the sharing they be-come one: for that while, one: for that little while at least, one: indivisible" (297). But open association of her body and sexual gratification with the land of the plantation makes "the chaste woman, the wife" seem different, her naked body "changed, altered" into "the composite of all woman-flesh," which Ike associates with mystical knowledge beyond his relational capacity: "*She already knows more than I with all the man-listening in camps. . . . They are born already bored with what a boy approaches only at fourteen and fifteen with blundering and aghast trembling. . . . She is lost. She was born lost. We were all born lost*" (299–300). Ike's desire for absolution from guilt for his family's and culture's sins becomes a wish for a return to original innocence through rejection of the female body, but the futility of this desire is revealed in the destruction of Ike's revered woods, his Delta Eden.

The encounter with Roth's mistress occurs, ironically enough, in the wil-derness where Ike had supposedly learned about truth, honor, and humility. Upon meeting the unnamed granddaughter of Tennie's Jim, Ike can think only that she has come to ambush Roth. He tells her, "You won't jump him here," and he repeatedly asks, "What do you want? What do you expect?" (340, 342). But she wants nothing more than to see Roth again before her trip back home, and thus exposes Ike's misguided thinking and "gives lie to the myth of women as castrators, entrappers, and betrayers."[36] The cycle of interracial, intrafamilial breeding continues, and Ike is once again trying to pay off the "black" side of his family, spouting platitudes like, "Go back North. Marry: a man in your own race. . . . You are young, handsome, almost white. . . . Then you will forget all this, forget it ever happened, that he ever existed." But Ike merely seems pathetic and bitter "in his huddle of blankets," as she "blazed silently down at him" before delivering her withering assessment of Uncle Ike's life: "'Old man,' she said, 'have you lived so long and forgotten so much that you don't remember anything you ever knew or felt or even heard about love?'" (346).

While men are revealed as the agents of destruction, women are the agents of (potential) salvation. The key trait in the struggle for future survival is endurance, a trait Faulkner identifies in three offspring of mixed heritage: the son of Roth and his cousin, the expected child of Natalie and George Wilkins, and the fyce that Ike saves from Old Ben. Faulkner says that the little dog represents "the indomitable spirit of man," and he calls it the antithesis of the bear: "[T]he fyce represents the creature who has coped with his environment and is still on top of it, you might say. That he has—instead of sticking with his breeding and becoming a decadent, degenerate creature, he has mixed himself up with the good stock where he picked and chose."[37] Running counter to Ike's fears of miscegenation, then, is Faulkner's belief that heterogeneous elements increase adaptability, which is essential for survival. The children of the Beauchamp line of the family, including Roth's illegitimate son, are most like the admirable fyce and offer the possibility of change and revitalization in the midst of a "clear-cut," "deswamped and denuded and derivered" Southern wasteland (347).

In fact, this combination of white and black is effectively the pastoral ideal translated into human terms. The combination of black and white blood embodies the pastoral combination of opposites, the harmonic balance of the middle ground, and it suggests a dialectic that moves beyond the antagonistic white/black relationships of the past. The young Ike who rejects his birthright aims to rectify past wrongs. Based on the ecological consciousness he learns from Sam Fathers, Ike envisions a more fluid society, less rigid in its hierarchies, if not exactly egalitarian. In "Delta Autumn," however, Faulkner introduces some significant changes. As an old man, Ike is horrified by the thought of race mixing and is appalled by the fact that people no longer seem to stay in their "proper" place:

This Delta, he thought. This Delta. This land which man has deswamped and denuded and derivered in two generations so that white men can own plantations and commute every night to Memphis and black men own plantations and ride in jim crow cars to Chicago to live in millionaires' mansions on Lakeshore Drive, where white men rent farms and live like niggers and niggers crop on shares and live like animals. . . . Chinese and African and Aryan and Jew, all breed and spawn together until no man has time to say which one is which nor cares. . . . No wonder the ruined woods I used to know don't cry for retribution! he thought: The people who have destroyed it will accomplish its revenge. (347)

Ike links environmental degradation to cultural decay, and he now defines the disruption of social categories and hierarchies as unnatural, which is why he expects nature itself to call for retribution.

Neil Evernden, in *The Social Creation of Nature,* shows how nature can be used as a concept to justify vastly different social alternatives. "Once we can say, and believe, that a thing is natural," Evernden writes, "it is beyond reproach: it is now in the realm of the absolute." Yet, as he points out, the natural can be defined both as competition that eliminates the weak and as compassionate cooperation.[38] Scientific evidence can be easily marshaled for either interpretation, while the social systems that may then be justified as natural will be quite different.

Rather than use the concept of "naturalness" to promote one or another ideology, Faulkner exposes this process as a purely cultural construction. The pastoral mode is itself dependent on such constructions in its pattern of retreat toward nature and critique of city culture from the supposedly more authentic, more "natural" viewpoint of the country. Rawlings can therefore use the pastoral to promote values of cooperation and interdependence that she perceives to be lacking from a distant urban society. At the same time, the authors of *I'll Take My Stand* can employ the pastoral to renounce the dissolution of fixed categories and call for a return to the supposed stability of an imagined golden age. Faulkner, in a sense, utilizes the pastoral impulse on the pastoral mode itself, pulling back to a critical distance from which he can more clearly survey the territory. Thus, his postpastoral text reveals the inadequacies of Ike's pastoral retreat to the wilderness and return to the town.

Ike's act of relinquishment is a withdrawal from life, and in "Delta Autumn" he is alienated from both culture and nature, from his fellow hunters and from the wilderness he once revered. Reintegration of culture and nature would mean reinvigoration with life, and Faulkner suggests, through the example of Ike, that a new version of the pastoral quest for a harmonic middle ground is necessary. Ike rejects the tainted history of the plantation but offers no alternative in its place. Instead, the novel leaves final images of death and devastation but also all the promise and possibilities of future life.

The cycles of destruction and renewal in *Go Down, Moses* reflect the tentative beginnings of ecological renewal in Mississippi just prior to, but especially after, the novel's publication. After the heyday of the logging industry ended in the 1920s, there were sporadic efforts at reforestation, and by the late 1930s young forests were beginning to reappear on the Mississippi landscape.[39] The New Deal also created the Civilian Conservation Corps (CCC), which planted trees on over 160,000 acres of worn-out farmland, mostly in the South.[40] Abandoned farmland in north Mississippi even began to return to various forest types on its own, and the Forest Service planted over 600,000 acres of trees in Mississippi, including some 39 million young pine trees in Lafayette County alone from 1949 to 1959. Such efforts led the mayor of Oxford in 1959 to issue a proclamation calling the town "The Reforestation Capital of the World," a claim that would have been unthinkable just thirty years earlier.[41]

Even the timber companies sought to preserve the smallest trees and encourage reforestation through organizations like the Southern Pulpwood Conservation Association. The railroad industry leaders also realized that better long-term forest management was in their best interests, lest hundreds of miles of tracks built primarily to move logs to mills sit idle.[42] Of course, the motives of the timber and railroad industries in encouraging reforestation are hardly altruistic, and their efforts are a reminder that the renewal of forests can easily engender a new period of massive logging and environmental exploitation. For instance, a 1996 article in *Pulp & Paper* reports that "a switch from short-sighted cut-and-run policies of the beginning of the century to long-range forest planning and management" in Mississippi has helped replenish the state's forests and revive the forest product industry to the point that timber is once again "the state's most valuable economic commodity." However, a 1997 *Audubon* article describes the continued use of skidders and other modern machinery in a sudden rise of logging in the South (especially in Georgia, Alabama, and Mississippi) "with a determination not seen in this area since the cut-and-run logging days of the early 1900s," and the timber industry's own literature estimated in 1997 that the removal rate would exceed growth in the South in only ten more years.[43] As these developments attest, Faulkner's cyclical view of history in *Go Down, Moses* entails the potential for both recovery and renewed destruction: repetition with revision or an unaltered repetition of the past.

The novel as a whole conveys a need to go beyond the traditional pastoral mindset in order to find a productive, principled method of combining Ike's understanding of nature with his moral consciousness. Or, as Faulkner says, there must be an alternative to Ike's willful nonparticipation: "What we need are people who will say, This is bad and I'm going to do something about it, I'm going to change it."[44] But *Go Down, Moses* does not reveal what an ethical Southern postpastoral relationship with nature might actually look like.

Conclusion

Ecopastoral and the Past, Present, and Future of Southern Literature

In his compelling book *The Organic Machine: The Remaking of the Columbia River* (1995), Richard White recounts the fascinating and often troubling history of human interaction with the Columbia River in the Pacific Northwest. In the Columbia Basin, a dozen dams have been built on the river and its tributaries, creating a vast power system that has never fulfilled its own goals. The development of the river "has largely destroyed a vast natural bounty of salmon and replaced it with an expensive and declining artificial system of hatcheries." The Hanford Nuclear Reservation that was built on the river regularly released poisonous and carcinogenic elements, creating "a radioactive geography . . . by the intersection of weather, water, soils, plants, animals, markets, specific radionuclides, and our own bodies."[1]

Yet White's purpose is not to denounce the development of the waterway he refers to as "a virtual river," where the human and the natural, the mechanical and the organic, have merged to the point that they can no longer be separated: "We can't treat the river as if it is simply nature and all dams, hatcheries, channels, pumps, cities, ranches, and pulp mills are ugly and unnecessary blotches on a still coherent natural system. These things are now part of the river itself." Ultimately, White argues that the history of the Columbia River teaches not "the need to leave nature alone," but that "there is no clear line between us and nature." The central insight of White's book, which Leo Marx calls "a compelling microhistory of the encounter between the forces of technology and nature in America," is that the separation between humans and nature exists to be crossed.[2] Coming to terms with the reality and implications of the idea that humanity and nature are inextricably bound within the same larger system is imperative for understanding our history and for plotting our future.

Throughout his book, White argues that the workers who helped create the organic machine of the river experienced an intimate bond with nature through labor (a notion often shunned in contemporary environmental movements).[3] As I have suggested throughout this study, the authors of eco-pastorals of the 1930s and 1940s posit the same idea in their fiction. Surely part of their impetus for doing so was a distrust of abstract labor like cotton and stock brokering that seemed responsible for national financial calamities and gross class inequities. Yet another part of the appeal of knowing nature through work was perhaps the somewhat contradictory allure of reconfirming "the deep, indestructible bond . . . between man and his environment," to use Faulkner's words, in order to establish a continuity with the Southern past, even while reinventing the idea of the South for the present and future.[4]

In the South of the Great Depression, work of any sort tends to be extolled, and the idea of knowing nature through labor appears time and again in different forms. For the authors considered in this project, knowing nature through work is a potential means for overcoming the apparent separation of the human and the natural. But it also can be both a catalyst for and model of more egalitarian social systems. The abusive (to both land and people) agricultural system of the South seems to have made Caldwell give up on the idea of productive labor in nature as a viable future alternative, at least for small independent farmers. Jeeter Lester is denied the chance to work the land by a combination of ecological, economic, and physiological factors, and the result is devastating, threatening even the humanity of the Lester family. Ty Ty Walden's labor is not necessarily productive, but his obsessive digging at least keeps him healthy and even happy. Will Thompson's story suggests that Caldwell feels any type of labor can be positive because of the lack of available work in the Depression-era South. Will finds the proper balance of nature and culture in the ivy-covered walls of the cotton mill, forsaking the inherently solitary labor of farming in favor of the mill work, which fosters a spirit of collective unity. But this more urban setting ultimately fails as well as a productive site for Southern workers, and in both novels Caldwell links the inability to work with death.

Rawlings presents the wilderness of the Florida scrub as outside the market forces that trap professional farmers. The subsistence farming of Lant and Penny permits a diversified knowledge of nature through labor. Lant makes moonshine in the forest and raises sunken logs from the river, while both men hunt and trap for subsistence, rather than for sport or pure profit, in ways that stress responsibility within an ecological network. Rawlings herself learned nature by hunting, running an orange grove, and growing small plots of food. She posits the interdependence of the human and the natural by linking Lant's and Penny's responsible relationships with their environments to their positive and healthy human relationships. In Rawlings's work, it is the crackers, people who use nature to make a living, who actually feel compelled to act responsibly, as members of a community. Nature is commodity, but it is also home. For those to whom nature is only a commodity or a source of recreation, there is no sense of being a part of nature—only of being apart from it. Rawlings, like Faulkner, Hurston, and Caldwell, suggests that estrangement from nature causes alienation from fellow human beings.

Hurston, in *Their Eyes*, distinguishes the labor that Janie is compelled to do by Logan Killicks and Jody Starks from the labor she chooses to do alongside Tea Cake. Portraying an intimate connection of inner and outer nature, Hurston suggests that Janie's work for her first two husbands is too much like slave labor—forced rather than chosen—to be fulfilling. Like former slaves, Janie associates Logan's farm with bondage and the more wild space of the muck with freedom. Even though she works in agriculture on the muck, she actively chooses this labor in order to spend more time with Tea Cake, the "bee-man" who is good for her inner nature. In *Seraph on the Suwanee*, Hurston develops a working-class pastoral that reveals that knowing nature through labor can be financially rewarding as well. She also shows the uneasy balance of culture and nature that constitutes the pastoral ideal, a balance that can be easily thrown out of whack by the prospect of material wealth.

Faulkner's Ike McCaslin has no real working connection with nature because of his repudiation of his family farm. His only work is transforming the processed trees of the forest into buildings in town as a carpenter. Unlike the benefit of a sense of collective power that Will Thompson gets from labor similarly removed from direct contact with nature, Ike's occupation symbolizes his alienation from everything: the land, his family, the society of the South, his wife, and himself. Ike's hunting is more recreation and a quest for personal enlightenment than the necessary labor and way of life that it is for Jobaker or Lant or Penny, a fact that ironically denies Ike the lasting and intimate bond with nature he seeks. Lucas Beauchamp farms, makes moonshine, and digs for gold in nature, and his fire on the hearth signifies a healthy home life, in stark contrast to Ike's cold, loveless, and childless marriage.

Despite these authors' positive views of labor in nature during the Depression, this idea meets fierce resistance in the popular notion of (some) contemporary environmental movements that nature is best and purest when untouched by humans. As critic Glen Love argues, and as I have discussed in my reading of Rawlings's work, wilderness has come to replace the pastoral middle ground "as the locus of stability and value, the seat of instruction."[5] This shift is due in some part to works like these ecopastorals, which reveal the traditional pastoral version of nature to be a simplified version of civilization. Thus, wilderness is posited as the site of "real" nature, and any signs of human influence are seen as artificial, debasing intrusions. As defined in the Wilderness Act of 1964, wilderness is "an area where the earth and its community of life are untrammeled by man, where man himself is a visitor who does not remain."[6] Ike McCaslin's example shows, however, that condemning humans for spoiling the wilderness leaves Ike powerless to prevent its further destruction. On the other hand, Rawlings's work suggests that humans can live responsibly alongside or even in wilderness, supporting both themselves and their natural environment.

The conventional understanding of wilderness reflected in the legal definition quoted above preserves the dichotomy of humans and nature, as opposed to the network model put forth in ecopastorals. J. Baird Callicott argues that we need a third alternative to bridge the "notorious Schism" in the American conservation movement rent by former allies Gifford Pinchot and John Muir. Callicott describes the split and argues in favor of Aldo Leopold's vision of "harmony between man and land" as a corrective to "Pinchot's brazenly anthropocentric, utilitarian definition of conservation as efficient exploitation of 'resources' and Muir's anti-anthropocentric definition of conservation as saving innocent 'Nature' from inherently destructive human economic development." This suggests the continuing relevance of pastoral in general and ecopastoral in particular in the future as a vision of that third way, a model of sustainable development, that may help us, as Callicott says, "reconcile and integrate human economic activities with biological conservation."[7]

Work in nature is contact with the natural for cultural reasons, an activity that potentially bridges the human-nature divide in a sustainable way. Of course, as Caldwell shows in *Tobacco Road* and Hurston shows in *Seraph*, the tricky balance of sustainability can be tipped toward exploitation. A knowledge of nature can be gained through destructive as well as constructive work, and some forms of labor may be both. But some of Jim's ventures in *Seraph*, as well as Lant's in *South Moon Under*, show that mutually beneficial work with nature is possible. While all four authors convincingly demonstrate that the traditional Southern pastoral mode has outlived its usefulness, their revisions of the pastoral suggest its inherent value for discovering ethical and sustainable models of a natural network in which humans play an integral and responsible role. Working in nature, in Richard White's words, "imparts a bodily knowledge and a social knowledge, part of what Pierre

Bourdieu calls habitus."[8] And the way we treat nature conditions the way we treat our fellow humans. Since work in nature has always been the foundation of the pastoral, new forms of this complex literary mode will continue to be significant ways of imagining our place in the world.

The idea of knowing nature through labor can be a useful way for ecopastoral literature to reject the limiting dualisms of nature/culture and nature/human in favor of the network model. As White argues, the difference may have profound ramifications for contemporary environmental debates:

> Environmentalists must come to terms with work because its effects are so widespread and because work itself offers both a fundamental way of knowing nature and perhaps our deepest connection with the natural world. If the issue of work is left to the enemies of environmentalism . . . then work will simply be reified into property and property rights. . . . Given the tendency of environmentalists to exaggerate boundaries, to make humans and nature opposing sides in a bitter struggle, any attempt to stress the importance of work needs to begin by blurring the boundaries and stressing human connections with nature.[9]

The attitude of many environmentalists that nature should be protected for leisure may make environmentalism itself appear trivial or incapable of addressing pressing and serious issues aside from conservation. The sense of habitus engendered by work may create a stronger connection between people and places, thus encouraging choices that are in the interests of the place as whole, including its human inhabitants.

The important links between the pastoral and environmentalism suggest that Southern literary studies could benefit from more ecocritical approaches. Current debates among environmental thinkers over the idea of wilderness, for instance, are anticipated by many of the texts examined in this study. Callicott and Cronon worry that the wilderness concept reinforces the separation of humans and nature, thereby perpetuating a harmful and false dichotomy. Holmes Rolston III, Donald Waller, and Reed Noss, on the other hand, adamantly defend the importance of wilderness without humans or with minimal human intrusion.[10] The works of Faulkner, Rawlings, and Hurston bring different viewpoints to this debate, and understanding their works as part of an ongoing conversation about conservation can illuminate them in new ways.

Taken together, these ecopastorals represent an important development in Southern literature. While the literature of this Southern Renaissance era has often been discussed as emblematic of the momentous changes occurring in the South, I think the importance of Southern writers' interrogation and redefinition of the relationship of Southerners to land and nature has been overlooked. Daniel Singal, for instance, writes about the change from Victorianism to modernism in *The War Within*, while Richard King talks mainly of the scrutiny and revision of the "Southern family romance" in *A Southern Renaissance*. The revisions of the pastoral and the changes in attitudes toward the natural environment, because of the ways they implicate matters of race, class, and gender, can be juxtaposed in illuminating ways with the approaches of Singal, King, and many others. The sense that society and culture were sick in the Depression extends to nature and how humans have treated it historically. What W. J. Cash and Lillian Smith did for the Southern psyche, the ecopastorals do for the Southern garden. They uncover buried truths and make clear unseen connections.

These ecopastoral works, and others like them, mark the beginning of the repossession of pastoral for an environmentally aware era. This does not mean, as detailed in the preceding chapters, that ecopastorals necessarily champion environmentalism and decry business or commercial interests. These pastorals seek to balance the often competing interests of nature and culture, but in a way that takes the natural world seriously, as more than resource or commodity or scenic background. Nature is seen as home, a place where people live and work, and this is a more ecocentric view that continues and increases in the late twentieth and early twenty-first centuries.

From the critic's perspective, a focus on the natural environment can also establish unexpected ties between seemingly disparate writers, as I have tried to demonstrate in this project. The different varieties of ecopastoral suggested here could be applied to other authors and texts from a variety of eras. Caldwell's antipastoral, for instance, has clear connections with works like John Steinbeck's *The Grapes of Wrath* (1939) and James Agee and Walker Evans's *Let Us Now Praise Famous Men* (1941), as well as with valuable, less canonical works like John Faulkner's *Dollar Cotton* (1942) and George Sessions Perry's *Hold Autumn in Your Hand* (1941). Perhaps Caldwell's novels are simply the best known of a whole category of antipastoral works that emerges in Southern literature during the Depression, including other sagas of the soil like Harry Kroll's *Cabin in the Cotton* (1931), Caroline Miller's Pulitzer Prize–winning *Lamb in His Bosom* (1934), Caroline Gordon's *The Garden of Adonis* (1937), Charles Curtis Munz's *Land without Moses* (1938), and Robert Ramsey's *Fire in Summer* (1942).

Richard Wright's treatments of race and nature obviously would compare in interesting ways with Hurston's, but a story like "Big Boy Leaves Home" might also be seen as a different version of antipastoral. Wright's country setting in that story is a landscape of fear, where young, black males are banned from a white-dominated garden and Big Boy literally curls up in the body of the earth in a refuge of sorts from which to criticize the larger, white society. All of the issues that the Depression-era ecopastorals grapple with resonate well beyond the 1930s and 1940s to the present, when environmental issues and the discourses about them are perhaps more prominent and important than ever before. New versions of the ecopastoral and postpastoral continue to spring up on the landscape of Southern literature, and as the struggle to blend nature and culture productively continues, the pastoral will remain a viable literary mode.

Some of the most interesting recent and contemporary works that utilize and revise the pastoral are books, like those of the authors I cover here, that focus on poor, rural "crackers" who are consigned to live on the fringes of society, closer to nature. The novels of Harry Crews, for instance, have much in common with Caldwell's antipastoral, as does a novel like Dorothy Allison's *Bastard out of Carolina* (1992), an antipastoral coming-of-age tale set in Greenville, South Carolina, which is both physically and metaphysically close to Caldwell's bleak environments. Allison's main characters are poor white Southerners who live in a series of bland rented houses with dirt yards. The utter lack of vitality in their environments is striking but appropriate for this story of families falling apart amid self-destructive drinking, brutal violence, and horrifying child sexual abuse. The rare instances of natural imagery are therefore all the more noticeable, highlighting how Bone's alienation from all the people in her life goes hand in hand with her estrangement from the natural world.

It is at her Aunt Raylene's house where Bone finds rare opportunities to engage with nature and, not coincidentally, to discover more and more about herself. Bone plays in the river that runs near the house, discovers strength in the roots of plants as she works in her aunt's garden, and finds sustenance in both food and the love of the novel's strongest female role model. Raylene, who reveals that she is a lesbian in the final chapter, is perhaps the only woman who is not man-defined, and the fact that she takes over for Bone's mother provides hope in an otherwise bleak ending to the book. A dream that Bone has at Raylene's house suggests her desire for a pastoral retreat, a restorative journey into nature that would provide both escape and critical distance from the complications of her city life: "In the half-sleep that preceded full sleep I began to imagine the highway that went north. No real road, this highway was shadowed by tall grass and ancient trees. Moss hung low and tiny birds with gray-blue wings darted from the road's edge to the trees. Cars passed at a roar but did not stop, and the north star shone above their headlights like a beacon. I walked that road alone, my legs swinging easily as I covered the miles. No one stopped. No one called to me. Only the star guided me, and I was not sure where I would end."[11] This image counters the desultory, second-floor downtown apartment Bone has just left to come to Raylene's, and it also echoes the longing for a return to childhood innocence that resonates throughout the novel. Interestingly, the passage also suggests an escape from slavery, underscoring both how Bone is trapped in a hellish existence and her family's marginalization as poor white trash. Ironically, though, Bone's escape at the novel's end is to a farm, not away from one. Raylene's small patch of land is a hopeful new beginning in a natural setting.

The critical considerations of gender that Allison employs also align her novel with Rawlings's and Hurston's pastorals, as well as with a tradition of novels that construct women's relationships with nature and/or wilderness as empowering. Ellen Glasgow's *Barren Ground* (1925) employs critiques of gender similar to Rawlings's works and also resembles Hurston's personal pastorals as its female protagonist forges an independent identity through her association with nature. Dorinda Oakley's inner self is compared to a hidden field early in the novel, neglected but with "a smothered fire, like the wild grass, running through it." The soil of the farm she takes over has been impoverished by tenant farming, but it can be brought back to health by being cared for "like a doctor treats an undernourished human body." Dorinda also needs revival, and she cultivates a strong sense of self, merging her consciousness with "the consciousness of nature."[12] These sorts of recurring ecopastoral patterns can link Rawlings, Hurston, and Glasgow's work with other and more modern varieties of ecopastoral, including Allison's novel, many of Eudora Welty's stories and novels, Willa Cather's Virginia-based final novel *Sapphira and the Slave Girl* (1940), Alice Walker's *The Color Purple* (1992), several of Toni Morrison's novels, Connie May Fowler's *River of Hidden Dreams* (1994), set in the Florida Everglades, Lane von Herzen's east Texas–based *Copper Crown* (1991), and Janisse Ray's *Ecology of a Cracker Childhood* (1999), a book structurally and thematically very similar to Rawlings's *Cross Creek*.

Ray, a naturalist, recounts growing up in her parents' Georgia junkyard, where decaying hulls of old cars and household appliances mixed with plants, insects, and wild goats to create a postmodern wilderness pastoral: "A junkyard is a wilderness. Both are devotees of decay. The nature of both is random order."[13] Like *Cross Creek*, Ray's book interweaves short chapters about family and friends with others focused on the natural world to describe how she came to work to preserve the longleaf pine ecosystems that have almost completely vanished from the South. Ray, who cites Rawlings as one of the few authors she read in high school, confronts the roles of her family and the crackers with whom she identifies in the destruction of the forests and eco-systems that she has come to love. But, like Rawlings, she also connects the treatment of the land to wider social and cultural developments: "Our rela-tionship with the land wasn't one of give and return. The land itself has been the victim of social dilemmas—racial injustice, lack of education, and dire poverty. It was overtilled; eroded; cut; littered; polluted; treated as a com-modity, sometimes the only one, and not as a living thing. Most people wor-ried about getting by, and when getting by meant using the land, we used it. When getting by meant ignoring the land, we ignored it" (164–65). Ray's book is a contemporary example of ecopastoral in that it confronts head-on the dilemmas of the pastoral middle state, even more so perhaps than Rawlings, who tends to incorporate the escapist tendencies of traditional pastoral. Ray recognizes the imprint of human culture in everything natural around her. In fact, there are echoes of Caldwell, Hurston, and Faulkner, as well as Rawl-ings, in passages like this from Ray's book. The problems of the Depression-era South are still the problems of the twenty-first-century South, and the pastoral continues to be one of the primary literary modes for negotiating the boundaries of nature and culture.

Hurston's treatments of gender, race, and nature clearly link her with Walker, Morrison, and others, but it might prove equally compelling to jux-tapose *Seraph on the Suwanee* with white authors' treatments of black farm-ers, like Gilmore Millen's *Sweet Man* (1930), Robert Rylee's *Deep Dark River* (1935), and Lyle Saxon's *Children of Strangers* (1937). Greater attention to au-thors' representations of nature could also supply new relevance to margin-alized texts by black authors. Works like George Wylie Henderson's *Ollie Miss* (1935) and William Attaway's *Blood on the Forge* (1941), for instance, make connections between rural life and labor unrest. Attaway's novel is an interesting variety of proletarian fiction—part Caldwell, part Richard Wright—that follows three brothers from a Kentucky plantation to the Pitts-burgh steel mills where they become embroiled in the labor movement while navigating a multiethnic subculture.

The issue of people who work the land in order to get by recalls the com-plexities of reading Jim Meserve's actions in *Seraph on the Suwanee*, and it remains a thorny problem in contemporary environmentalism. How can the preservation of species and ecosystems coexist with the need for people to earn a living and support their families? When, exactly, does knowing na-ture through labor become exploiting nature for profit? Larry Brown's char-acters, for instance, are often endangered species themselves and understandably have little concern for ethical debates about interacting responsibly with nature. In *Joe* (1991), for example, the title character's job is to inject poison into trees so that a lumber company can plant more profitable pine in their place for later harvesting. But while Ray's book has entire chapters that ruminate on the effects of logging, Brown's Joe Ransom only once briefly voices his ambivalent feelings about how he and his crew make a living: "He didn't feel good about being the one to kill it [the forest]. He guessed it had never occurred to any of them what they were doing. But it had occurred to him."[14] Joe also knows he is destroying himself but does nothing to stop that either.

Although nature is peripheral through much of the novel, mainly appearing as passing landscape as Joe drunkenly pilots his pickup truck, Brown's story exhibits the central pastoral impulse to combine nature and culture. Joe himself is disconnected from everything, both natural and human, and Brown's portrait of him shows his lack of connection to the world around him—his isolation from friends, family, and, indeed, life itself. Joe's attachment to his truck indicates his alienation from nature, and he is a sort of Dude Lester with a six-pack as he drunkenly careens down country roads. As in *Tobacco Road,* the automobile symbolizes life out of control, wanton destruction, the machine in the garden. In this case, though, the truck as machine in the garden is not an unambiguous metaphor for the evil intrusions of man into pristine nature. The battered and beat-up old pickup clearly represents Joe himself, and when he basically gives it to young Gary, it represents giving of himself, bringing Joe back into contact with the world, as is made clear when he sacrifices his freedom for the sake of Gary and his sister at the end of the novel. The barely working truck represents for Gary independence through mobility, which, like his wages from poisoning trees, provides him a chance to leave his hellish poverty in the rearview mirror. Here, then, is a new version of the working-class pastoral, wherein working in nature is a means of economic advancement. As readers, we are inclined to root for Gary to escape his wretched poverty and abusive father. Does it matter that he poisons trees for a lumber company to do it? Should we demand that the working poor refuse certain jobs because they may damage the environment? Brown's gritty pastoral raises these sorts of ethical quandaries but provides no easy answers.

Ray's memoir does, in fact, address this very issue, at least briefly, in a chapter titled "The Kindest Cut." She offers a postpastoral, environmentally friendly, and financially profitable view of logging from "ecological forester" Leon Neel: "Known as single-tree selection or uneven-aged management, Leon's silviculture selects by hand individual trees to be harvested and leaves multigenerational or multispecies growth in a handsome, functioning grove. It is an innovative alternative to clear-cutting, proving endangered species can exist in a working landscape" (251). However, this quick mention is more of an aside than a genuine effort to reconcile environmental and business interests. Ray's version of the ecopastoral prefers wilderness to an inhabited middle state, as her call to arms in the book's afterword makes clear: "When we say the South will rise again we can mean that we will allow the cutover forests to return to the former grandeur and pine plantations to grow wild" (272).

One recent novel that does attempt to provide some answers about how to craft an environmentally responsible yet economically viable pastoral is Barbara Kingsolver's *Prodigal Summer* (2000), perhaps the most fully realized postpastoral Southern novel. Kingsolver, a Kentucky native, intertwines the stories of Deanna Wolfe, Lusa Maluf Landowski, and Garnett Walker in rural southern Appalachia. All three characters are intimately connected to their natural environments, emotionally, materially, metaphorically, and economically. Deanna lives and works in a National Forest, monitoring the tentative return of coyotes to the area; in the valley below, Lusa, a recent émigré from the "big city" of Lexington, inherits her husband's family farm; and Garnett's lifework is attempting to restore the American chestnut tree, which has been virtually wiped out by blight. Unlike *Joe*, this novel explicitly examines the interdependences of people and their environments, showing how they are part of the same system.

The health of people and the land are inseparable, and Kingsolver depicts a new, viable, ethical postpastoral: humans in kinship with their natural environment, ending the use of pesticides on crops, halting the ineffectual slaughter of predators, yet finding other ways of ordering the environment for the benefit of human inhabitants without doing unnecessary harm to the other species that share the space. Lusa, for example, strives to find a balance between nature and culture as she tries to keep her farm solvent. She at first is too idealistic and philosophical in wanting to grow tomatoes instead of tobacco. As she quickly learns, the realities of the market make tobacco a more practical crop (it's easy to store and ship, unlike tomatoes). Because of her ethical objections to growing tobacco (as every other farmer in the area does), Lusa finds an ecologically friendly, ethically satisfying alternative: raising goats. Significantly, her success depends on the culture/city side of the pastoral equation: she arranges to sell her goats to her cousin, a butcher in New York City, and times their births so that they are ready for sale at the times of the major Muslim, Christian, and Jewish holidays, when prices for goat meat in New York are highest. Lusa's neighbors think her ideas are crazy, but her success shows that a profit can be made on the farm while agribusiness is driving others out of business, forcing them to work other jobs or give up family land.

Like Lusa, Deanna and Garnett come to reject (or at least revise) the conventional wisdom of the past as they discover how to live as parts of an interdependent network of life. Garnett, for example, is shown by his neighbor how the use of insecticide not only fails to give humans more control over nature, but actually results in the opposite of its intended effect:

> When you spray a field with a broad-spectrum insecticide like Sevin, you kill the pest bugs *and* the predator bugs, bang. If the predators and prey are balanced out to start with, and they both get knocked back the same amount, then the pests that survive will *increase* after the spraying, fast, because most of their enemies have just disappeared. And the predators will *decrease* because they've lost most of their food supply. So in the lag between sprayings, you end up boosting the numbers of the bugs you don't want and wiping out the ones you need. And every time you spray, it gets worse.[15]

This same idea is echoed in Deanna's story, as she explains to her love interest, Eddie Bondo, how hunting coyotes actually increases their numbers, not to mention increasing the numbers of rodents that coyotes feed on. Recalling the emphasis on unintended and long-term consequences in *Go Down, Moses*, Deanna persuades Eddie, who sometimes hunts coyotes, that killing a top carnivore is not the same as stepping on a bug:

> "When you get a coyote in your rifle sight and you're fixing to pull the trigger, what happens? Do you forget about everything else in the world until there's just you and your enemy? . . . The idea that there's just the two of you left, alone in the world?"
>
> "I guess." He shrugged.
>
> "But that's wrong. There no such thing as *alone*. That animal was going to do something important in its time—eat a lot of things, or be eaten. There's all these connected things you're about to blow a hole in. They can't *all* be your enemy, because one of those connected things is you." (320)

Kingsolver's characters see their lives as connected to everything else that inhabits the same place, and it is no coincidence that as they find ways to responsibly live as part of their natural environment their relationships with their fellow humans become deeper, more intimate, and more meaningful.

Sam Fathers has the same awareness that Kingsolver's characters do, that pain, death, and killing are integral parts of nature's balance. Thus, Sam nurtures and raises Lion even though he has the foreknowledge that the dog will kill that symbol of wilderness, Old Ben. Ike cannot fully accept destruction as part of nature, clinging to a Grecian urn fantasy of permanence, and his estrangement from nature results in a lifelong lack of meaningful personal relationships, epitomized in the novel's famous opening description of him as "uncle to half a county and father to no one" (3). *Go Down, Moses* shows the divisions that can be created by the binary modes of thought that characterize traditional Southern pastoral, implicitly arguing for the necessity of new ways of conceptualizing and relating to our natural environments and all the life forms that live with us. *Prodigal Summer* works toward one fictional model of a Southern postpastoral that fulfills the hope that suffuses the ecopastorals of the Depression, to work and live productively in nature by recognizing that the way we treat nature is the way we treat ourselves. But a novel like *Prodigal Summer* represents not the culmination of a quest but rather the ongoing desire for a pastoral sense of balance and harmony in people's relationships with one another and with nature.

What is so revolutionary and compelling about the ecopastorals of the Southern Renaissance and Great Depression is their prescience in articulating environmental issues that are still pressing and unresolved, as well as their skillful adaptation of traditional conventions and themes for a new era. Although the pastoral is often still castigated as shopworn, dated, sentimental, and escapist, the ecopastorals illustrate that the pastoral is in fact adaptable and complex, able to interconnect issues of the environment, race, class, and gender. Understanding how these various strands intertwine and affect one another is an integral part of fashioning the South, indeed the world, of the twenty-first century. For such a daunting task, learning from the past is imperative. The authors of ecopastorals in the Depression seem to have embraced Lewis Simpson's characterization of the South as the dispossessed garden, and their new versions of pastoral do not seek to return to an imagined lost Eden. They show instead that the pastoral may yet represent the best hope for imagining and creating a healthy, responsible, and productive future.

Notes

Introduction

1. Singal, *The War Within*, 9–10.

2. Alpers, *What Is Pastoral?*, ix, 8, 418.

3. Buell, "American Pastoral Ideology Reappraised"; Gifford, *Pastoral*, 2. Marx's *The Machine in the Garden* remains one of the best examinations of the appeal of the pastoral in America.

4. Bakker cites Hinton Helper in the 1860s, along with Louis Rubin and Lucinda MacKethan in the 1970s and 1980s, as critics who too quickly dismiss antebellum authors. See *Pastoral in Antebellum Southern Romance*, 5.

5. Ibid., 3–4.

6. MacKethan, *The Dream of Arcady*, 10, 9.

7. Mitchell, *Gone With the Wind*, 821. Subsequent references will be cited parenthetically in the text.

8. Bakker, *Pastoral in Antebellum Southern Romance*, 9.

9. For example, the number of farms in Mississippi rises every decade until a drop of 0.8 percent from 1910 to 1919. After a 15 percent increase in the relatively prosperous 1920s, the total decreases 7 percent in the 1930s, 13.6 percent in the 1940s, and 45 percent in the 1950s. In Georgia, there is a steady increase in the number of farms until a 15.8 percent drop in the 1920s, followed by a 15.5 percent decrease in the 1930s, another 8.2 percent in the 1940s, and a 46.3 percent plunge in the 1950s. The losses were mainly small farms and were accompanied by a rise in urban populations throughout the South. See Dodd and Dodd, *Historical Statistics of the South*, 14–15, 18–19, 34–37.

10. See Kirby, *Rural Worlds Lost*, 276, who also notes that the alteration of farming practices virtually destroyed a seventy-five-year-old sharecropping system, mechanized agricultural labor, and "convulsed" the region by dispersing millions of people to cities (51).

11. Walter, *Placeways*, 121; Entrikin, *The Betweenness of Place*, 7.

12. See Vance, *Human Geography of the South*. Vance's bibliography reveals a spate of books in the previous decade alone that examine the effects of humans on the natural world, and vice versa, on a national scale, including Thomas Brues's *Insects and Human Welfare* (1920), O. D. Von Englin's *Inheriting the Earth; or, The Geographic Factor in National Development* (1922), Ellsworth Huntington's *Civilization and Climate* (1924), Lucien Febvre's *A Geographical Introduction to History* (1925), Milton Whitney's *Soil and Civilization* (1925), and Franklin Thomas's *The Environmental Basis of Society* (1925).

13. Wittenberg, "*Go Down, Moses* and the Discourse of Environmentalism," 56.

14. In the 1930s and 1940s, ecologists still uniformly held a holistic conception of nature. Barbour, in "Ecological Fragmentation in the Fifties," explains that in the 1950s this interdependent view began to be challenged and disputed, ushering in profound change in the field: "The ecologists of the 1950s were actors in the long-running story of holism yielding to reductionism, a theme in the history of science" (233). The debate continues to this day (254–55).

15. Cowdrey, *This Land, This South*, 127–30.

16. See ibid., 71–79; and Vance, *Human Geography of the South*, 95–97. For other contemporaneous assessments of Southern agricultural practices, particularly in the dominant cotton industry, also see Vance, *Human Factors in Cotton Culture;* Gray, *History of Agriculture in the Southern United States to 1860;* and Johnson, Embree, and Alexander, *The Collapse of Cotton Tenancy.*

17. Doyle, *Faulkner's County*, 300.

18. Cowdrey, *This Land, This South*, 114; Tindall, *The Emergence of the New South*, 405; Worster, *Dust Bowl*, 5; Pells, *Radical Visions and American Dreams*, 72.

19. Wittenberg, "*Go Down, Moses* and the Discourse of Environmentalism," 56. Also see chapter 5 of Buell's *Writing for an Endangered World*, where Buell, like Wittenberg, makes an extensive comparison of the ecological ethics of Leopold and Faulkner (particularly as expressed in *Go Down, Moses*).

20. Tindall, *The Emergence of the New South*, 405; Fickle, *Mississippi Forests and Forestry*, 160–63.

21. Barry Commoner first articulated this law in these words in *Making Peace with the Planet.*

22. Campbell, "The Land and Language of Desire," 207. As Joseph Meeker puts it in *The Comedy of Survival*, "[T]he profound insight at the heart of the science of ecology is that nature is indivisible, and therefore it cannot be comprehended by studying only its isolated fragments" (10).

23. Kroeber, *Ecological Literary Criticism*, 7.

24. These quotes are taken from a piece by David Griffin rather than directly from Whitehead, "the ecological philosopher par excellence," as Griffin has helpfully consolidated Whitehead's theories of nature from various works into his article "Whitehead's Contributions to a Theology of Nature."

25. For an analysis of how the shift in scientific thought to a mechanistic model of nature sanctions both environmental abuse and the subjugation of women, people

of color, and other minorities, see Merchant, *The Death of Nature*. Merchant's overview traces the ascent of the modern scientific conception of a passive natural world that Whitehead's philosophy controverts: "Nature as purely objective, was given only instrumental value for man, who, as a subject, was given absolute value as an end in himself. Any amount of exploitation could be justified if it gave even the slightest benefit to man" (Griffin, "Whitehead's Contributions to a Theology of Nature," 8).

26. Buell, *The Environmental Imagination*, 52.

27. Patterson, *Pastoral and Ideology*, 7; Alpers, *What Is Pastoral?* 11.

28. In formulating these central pastoral features, I have culled from a wide range of pastoral scholars, including Marx, Buell, Alpers, Patterson, Bakker, MacKethan, Gifford, Lewis Simpson, Raymond Williams, William Empson, Elizabeth Jane Harrison, Melvin Dixon, Annette Kolodny, and Louise Westling.

29. Marx, *The Machine in the Garden*, 70.

30. MacKethan, *The Dream of Arcady*, 10.

31. Twelve Southerners, *I'll Take My Stand*, xxxvii–xxxviii, 3.

32. Love, "*Et in Arcadia Ego*," 202, 203.

33. Simpson, *The Dispossessed Garden*, 69.

34. Love, "*Et in Arcadia Ego*," 202–3.

35. Stein, *Shifting the Ground*, 17.

36. While the terms "personal pastoral" and "wilderness pastoral" are my own, I borrow "antipastoral" and "postpastoral" from Gifford, altering and expanding his definitions within a new context.

37. Marx, "Pastoralism in America," 66; Buell, *The Environmental Imagination*, 51.

38. Ching and Creed, *Knowing Your Place*, 3; Buell, *The Environmental Imagination*, 36.

39. Walter, *Placeways*, 121.

40. Gifford, *Pastoral*, 148.

Chapter 1

1. Miller, *Erskine Caldwell*, 197–202.

2. Westling, *The Green Breast of the New World*, 101, 52. See also Carolyn Merchant's *The Death of Nature* for a historical account of the rise to dominance in the Western world of the conception of science as masculine and nature as its feminine object of study.

3. Caldwell and Bourke-White, *You Have Seen Their Faces*, 29, 76. Subsequent references will be cited parenthetically in the text.

4. Renek, "'Sex Was Their Way of Life,'" 68.

5. Lee, "Relocating Location," 127, 132. See also Bourdieu, *Distinction*.

6. McElvaine, *The Great Depression*, 201, 202.

7. See Pells, *Radical Visions and American Dreams*, 98, who also cites a 1934 essay in *New Masses* by Rebecca Pitts, "Something to Believe In," as the best expression of the mood and attitudes of American writers, and her description is accurate for

Caldwell's fiction. The fundamental dilemma of the 1930s, Pitts says, is how to become part of a social group or gain satisfaction in a collective cause without sacrificing one's "personal integrity . . . individuality and self-awareness" (117).

8. Cowley, "The Two Erskine Caldwells"; Brinkmeyer, "Is That You in the Mirror Jeeter?" 370.

9. Mixon, *The People's Writer*, 44.

10. Caldwell, *Tobacco Road*, 22. Subsequent references will be cited parenthetically in the text.

11. Vance, *Human Geography of the South*, 95. See also 93–106.

12. As McElvaine, *The Great Depression*, notes, one of the bitterest ironies of the Depression is that warehouses of goods sat idle and tons of "surplus" food was destroyed even as millions starved and lacked basic necessities.

13. In his introduction to the 1940 Modern Library edition of *Tobacco Road*, Caldwell demonstrates his familiarity with the South's history of soil problems: "Their forefathers had seen tobacco come and flourish on these same plots of earth. But after its season it would no longer grow in the depleted soil. . . . Then came cotton. Cotton thrived in abundance for several generations, and then it, too, depleted the soil of its energy until it would no longer grow" (ii).

14. The National Emergency Council's *The Report on Economic Conditions of the South* notes that despite having "more than half of the Nation's farm people," the South raises less than one-third of the country's pigs and cattle, "one-fifth of the country's eggs, milk, and butter [and] . . . one-eighth of the potatoes." The report also explains that "[b]ecause they have concentrated on cash crops" Southern farmers have failed to plant cover crops "that add fertility to the soil" and protect against erosion (70). This hard-to-find, out-of-print 1938 report is reprinted in Carlton and Coclanis, *Confronting Southern Poverty*.

15. Kirby, in *Rural Worlds Lost*, cites evidence that Caldwell's figures are no exaggeration. He notes that during the late 1920s and early 1930s Arthur Raper surveyed two rural Georgia counties and found "landlords and merchants charging 10 percent interest on advances for three and a half months. Four-month money cost 25 percent, and the actual annual rate was about 35 percent" (149).

16. Cowdrey, *This Land, This South*, 79.

17. For more on the decline of diversified farming and the rise of staple crops in the South, see Vance, *Human Geography of the South*, 154–59; Vance, *Human Factors in Cotton Culture*, 179–92; and Tindall, *The Emergence of the New South*, 124–27. Tindall also shows that "the Jeffersonian vision of the independent yeoman farmer" persists in the South, despite the rise in tenancy rates from 36.2 percent of all Southern farms in 1880 to 55.5 percent in 1930: "It was a perennial irony that such invocations of the agrarian myth accompanied the steady drift of farmers into the dependent status of tenancy and sharecropping" (125).

18. Broadwell and Hoag, "'A Writer First.'"

19. Byrd finds North Carolina to be populated by "indolent wretches" who live in "a dirty state of nature," disdainfully concluding that "'tis a thorough Aversion to Labor that makes People file off to N Carolina, where Plenty and a Warm Sun confirm

them in their Disposition to Laziness for their whole Lives" (*William Byrd's Histories of the Dividing Line betwixt Virginia and North Carolina,* 92). This characterization can even be found in colonial writings by John Smith, William Strachey, and Robert Beverly, who concludes in *The History and Present State of Virginia* that the "Liberality of Nature" itself is responsible for the colonists' "slothful Indolence" (314). For an extended analysis of literary representations of poor whites, see Cook, *From Tobacco Road to Route 66.*

20. Broadwell and Hoag, " 'A Writer First,' " 90.

21. Lytle, "The Hind Tit," 202.

22. Jay Watson has called this repetitive style of Caldwell's "the exhaustion of rhetoric," and he argues that this experimental dialogue evolves from and complements the subject matter of exhausted soil and lives. See "The Rhetoric of Exhaustion and the Exhaustion of Rhetoric."

23. Gold, "Go Left, Young Writers!"

24. The Lester domicile, however, has none of the activity and vitality that authors like Eudora Welty and Marjorie Kinnan Rawlings show can be as rich, varied, and meaningful as typically male spheres of action.

25. The famous Gastonia, North Carolina, strike is Caldwell's model for these events. This six-month, often violent dispute between the Communist-led National Textile Workers Union on one side and the mill owners, police, and National Guard on the other was played out in the national press. When police raided a tent colony of evicted workers, gunfire erupted and Chief D. A. Aderholt was killed. Protests during the ensuing trial ended with Ella May Wiggins, a balladeer from the tent colony, shot to death as well. Cook, in *From Tobacco Road to Route 66,* 85–97, notes that at least six novels were inspired by the insurrection. Generally considered the best account of the strike is Liston Pope's *Millhands and Preachers.*

26. Caldwell, *God's Little Acre,* 96. Subsequent references will be cited parenthetically in the text.

27. McDonald, *Erskine Caldwell,* 64.

28. Devlin, *Erskine Caldwell,* 54–55; Kubie, "*God's Little Acre*: An Analysis."

29. Vance, *Human Geography of the South,* explains how the monocrop culture of nineteenth-century Southern agriculture fostered a pattern of farmers exhausting their land and then moving on to other areas and repeating the process (just as Ty Ty digs a deep hole and moves on without ever filling it in or repairing the damage). The boom in commercial fertilization from 1840 to 1860 was a temporary solution that eventually worsened soil erosion. Vance sees the same dependence on fertilizer returning in the 1920s (over 70 percent of fertilizer in 1929 is used by Southern states) and warns his audience of an impending crisis.

30. Devlin, *Erskine Caldwell,* 65; Cook, *From Tobacco Road to Route 66,* 73.

Chapter 2

1. Rawlings commented in a 1939 paper for the National Council of Teachers of English titled "Regional Literature of the South" that the term *regional literature* usu-

ally referred to "futile outpourings of bad writing whose only excuse is that they are regional, regionalism being at the moment a popular form of expression." Quoted in Bigelow, *Frontier Eden*, 71.

2. Rawlings, *Cross Creek*, 3. Subsequent references will be cited parenthetically in the text.

3. Cross Creek is about one hundred miles north of Orlando and twenty miles southeast of Gainesville, isolated on a small strip of land between two large lakes that are connected by the creek that gives the town its name.

4. Bigelow, *Frontier Eden*, 11, 70.

5. The Florida scrub is a distinctive, desertlike ecosystem of sandy soil, shrubs, and small trees found on coastal and inland ridges throughout Florida. The largest area of scrub in the state is around Cross Creek and the Ocala National Forest.

6. Derr, *Some Kind of Paradise*, 313, 338.

7. Barbour, *That Vanishing Eden*, 3.

8. See Harrison's introduction to *Female Pastoral*; and Dixon's *Ride Out the Wilderness*, where he discusses how slaves (and later free blacks) were kept outside the plantation boundaries, excluded from the pastoral scene, and associated with chaotic, wild nature but not the improved garden.

9. Phillips, for instance, argues in *The Truth of Ecology* that ecology is more of "a fuzzily defined and value-ridden 'point of view'" than it is "a coherent scientific enterprise in its own right." Many scientists, including a "growing number" of ecologists, Phillips says, are critical of ecology's methods and assumptions: "The values to which ecology dedicated itself early on—especially balance, harmony, unity, and economy—are now seen as more or less unscientific, and hence as 'utopian' in the pejorative sense of the term" (42–43). Needless to say, not everyone agrees with Phillips. Rather than enter debates on the merits of ecology and on the way nature actually works, I want instead to focus on how authors utilize a particular conception of nature, including the ecological values Phillips mentions, in order to present certain social and cultural systems as more natural than others.

10. Harrison, *Female Pastoral*, 14–15.

11. Bigelow notes that Rawlings was "horrified" when someone once compared her characters to the "hideous" ones in *Tobacco Road* (*Frontier Eden*, 101). Moreover, the absence of food that signals estrangement from nature and a lack of spiritual sustenance in Caldwell's work is contrasted by Rawlings's frequent lush descriptions of preparing and eating food.

12. Letter dated March 1930 in Bigelow and Monti, *Selected Letters of Marjorie Kinnan Rawlings*, 37.

13. Bakker, *Pastoral in Antebellum Southern Romance*, 10.

14. Letter dated October 24, 1936, in Bigelow and Monti, *Selected Letters*, 122.

15. Pells, *Radical Visions and American Dreams*, 101. Thus Bigelow also overstates the case, and somewhat misses the point, when he claims that "while most of the action in *South Moon Under* takes place in the Roaring Twenties, almost nothing of that roar penetrates the silence of the scrub" (*Frontier Eden*, 109). As Pells suggests, the withdrawal from mainstream American society and the refusal to suggest how to fix

an apparently broken capitalist system may be a direct reaction and response to current social crises.

16. Bigelow, *Frontier Eden*, 7. These poems are collected in Tarr, *The Poems of Marjorie Kinnan Rawlings.*

17. Letter dated November 11, 1933, in Bigelow and Monti, *Selected Letters*, 80.

18. Harrison, *Female Pastoral*, 11.

19. See Merchant's *The Death of Nature;* Westling's *The Green Breast of the New World;* Kolodny's *The Lay of the Land;* and Harrison's *Female Pastoral.*

20. Standpoint theory makes a basic assumption that members of an oppressed group are in an epistemically privileged position to have a more immediate, thorough, and critical knowledge about the nature of their oppressions. Some standpoint theorists claim that this knowledge extends beyond the immediate situation to an understanding of other oppressed groups. For a discussion of the variety of standpoint theories and their differences and connections with ecofeminism, see Slicer, "Toward an Ecofeminist Standpoint Theory."

21. Salleh, "The Ecofeminism/Deep Ecology Debate," 199.

22. Rawlings, *South Moon Under*, 1. Subsequent references will be cited parenthetically in the text.

23. MacKethan, *The Dream of Arcady*, 10.

24. In the first chapter of *Cross Creek*, Rawlings reveals her ambivalence toward the pastoral ideal of order. She recalls her initial desire for a white picket fence around her new home, but seems uncomfortable with the psychological separation that such a fence would bring, preferring the appearance of continuity with the surrounding landscape: "[A]n elegant fence would bring to the Creek a wanton orderliness that is out of place" and "would interfere with the feeling one has inside the house of being a part of the grove" (9).

25. Harrison, *Female Pastoral*, 10–11.

26. See Lutwack, *The Role of Place in Literature.* Lutwack goes on to astutely note that "all of the attributes of enclosed places are easily transferred to woman" (95–96).

27. Appropriately, Lant and the others use their superior hunting and tracking skills, using the wilderness as cover to launch a campaign of harassment against their common enemy (141–46).

28. Pells, *Radical Visions and American Dreams*, 98–99.

29. Sutter, *Driven Wild*, 24.

30. Rogers, "The Great Depression," 317–19; Derr, *Some Kind of Paradise*, 320.

31. Sutter, *Driven Wild*, 16. As Sutter explains, the histories of roads and wilderness preservation are deeply intertwined. The original purposed of National Parks was not conservation as we understand it today, but rather to provide automobile-based recreation for tourists, as well as access for logging companies.

32. Lee, "Relocating Location," 126.

33. The Ocala National Forest actually already existed but thousands of acres were added to it in the 1930s by the federal government.

34. Cronon, "The Trouble with Wilderness," 80.

35. Ibid., 80–81.

36. Brinkley, *Voices of Protest*, 144.

37. Letter dated November 4, 1931, in Bigelow and Monti, *Selected Letters*, 49.

38. Tarr, *Max and Marjorie*, 58.

39. Salleh, "The Ecofeminism/Deep Ecology Debate," 208.

40. Rogers, "The Great Depression," 317.

41. Derr, *Some Kind of Paradise*, 116.

42. Kuehl and Breyer, *Dear Scott/Dear Max*, 244.

43. Morris, "Engendering Fictions," defines "woman's story" in this context as one of "a woman striving to surpass narrow definitions of female self constituted through or in tension with marriage and motherhood to achieve a sense of self-possession or self-expansion," a familiar pattern in Southern women's texts in the years between the wars (29).

44. Ibid., 31.

45. Ibid., 29.

46. Rawlings, *The Yearling*, 10. Subsequent references will be cited parenthetically in the text.

47. For an analysis of Penny's and Jody's maternal qualities, as well as of sexual desire in the novel, see Vallone, "Gender and Mothering in *The Yearling*."

48. Silverthorne notes in *Marjorie Kinnan Rawlings* that Rawlings was very close to her own father, who died from a kidney infection when she was seventeen (12–14, 24–25).

49. Later in the novel, after seven days of constant rain that has destroyed most of their crops, Penny voices this sentiment, saying the only "good" result of the storm is "to remind a man to be humble, for there's nary thing on earth he kin call his own" (236).

50. Lowe, "The Construction and Deconstruction of Masculinity in *The Yearling*," 232; Tarr, "In 'Mystic Company.'" Tarr also agrees that Jody's rite of passage is not a consequence of killing Flag: "Jody does not suddenly become a man the instant he shoots his deer. Rather, he is slowly growing up all the way through the novel" (32).

51. See Lesnik-Oberstein, "Children's Literature and the Environment," 210, where she prudently qualifies the universality of this relationship, noting that its prevalence in Anglo-American culture is not necessarily matched in other cultures. For a broader analysis of literary representations of children, see her full-length study *Children's Literature*.

52. Lesnik-Oberstein, "Children's Literature and the Environment," 212.

53. Lowe, "The Construction and Deconstruction of Masculinity in *The Yearling*," 244.

54. Peggy Prenshaw has read this use of "We" as "commanding," that is, as evidence of Rawlings's growing mastery of her craft and her self-confidence as an artist. See "The Otherness of Cross Creek."

55. Harvey, *Justice, Nature and the Geography of Difference*, 153.

56. Whitehead, *Science and the Modern World*, 206.

57. Marx, *The Machine in the Garden,* 127.

58. Glisson, *The Creek,* 85.

59. Jones, "Race and the Rural," 218.

60. Ibid., 221–22.

61. The system of slavery and the virtual servitude that followed, Rawlings says, have conditioned African Americans to work because they are required to work and to view any amount of freedom as a chance "to escape for the moment the lowliness and the poverty and the puzzle of living," thereby causing them to appear irresponsible and undisciplined to whites (181).

62. Bigelow and Monti, *Selected Letters,* 223–24.

63. Parker, *Idella,* 87–88.

64. Tarr, *Max and Marjorie,* 496; Jones, "Race and the Rural," 227–28.

65. See Prenshaw, who says that in this section of the book (the last six chapters) Rawlings "most fully foregrounds the self." She reads this strong "I" as evidence of Rawlings having overcome the immanence of the everyday, her ability to "subordinat[e] the daily life" in order "to see and write about larger, transcendent patterns" ("The Otherness of Cross Creek," 21). I would also add that Rawlings sometimes must subordinate the self to the otherness of nature in order to rediscover her subjective identity.

66. Gifford, *Pastoral,* 80.

67. Love, "*Et in Arcadia Ego,*" 202–3.

68. Buell, *The Environmental Imagination,* 44, 50.

69. Glisson, *The Creek,* 39.

Chapter 3

1. Dodd and Dodd, *Historical Statistics of the South,* 14–18, 34–36.

2. I am following Leslie G. Desmangles's spelling in order to differentiate this complex Haitian religion from the erroneous portrayals of "voodoo" in Hollywood movies and popular culture. The commonly (mis)used term *voodoo* "is a deterioration of the Dahomean term *vodu* or *vodun,* meaning 'deity' or 'spirit,'" as Desmangles explains in his excellent study *The Faces of the Gods,* 2. Daphne Lamothe also adopts the Creole spelling "Vodou" from Desmangles because the more familiar "voodoo" and "hoodoo" are "saddled with misleading and defamatory meaning" ("Vodou Imagery, African American Tradition, and Cultural Transformation in Zora Neale Hurston's *Their Eyes Were Watching God,*" 183).

3. For a detailed account of Hurston's anthropological training and fieldwork, see Hemenway, *Zora Neale Hurston,* 84–135.

4. See Lowe's "Seeing Beyond Seeing" for a more extensive appraisal of Hurston's religious influences and beliefs.

5. Lowe notes that Hurston "was increasingly drawn to a form of Deism, if not agnosticism" (ibid., 77) and that "she did not actively practice any set religion in her personal life" (85).

6. Rachel Stein, in *Shifting the Ground,* has demonstrated many of the important connections between Hurston's natural world in *Their Eyes* and principles of Vodou. Similarly, Daphne Lamothe's essay "Vodou Imagery, African American Tradition, and Cultural Transformation in Zora Neale Hurston's *Their Eyes Were Watching God"* identifies some specific associations of Vodou deities with characters and events in *Their Eyes.* While I will be relying on these critics' insights, as well as on some of the same ecofeminist approaches utilized by Stein in particular, I also examine Hurston's ideas about nature within the context of the Southern pastoral tradition. Other treatments of Hurston's use of Vodou include Southerland, "The Influence of Voodoo on the Fiction of Zora Neale Hurston"; Dutton, "The Problem of Invisibility: Voodoo and Zora Neale Hurston"; Collins, "The Myth and Ritual of Ezili Freda in Hurston's *Their Eyes Were Watching God"*; and Menke, "'Black Cat Bone and Snake Wisdom.'"

7. The lack of direct commentary on the effects of the Depression in Hurston's fiction might also be related to an apparent absence of worsening conditions in Eatonville. Hoyt Davis, who grew up in Eatonville around the same time as Hurston, was asked by an interviewer if there were hard times during the 1930s: "To tell you the truth, I don't know of one person being hungry at that time in Eatonville. Everybody out here planted gardens and they grew chickens. They could eat chickens whenever they wanted and they fished. So I never heard of anybody asking for food" (quoted in Lillios, "Excursions into Zora Neale Hurston's Eatonville," 21).

8. Bakker, *Pastoral in Antebellum Southern Romance,* 10; Empson, *Some Versions of Pastoral,* 23.

9. Hathaway, "The Unbearable Weight of Authenticity," 185.

10. Hemenway, *Zora Neale Hurston,* 237.

11. Hurston, *Their Eyes Were Watching God,* 15–16. Subsequent references will be cited parenthetically in the text.

12. Or as Dixon puts it in *Ride Out the Wilderness,* "[S]he perceives an irony about landscape that had eluded Nanny's vigilance: the lowlands can be high ground" (88).

13. Stein, *Shifting the Ground,* 54. More broadly, Vodou effaces the fundamental division between humans and the physical world, a split reinforced by the Judeo-Christian separation of spirit and body. See also Lowe's *Jump at the Sun* for more on Hurston's treatment of this separation in *Jonah's Gourd Vine:* "White-dominated society seeks to create a boundary between the body and soul, the sexual and the sacred" (97).

14. Kaufman, *The Theological Imagination,* 226.

15. Trefzer, "Possessing the Self," 305.

16. Hurston, *Tell My Horse,* 234. Subsequent references will be cited parenthetically in the text.

17. This scene also has some odd parallels with the scene in *God's Little Acre* where Will performs a similar ritual on Griselda in order to tap into the life force through the "mysterious source of life."

18. Stein, *Shifting the Ground,* 64.

19. Combinations of opposites abound in Haitian Vodou. The religion itself is referred to by scholars as syncretistic, a fusion of the officially sanctioned Catholic Church and the underground African religious traditions of the lower classes (although Desmangles argues that it is not technically syncretistic but symbiotic [*The Faces of the Gods,* 7–8]). Vodou deities may have two or more personalities, often with nearly opposite characteristics. For example, the goddess Ezili includes the personae of Ezili Freda, an upper-class, light-skinned or mulatta love goddess, and Ezili Danto, a working-class, dark-skinned goddess who represents motherhood and especially maternal rage (see Lamothe, "Vodou Imagery, African American Tradition, and Cultural Transformation in Zora Neale Hurston's *Their Eyes Were Watching God*"; and Collins, "The Myth and Ritual of Ezili Freda in Hurston's *Their Eyes Were Watching God,*" who make extensive comparisons of Janie and Ezili). While such inverse personae may seem to reproduce the binary oppositions that I am claiming Hurston and Vodou transcend, "Vodouisants do not understand them to represent two distinct divine entities, the one symbolizing beneficence and creativity and the other maleficence and destruction." Instead, both personalities are understood to be attributes of the same divine being, and the opposition is "reconciled (or rather transcended)," as Desmangles says, by the vital force of Bondye (derived from the French *Bon Dieu*), the Godhead or creator of the universe (*The Faces of the Gods,* 95–97).

20. Dixon, *Ride Out the Wilderness,* 87; Meisenhelder, *Hitting a Straight Lick with a Crooked Stick,* 62; Lowe, *Jump at the Sun,* 157–97.

21. See Haurykiewicz, "From Mules to Muliebrity," for an extended analysis of Hurston's use of mules as figures of both degradation and resistance.

22. Hemenway, *Zora Neale Hurston,* 222.

23. The talking buzzards that swoop in to devour the carcass seem to parody the parody that the townspeople have just performed, including the lead buzzard that stands on the dead mule like Jody. These talking animals do not seem to be related to any Vodou rituals or deities and are perhaps more like the animal tales in *Mules and Men.*

24. For example, Meisenhelder says his "feminized" nickname promises a "sweeter" and gentler masculinity and that his surname suggests "a healthy black identity compared to the sterility implied in Joe's" (*Hitting a Straight Lick with a Crooked Stick,* 68), and Lowe notes the connection to Virbius, King of the Woods, as well as parallels with Christ: "Tea (red, like blood) Cake (the body)" (*Jump at the Sun,* 199n5, 204n30).

25. Grant and Ruzich take this position in their article "A Rhetoric of Roads," 18.

26. During her visit to Jamaica (before going to Haiti), Hurston was struck by the extreme intraracial color consciousness of the island's black population. In chapter 1 of *Tell My Horse,* she lampoons the Jamaicans who trace their ancestry through white fathers while never mentioning their black mothers, saying the island is a place where roosters lay eggs.

27. Derr, *Some Kind of Paradise,* 326.

28. McCally, *The Everglades,* 144.

29. Derr, *Some Kind of Paradise,* 327.

30. McCally, *The Everglades,* 140–46.

31. Derr, *Some Kind of Paradise,* 172–73.

32. Hurston also lived through a 1929 hurricane while in Nassau, the Bahamas. See Lowe, *Jump at the Sun* (202–3); and Lillios, "'The Monstropolous Beast.'"

33. Derr, *Some Kind of Paradise,* 166–67, 196. After the 1928 hurricane, the Hoover Dike is built around the south shores of the lake—34 to 38 feet high and 125–50 feet wide at the base—dropping the lake's level another 10 feet (327).

34. Cassidy, "Janie's Rage," 262.

35. Interestingly, Hurston explains that this form of possession often results in the cheval ridiculing, insulting, or criticizing prominent officials or other persons with authority and social status. In this sense, possession is similar to Bahktinian "carnivalesque" and other masked forms of social critique. While Hurston does not employ this aspect in Tea Cake's "possession" episode, the hurricane does have the effect of unmasking white authority. One might even claim that the entire novel, or perhaps Hurston's entire body of work, is a form of cleverly masked criticism and ridicule of various forms of authority and power. See *Tell My Horse,* 232–50, for more of Hurston's experiences with possession rituals in Haiti.

36. Lowe notes the affinities between Janie and the Egyptian goddess Isis, who is associated with floods and whose symbol is the cow, and details Hurston's use of Isis in other work (*Jump at the Sun,* 195).

37. See Huxley, *The Invisibles.* Huxley explains that "the nape of the neck is important in voodoo: loa perch there when whispering secrets in your ear, a candle is stubbed out there during initiation, to seat the soul firmly in its place, and possession is often heralded by discomfort in that region" (126).

38. Cassidy, "Janie's Rage," 264.

39. Hemenway relates that Hurston was broke in Honduras while composing the novel and desperately needed money to facilitate an expedition to find a lost Mayan city (*Zora Neale Hurston,* 301–7).

40. Ibid., 307, 314; Washington, "A Woman Half in Shadow," 21. St. Clair, calls Arvay a woman who "resists victimization" and "chooses the burden she will carry" ("The Courageous Undertow of Zora Neale Hurston's *Seraph on the Suwanee,*" 39).

41. Meisenhelder, *Hitting a Straight Lick with a Crooked Stick,* 92. See also Lowe's *Jump at the Sun* and Tate's "Hitting 'A Straight Lick with a Crooked Stick.'"

42. Bakker, *Pastoral in Antebellum Southern Romance,* 3; St. Clair, "The Courageous Undertow of Zora Neale Hurston's *Seraph on the Suwanee,*" 38, 42; Buell, *The Environmental Imagination,* 52.

43. Marx, *The Machine in the Garden,* 127.

44. Hurston, *Seraph on the Suwanee,* 1. Subsequent references will be cited parenthetically in the text.

45. Hurston expresses this opinion in her review of Wright's *Uncle Tom's Children,* "Stories of Conflict," *Saturday Review,* April 2, 1938, 32.

Meisenhelder, *Hitting a Straight Lick with a Crooked Stick,* 96; Alice Walker, foreword to Hemenway's *Zora Neale Hurston,* xvi.

46. Meisenhelder, *Hitting a Straight Lick with a Crooked Stick,* 102.

47. Ettin, *Literature and the Pastoral,* 113–14.

48. Meisenhelder, *Hitting a Straight Lick with a Crooked Stick,* 102.

49. For a related discussion, see Tate on the white characters' use of black vernacular ("Hitting 'A Straight Lick with a Crooked Stick,'" 387–91).

50. Kaplan, *Zora Neale Hurston,* 557–58.

51. Lowe, *Jump at the Sun,* 294.

52. Lee, "Relocating Location," 127, 132.

53. Bordelon, *Go Gator and Muddy the Water,* 14. Bordelon discusses the "lengthy and humiliating process" Hurston had to endure of being certified as indigent prior to being hired.

54. Gifford, *Pastoral,* 52.

55. See especially Kaplan, *Zora Neale Hurston,* 611–15; and Hemenway, *Zora Neale Hurston,* 333–37, on Hurston's opposition to Communism.

56. *The Report on Economic Conditions of the South,* published by the federal government in 1938, blames Southern farmers for failing to plant crops like alfalfa, clover, field peas, and soybeans "that add fertility to the soil and at the same time protect fields against washing and gullying" (Carlton and Coclanis, *Confronting Southern Poverty,* 70).

57. Meisenhelder, *Hitting a Straight Lick with a Crooked Stick,* 113.

58. As a common joke says, suburbs are where they cut down all the trees and name the streets after them.

59. Hemenway, *Zora Neale Hurston,* 311.

60. As Lowe notes of this scene, "[T]he true psychological breakthrough here lies in Arvay's understanding that all these years when she thought the mulberry tree was her 'sign,' the ramshackle cabin of her familial and personal past has ruled in its place" (*Jump at the Sun,* 325).

61. Hurston actually lived on a houseboat for about four years, beginning in 1943 (she even sailed from Florida to New York in 1944), and in a letter to Rawlings she praises the atmosphere of the unsegregated Florida boatyards: "[A]ll the other boat owners are very nice to me. Not a word about race" (Kaplan, *Zora Neale Hurston,* 495).

62. Meisenhelder, *Hitting a Straight Lick with a Crooked Stick,* 112.

63. Ibid.

64. Ward, "From the Suwanee to Egypt," 79.

65. Harrison, *Female Pastoral* 10–11.

Chapter 4

1. Meriwether and Millgate, *Lion in the Garden,* 72.

2. Blotner, *Faulkner,* 633.

3. Faulkner, *Absalom, Absalom!* 4.

4. Gifford, *Pastoral*, 148.

5. Lutwack, *The Role of Place in Literature*, 44–55; Elder, *Imagining the Earth*, 43–44; Kolodny, *The Lay of the Land*, 140–45; Wittenberg, "*Go Down, Moses* and the Discourse of Environmentalism," 52, 57–59; Buell, *Writing for an Endangered World*, 187.

6. Meriwether and Millgate, *Lion in the Garden*, 255.

7. Dodd and Dodd, *Historical Statistics of the South*, 34–37. The approximately 1.75 million rural residents of Mississippi in 1940 were having increasing difficulty making their living from the land, as the number of farms fell nearly 7 percent statewide in the 1930s and 13.6 percent in the 1940s (34–35).

8. Aiken, in "Faulkner's Yoknapatawpha County" and "A Geographical Approach to William Faulkner's 'The Bear,'" demonstrates the amazing amount of specific similarities between the "actual" and the "apocryphal" (to use Faulkner's terms), including the geographic formulation of the county, the locations of settlements, rivers, soil types, bridges, railroads, stores, and public buildings.

9. Doyle, *Faulkner's County*, 300.

10. Faulkner, *The Hamlet*, 190.

11. Doyle, *Faulkner's County*, 297–98.

12. Ibid., 297.

13. See Hickman, "Mississippi Forests," 221.

14. Cowdrey, *This Land, This South*, 112, 114.

15. Hickman, *Mississippi Harvest*, 71–84. Other states were selling similar land at the time for $19 per acre (97), perhaps suggesting why Mississippi's forests fell into the hands of a few large syndicates that then could level hundreds of thousands of forest acres in a relatively short period.

16. Hickman, *Mississippi Harvest*, 153; Doyle, *Faulkner's County*, 299.

17. Hickman, *Mississippi Harvest*, 155. In 1908, when Faulkner was eleven years old, a report compiled by U.S. government foresters concluded that "more than half of the longleaf pineland of Mississippi had already been converted into stumps" (261).

18. Ibid., 165–66.

19. Faulkner, *Go Down, Moses*, 325. Subsequent references will be cited parenthetically in the text.

20. Fickle, *Mississippi Forests and Forestry*, 77, 98, 66.

21. Gifford, *Pastoral*, 152–65, 151; Buell, *The Environmental Imagination*, 52.

22. Gifford, *Pastoral*, 152.

23. Buell, *The Environmental Imagination*, 179; Cronon, "The Trouble with Wilderness," 81.

24. Doyle, *Faulkner's County*, 50–51. Doyle explains that the 1837 sale was of collectively owned lands (some 4 million of a total 6.4 million acres) in the area that includes Oxford. The rest of the territory (often the best land) was allotted to individual heads of families who negotiated its sale themselves, as Ikkemotubbe does in *Go Down, Moses* (45–46).

25. Moore, *Agriculture in Ante-bellum Mississippi*, 37, 38, 41–42.

26. Cowdrey, *This Land, This South*, 71, 3.

27. Blotner, *Faulkner*, 327.

28. Vance, *Human Geography of the South*, 11.

29. Lee, "Relocating Location," 133.

30. For more on Faulkner's repetition and revision in *Go Down, Moses*, see Grimwood, *Heart in Conflict*, 223–98; and Moreland, *Faulkner and Modernism*, 158–93.

31. Slatoff's formalist study *Quest for Failure* explores Faulkner's "polar imagination," defined as an inherent tendency to view the world as composed of pairs of opposed entities. Slatoff compiles a lengthy catalogue of examples of this technique from virtually all of Faulkner's major works and finds a syntactic and thematic emphasis on antitheses. Although Faulkner frequently "unites" these poles, Slatoff argues, the oppositions "remain in a state of deadlock where they can neither be separated nor reconciled" (83). Thus the mediating position between the poles is an unstable condition more often defined by what it is not than by its own characteristics. The repeated use of negative terms (describing something or someone by what they are not) is a hallmark of Faulkner's style that automatically invokes its opposite state. Faulkner writes, for instance, that Old Ben "didn't walk into the woods," which immediately conjures up its counterpoint of walking. Yet the bear's actual movement falls somewhere in between these poles, paradoxically joining and opposing, while neither reconciling nor separating, the conditions of walking/not walking in an indeterminate state of movement without action: "It faded, sank back into the wilderness without motion" (200). The same process is at work as Faulkner shows wilderness to be a fluctuating combination of nature and culture.

32. Cronon, "The Trouble with Wilderness," 80.

33. See particularly chapter 4 of Atkinson, *Faulkner and the Great Depression*.

34. Gwynn and Blotner, *Faulkner in the University*, 246.

35. Westling, *The Green Breast of the New World*, 122, 5, 116.

36. Ibid., 123.

37. Gwynn and Blotner, *Faulkner in the University*, 280, 37.

38. Evernden, *The Social Creation of Nature*, 24, 27.

39. Hickman, *Mississippi Harvest*, 265–66.

40. See Cowdrey, *This Land, This South*, 160, who adds that "eight years of CCC work advanced state and national conservation by twenty-five to forty years."

41. Prewitt, "Return of the Big Woods," 214.

42. The Illinois Central Railroad helped design and manufacture a mechanical tree planter that they demonstrated throughout Mississippi in the 1950s, giving away blueprints of the machine at no cost to any interested parties. See Fickle, *Mississippi Forests and Forestry*, 185–94.

43. Cross, "Timber Renewal in Ole Miss," 31; and Luoma, "Whittling Dixie," 38.

44. Gwynn and Blotner, *Faulkner in the University*, 246.

Conclusion

1. White, *The Organic Machine*, 108, 87.

2. Ibid., 109. Marx's comment appears on the cover of White's book.

3. One particularly interesting example is White's defense of dam builders: "It is foolish to think that the danger and exhilaration of a man dangling from a cliff with a jackhammer somehow differs from that of rock climbers who also dangle from cliffs. We need to take the work and its intent seriously" (ibid., 61).

4. Meriwether and Millgate, *Lion in the Garden*, 72.

5. Love, "*Et in Arcadia Ego*," 203.

6. Quoted in Nash, *Wilderness and the American Mind*, 5.

7. Callicott, "The Wilderness Idea Revisited," 345.

8. White, "'Are You an Environmentalist or Do You Work for a Living?'" 179.

9. Ibid., 174.

10. These issues are debated in essays gathered in Callicott and Nelson, *The Great New Wilderness Debate;* see especially 337–567.

11. Allison, *Bastard out of Carolina*, 259.

12. Glasgow, *Barren Ground*, 12, 111, 131.

13. Ray, *Ecology of a Cracker Childhood*, 268. Subsequent references will be cited parenthetically in the text.

14. Brown, *Joe*, 203.

15. Kingsolver, *Prodigal Summer*, 275. Subsequent references will be cited parenthetically in the text.

Bibliography

Aiken, Charles S. "Faulkner's Yoknapatawpha County: Geographical Fact into Fiction." *Geographical Review* 67 (January 1977): 1–21.

———. "A Geographical Approach to William Faulkner's 'The Bear.'" *Geographical Review* 71 (October 1981): 446–59.

Allison, Dorothy. *Bastard out of Carolina.* 1992. Reprint, New York: Plume, 1993.

Alpers, Paul. *What Is Pastoral?* Chicago: University of Chicago Press, 1996.

Atkinson, Ted. *Faulkner and the Great Depression: Aesthetics, Ideology, and Cultural Politics.* Athens: University of Georgia Press, 2006.

Bakker, Jan. *Pastoral in Antebellum Southern Romance.* Baton Rouge: Louisiana State University Press, 1989.

Barbour, Michael G. "Ecological Fragmentation in the Fifties." In *Uncommon Ground: Toward Reinventing Nature,* edited by William Cronon, 233–55. New York: Norton, 1995.

Barbour, Thomas. *That Vanishing Eden: A Naturalist's Florida.* Boston: Little, Brown, 1944.

Bellman, Samuel I. *Marjorie Kinnan Rawlings.* New York: Twayne, 1974.

Beverly, Robert. *The History and Present State of Virginia.* Edited by Louis B. Wright. Chapel Hill: University of North Carolina Press, 1947.

Bigelow, Gordon. *Frontier Eden: The Literary Career of Marjorie Kinnan Rawlings.* Gainesville: University of Florida Press, 1966.

Bigelow, Gordon, and Laura V. Monti, eds. *Selected Letters of Marjorie Kinnan Rawlings.* Gainesville: University of Florida Press, 1983.

Blotner, Joseph. *Faulkner: A Biography.* 2 vols. New York: Random, 1974.

Bordelon, Pamela, ed. *Go Gator and Muddy the Water: Writings by Zora Neale Hurston from the Federal Writers' Project.* New York: Norton, 1999.

Bourdieu, Pierre. *Distinction: A Social Critique of the Judgement of Taste.* Translated by Richard Nice. Cambridge, Mass.: Harvard University Press, 1984.

Brinkley, Alan. *Voices of Protest: Huey Long, Father Coughlin and the Great Depression.* New York: Vintage, 1983.

Brinkmeyer, Robert, Jr. "Is That You in the Mirror Jeeter? The Reader and To-
    bacco Road." In *Critical Essays on Erskine Caldwell,* edited by Scott MacDonald,
    370–74. Boston: G. K. Hall, 1981. (Originally published in *Pembroke* 11 (1979):
    47–50.)

Broadwell, Elizabeth Pell, and Ronald Wesley Hoag. "'A Writer First': An Interview
    With Erskine Caldwell." *Georgia Review* 36 (Spring 1982): 83–101.

Brown, Larry. *Joe.* 1991. Reprint, Chapel Hill, N.C.: Algonquin, 2003.

Buell, Lawrence. "American Pastoral Ideology Reappraised." *American Literary His-
    tory* 1 (1989): 23.

———. *The Environmental Imagination: Thoreau, Nature Writing and the Formation
    of American Culture.* Cambridge, Mass.: Belknap, 1995.

———. "Forum on Literatures and the Environment." *PMLA* 114 (October 1999):
    1090–92.

———. *Writing For an Endangered World: Literature, Culture and Environment in
    the U.S. and Beyond.* Cambridge, Mass.: Belknap, 2001.

Byrd, William. *William Byrd's Histories of the Dividing Line betwixt Virginia and
    North Carolina.* 1728. Reprint, New York: Dover, 1967.

Caldwell, Erskine. *God's Little Acre.* 1933. Reprint, New York: Modern Library, 1934.

———. *Tobacco Road.* 1932. Reprint, New York: Modern Library, 1940.

Caldwell, Erskine, and Margaret Bourke-White. *You Have Seen Their Faces.* New
    York: Viking, 1937.

Callicott, J. Baird. "The Wilderness Idea Revisited: The Sustainable Development
    Alternative." In *The Great New Wilderness Debate,* edited by J. Baird Callicott
    and Michael P. Nelson, 337–66. Athens: University of Georgia Press, 1998.

Callicott, J. Baird, and Michael P. Nelson, eds. *The Great New Wilderness Debate.*
    Athens: University of Georgia Press, 1998.

Campbell, SueEllen. "The Land and Language of Desire: Where Deep Ecology and
    Post-structuralism Meet." *Western American Literature* 24 (November 1989):
    199–211.

Carlton, David L., and Peter A. Coclanis, eds. *Confronting Southern Poverty in the
    Great Depression: The Report on Economic Conditions of the South with Related
    Documents.* New York: Bedford, 1996.

Cash, W. J. *The Mind of the South.* 1941. Reprint, New York: Vintage, 1991.

Cassidy, Thomas. "Janie's Rage: The Dog and the Storm in *Their Eyes Were Watch-
    ing God.*" *CLA Journal* 36 (March 1993): 260–69.

Ching, Barbara, and Gerald W. Creed, eds. *Knowing Your Place: Rural Identity and
    Cultural Hierarchy.* New York: Routledge, 1997.

Collins, Derek. "The Myth and Ritual of Ezili Freda in Hurston's *Their Eyes Were
    Watching God.*" *Western Folklore* 55 (Spring 1996): 137–54.

Commoner, Barry. *Making Peace with the Planet.* New York: Pantheon, 1975.

Cook, Sylvia Jenkins. *Erskine Caldwell and the Fiction of Poverty: The Flesh and the
    Spirit.* Baton Rouge: Louisiana State University Press, 1991.

———. *From Tobacco Road to Route 66: The Southern Poor White in Fiction.* Chapel Hill: University of North Carolina Press, 1976.

Cowdrey, Albert E. *This Land, This South: An Environmental History.* Lexington: University Press of Kentucky, 1983.

Cowley, Malcolm. "The Two Erskine Caldwells." In *Critical Essays on Erskine Caldwell,* edited by Scott MacDonald, 198–200. Boston: G. K. Hall, 1981. (Originally published in *New Republic,* November 6, 1944.)

Cronon, William. "The Trouble with Wilderness; or, Getting Back to the Wrong Nature." In *Uncommon Ground: Toward Reinventing Nature,* edited by William Cronon, 69–90. New York: Norton, 1995.

Cross, Tristan. "Timber Renewal in Ole Miss." *Pulp & Paper* 70 (September 1996): 31–33.

Derr, Mark. *Some Kind of Paradise: A Chronicle of Man and the Land in Florida.* New York: William Morrow, 1989.

Desmangles, Leslie G. *The Faces of the Gods: Vodou and Roman Catholicism in Haiti.* Chapel Hill: University of North Carolina Press, 1992.

Devlin, James E. *Erskine Caldwell.* Boston: Twayne, 1984.

Dixon, Melvin. *Ride Out the Wilderness: Geography and Identity in Afro-American Literature.* Urbana: University of Illinois Press, 1987.

Dodd, Donald B., and Wynelle S. Dodd. *Historical Statistics of the South, 1790–1970.* University: University of Alabama Press, 1973.

Doyle, Don H. *Faulkner's County: The Historical Roots of Yoknapatawpha.* Chapel Hill: University of North Carolina Press, 2001.

Dubek, Laura. "The Social Geography of Race in Hurston's *Seraph on the Suwanee.*" *African American Review* 30 (Fall 1996): 341–51.

Dutton, Wendy. "The Problem of Invisibility: Voodoo and Zora Neale Hurston." *Frontiers* 13 (Winter 1993): 131–53.

Elder, John. *Imagining the Earth: Poetry and the Vision of Nature.* Champaign: University of Illinois Press, 1985.

Empson, William. *Some Versions of Pastoral.* London: Chatto and Windus, 1935.

Entrikin, J. Nicholas. *The Betweenness of Place: Towards a Geography of Modernity.* Baltimore: Johns Hopkins University Press, 1991.

Ettin, Andrew. *Literature and the Pastoral.* New Haven: Yale University Press, 1984.

Evernden, Neil. *The Social Creation of Nature.* Baltimore: Johns Hopkins University Press, 1992.

Faulkner, William. *Absalom, Absalom!* 1936. Reprint, New York: Vintage, 1990.

———. *Go Down, Moses.* 1942. Reprint, New York: Vintage, 1990.

———. *The Hamlet.* 1940. Reprint, New York: Vintage, 1990.

Fickle, James E. *Mississippi Forests and Forestry.* Jackson: University Press of Mississippi, 2001.

Gaard, Greta, and Patrick D. Murphy, eds. *Ecofeminist Literary Criticism: Theory, Interpretation, Pedagogy.* Chicago: University of Illinois Press, 1998.

Gifford, Terry. *Pastoral.* New York: Routledge, 1999.

Glasgow, Ellen. *Barren Ground.* Garden City, N.Y.: Doubleday, 1925.

Glisson, J. T. *The Creek.* Gainesville: Florida University Press, 1993.

Glotfelty, Cheryll, and Harold Fromm, eds. *The Ecocriticism Reader: Landmarks in Literary Ecology.* Athens: University of Georgia Press, 1996.

Gold, Michael. "Go Left, Young Writers!" *New Masses* 4 (January 1929): 4.

Grant, A. J., and Connie Ruzich. "A Rhetoric of Roads: *Their Eyes Were Watching God* as Pastoral." *Interdisciplinary Literary Studies* 5 (Spring 2004): 16–28.

Gray, Lewis Cecil. *History of Agriculture in the Southern United States to 1860.* Vol. 2. Washington, D.C.: Carnegie Institution, 1942.

Gray, Richard. *The Literature of Memory: Modern Writers of the American South.* Baltimore: Johns Hopkins University Press, 1977.

Griffin, David. "Whitehead's Contributions to a Theology of Nature." *Bucknell Review* 20 (Winter 1972): 3–24.

Grimwood, Michael. *Heart in Conflict: Faulkner's Struggles with Vocation.* Athens: University of Georgia Press, 1987.

Gwynn, Frederick L., and Joseph L. Blotner, eds. *Faulkner in the University.* Charlottesville: University of Virginia Press, 1959.

Harrison, Elizabeth Jane. *Female Pastoral: Women Writers Re-visioning the American South.* Knoxville: University of Tennessee Press, 1991.

Harvey, David. *Justice, Nature and the Geography of Difference.* Cambridge, Mass.: Blackwell, 1996.

Hathaway, Rosemary V. "The Unbearable Weight of Authenticity: Zora Neale Hurston's *Their Eyes Were Watching God* and a Theory of 'Touristic Reading.'" *Journal of American Folklore* 117 (Spring 2004): 168–90.

Haurykiewicz, Julie A. "From Mules to Muliebrity: Speech and Silence in *Their Eyes Were Watching God.*" *Southern Literary Journal* 29 (Spring 1997): 45–60.

Hemenway, Robert E. *Zora Neale Hurston: A Literary Biography.* Urbana: University of Illinois Press, 1977.

Hickman, Nollie. "Mississippi Forests." In *A History of Mississippi,* edited by Richard McLemore, 2:212–32. Hattiesburg: University and College Press of Mississippi, 1973.

———. *Mississippi Harvest: Lumbering in the Long Leaf Pine Belt 1840–1915.* University: University of Mississippi, 1962.

Hurston, Zora Neale. *Seraph on the Suwanee.* 1948. Reprint, New York: Perennial, 1991.

———. *Tell My Horse.* Philadelphia: J. B. Lippincott, 1938.

———. *Their Eyes Were Watching God.* 1937. Reprint, New York: Perennial, 1990.

Huxley, Francis. *The Invisibles: Voodoo Gods and Haiti.* New York: McGraw Hill, 1966.

Jackson, Chuck. "Waste and Whiteness: Zora Neale Hurston and the Politics of Eugenics." *African American Review* 34 (Winter 2000): 639–59.

Johnson, Charles S., Edwin R. Embree, and W. W. Alexander. *The Collapse of Cotton*

Tenancy: Summary of Field Studies and Statistical Surveys, 1933–35. Chapel Hill: University of North Carolina Press, 1935.

Johnson, Gerald W. *The Wasted Land.* Chapel Hill: University of North Carolina Press, 1937.

Jones, Carolyn M. "Race and the Rural in Marjorie Kinnan Rawlings's *Cross Creek.*" *Mississippi Quarterly* 57 (Spring 2004): 215–30.

Jones, Suzanne W., and Sharon Monteith, eds. *South to a New Place: Region, Literature, Culture.* Baton Rouge: Louisiana State University Press, 2002.

Kaplan, Carla, ed. *Zora Neale Hurston: A Life in Letters.* New York: Doubleday, 2002.

Kartiganer, Donald M., and Ann J. Abadie, eds. *Faulkner and the Natural World: Faulkner and Yoknapatawpha.* 1996. Reprint, Jackson: University Press of Mississippi, 1999.

Kaufman, Gordon. *The Theological Imagination: Constructing the Concept of God.* Philadelphia: Westminster, 1981.

Kerridge, Richard, and Neil Sammells, eds. *Writing the Environment: Ecocriticism and Literature.* London: Zed, 1998.

King, Richard. *A Southern Renaissance: The Cultural Awakening of the American South, 1930–1955.* New York: Oxford University Press, 1980.

Kingsolver, Barbara. *Prodigal Summer.* New York: Harper Collins, 2000.

Kinney, Arthur F. *Go Down, Moses: The Miscegenation of Time.* New York: Twayne, 1996.

Kirby, Jack Temple. *Rural Worlds Lost: The American South, 1920–1960.* Baton Rouge: Louisiana State University Press, 1987.

Kolodny, Annette. *The Lay of the Land: Metaphor as Experience and History in American Life and Letters.* Chapel Hill: University of North Carolina Press, 1975.

Kroeber, Karl. *Ecological Literary Criticism: Romantic Imagining and the Biology of Mind.* New York: Columbia University Press, 1994.

Kubie, Lawrence S. "*God's Little Acre*: An Analysis." In *Critical Essays on Erskine Caldwell,* edited by Scott MacDonald, 159–66. Boston: G. K. Hall, 1981. (Originally published in *Saturday Review of Literature,* November 24, 1934, 305–6, 312.)

Kuehl, John, and Jackson Breyer, eds. *Dear Scott/Dear Max: The Fitzgerald-Perkins Correspondence.* New York: Scribner's, 1971.

Kuyk, Dirk, Jr. *Threads Cable-Strong: William Faulkner's "Go Down, Moses."* Lewisburg, Pa.: Bucknell University Press, 1983.

Lamothe, Daphne. "Vodou Imagery, African American Tradition, and Cultural Transformation in Zora Neale Hurston's *Their Eyes Were Watching God.*" In *Zora Neale Hurston's Their Eyes Were Watching God: A Casebook,* edited by Cheryl Wall, 165–87. New York: Oxford University Press, 2000.

Lee, Martyn. "Relocating Location: Cultural Geography, the Specificity of Place and the City Habitus." In *Cultural Methodologies,* edited by Jim McGuigan, 126–41. London: Sage, 1997.

Lesnik-Oberstein, Karin. "Children's Literature and the Environment." In *Writing the Environment: Ecocriticism and Literature,* edited by Richard Kerridge and Neil Sammells, 208–17. London: Zed, 1998.

———. *Children's Literature: Criticism and the Fictional Child.* Oxford: Clarendon, 1994.

Lillios, Anna. "Excursions into Zora Neale Hurston's Eatonville." In *Zora in Florida,* edited by Steve Glassman and Kathryn Lee Seidel, 13–27. Orlando: University of Central Florida Press, 1991.

———. "'The Monstropolous Beast': The Hurricane in Zora Neale Hurston's *Their Eyes Were Watching God.*" *Southern Quarterly* 36 (Spring 1998): 89–93.

Love, Glen A. "*Et in Arcadia Ego:* Pastoral Theory Meets Ecocriticism." *Western American Literature* 27 (Fall 1992): 195–207.

Lowe, John. "The Construction and Deconstruction of Masculinity in *The Yearling.*" *Mississippi Quarterly* 57 (Spring 2004): 231–46.

———. *Jump at the Sun: Zora Neale Hurston's Cosmic Comedy.* Urbana: University of Illinois Press, 1994.

———. "Seeing Beyond Seeing: Zora Neale Hurston's Religion(s)." *Southern Quarterly* 36 (Spring 1998): 77–87.

Luoma, Jon R. "Whittling Dixie," *Audubon* 99 (November–December 1997): 38–50.

Lutwack, Leonard. *The Role of Place in Literature.* Syracuse, N.Y.: Syracuse University Press, 1984.

Lytle, Andrew. "The Hind Tit." In *I'll Take My Stand: The South and the Agrarian Tradition,* by Twelve Southerners, 201–26. 1930. Reprint, Baton Rouge: Louisiana State University Press, 1977.

MacKethan, Lucinda Hardwick. *The Dream of Arcady: Place and Time in Southern Literature.* Baton Rouge: Louisiana State University Press, 1980.

Marx, Leo. *The Machine in the Garden: Technology and the Pastoral Ideal in America.* New York: Oxford University Press, 1964.

———. "Pastoralism in America." In *Ideology and Classic American Literature,* edited by Sacvan Bercovitch and Myra Jehlen, 36–69. Cambridge: Cambridge University Press, 1986.

Matthews, John T. "Touching Race in *Go Down, Moses.*" In *New Essays on "Go Down, Moses,"* edited by Linda Wagner-Martin, 21–47. New York: Cambridge University Press, 1996.

McCally, David. *The Everglades: An Environmental History.* Gainesville: Florida University Press, 1999.

McDonald, Robert, ed. *Erskine Caldwell: Selected Letters, 1929–1955.* Jefferson, N.C.: McFarland, 1999.

McElvaine, Robert S. *The Great Depression: America, 1929–1941.* New York: New York Times, 1984.

Meeker, Joseph. *The Comedy of Survival: Studies in Literary Ecology.* New York: Scribner's, 1974.

Meisenhelder, Susan Edwards. *Hitting a Straight Lick with a Crooked Stick: Race and*

Gender in the Work of Zora Neale Hurston. Tuscaloosa: University of Alabama
Press, 1999.

Menke, Pamela Glenn. "'Black Cat Bone and Snake Wisdom': New Orleanian Hoo-
doo, Haitian Voodoo, and Rereading Hurston's *Their Eyes Were Watching God.*"
In *Songs of the New South: Writing Contemporary Louisiana,* edited by Suzanne
Disheroon Green and Lisa Abney, 123–39. Westport, Conn.: Greenwood, 2001.

Merchant, Carolyn. *The Death of Nature: Women, Ecology and the Scientific Revolu-
tion.* San Francisco: Harper and Row, 1980.

Meriwether, James B., and Michael Millgate, eds. *Lion in the Garden: Interviews
with William Faulkner, 1926–1962.* Lincoln: University of Nebraska Press, 1968.

Miller, Dan B. *Erskine Caldwell: The Journey from Tobacco Road.* New York: Knopf,
1994.

Mitchell, Margaret. *Gone with the Wind.* New York: Macmillan, 1936.

Mixon, Wayne. *The People's Writer: Erskine Caldwell and the South.* Charlottesville:
University Press of Virginia, 1995.

Moore, John Hebron. *Agriculture in Ante-bellum Mississippi.* New York: Bookman,
1958.

Moreland, Richard C. *Faulkner and Modernism: Rereading and Rewriting.* Madison:
University of Wisconsin Press, 1990.

Morris, Rhonda. "Engendering Fictions: Rawlings and a Female Tradition of
Southern Writing." *Journal of Florida Literature* 7 (1996): 27–39.

Nash, Roderick. *Wilderness and the American Mind.* 3rd ed. New Haven: Yale University Press, 1982.

O'Brien, Michael. *The Idea of the American South, 1920–1941.* Baltimore: Johns Hopkins University Press, 1979.

Oelschlaeger, Max. *The Idea of Wilderness: From Prehistory to the Age of Ecology.*
New Haven: Yale University Press, 1991.

Parker, Idella. *Idella: Marjorie Kinnan Rawlings' "Perfect Maid."* Gainesville: Florida
University Press, 1993.

Patterson, Annabel. *Pastoral and Ideology: Virgil to Valery.* Berkeley and Los Ange-
les: University of California Press, 1987.

Pells, Richard H. *Radical Visions and American Dreams: Culture and Social Thought
in the Depression Years.* New York: Harper and Row, 1973.

Phillips, Dana. *The Truth of Ecology: Nature, Culture, and Literature in America.*
Oxford: Oxford University Press, 2003.

Pope, Liston. *Millhands and Preachers: A Study of Gastonia.* New Haven: Yale University Press, 1942.

Prenshaw, Peggy. "The Otherness of Cross Creek." *Journal of Florida Literature* 4
(1992): 17–24.

Prewitt, Wiley C., Jr. "Return of the Big Woods: Hunting and Habitat in Yoknapatawpha." In *Faulkner and the Natural World: Faulkner and Yoknapatawpha, 1996,*
edited by Donald M. Kartiganer and Ann J. Abadie, 198–221. Jackson: University
Press of Mississippi, 1999.

Rawlings, Marjorie Kinnan. *Cross Creek*. New York: Scribner's, 1942.

———. *South Moon Under*. New York: Scribner's, 1933.

———. *The Yearling*. 2nd ed. New York: Scribner's, 1940.

Ray, Janisse. *Ecology of a Cracker Childhood*. Minneapolis: Milkweed, 1999.

Renek, Morris. "'Sex Was Their Way of Life': A Frank Interview with Erskine Caldwell." In *Conversations With Erskine Caldwell*, edited by Edwin T. Arnold, 66–80.
Jackson: University Press of Mississippi, 1988.

Rogers, William W. "The Great Depression." In *The New History of Florida*, edited
by Michael Gannon, 304–22. Gainesville: University Press of Florida, 1996.

Salleh, Ariel. "The Ecofeminism/Deep Ecology Debate: A Reply to Patriarchal
Reason." *Environmental Ethics* 14 (1992): 195–216.

Silverthorne, Elizabeth. *Marjorie Kinnan Rawlings: Sojourner at Cross Creek*. Wood-
stock, N.Y.: Overlook, 1988.

Simpson, Lewis. *The Dispossessed Garden: Pastoral and History in Southern Literature*. Athens: University of Georgia Press, 1975.

Singal, Daniel. *The War Within: From Victorian to Modernist Thought in the South,
1919–1945*. Chapel Hill: University of North Carolina Press, 1982.

Slatoff, Walter J. *Quest for Failure: A Study of William Faulkner*. Westport, Conn.:
Cornell University Press, 1972.

Slicer, Deborah. "Toward an Ecofeminist Standpoint Theory: Bodies as Grounds."
In *Ecofeminist Literary Criticism: Theory, Interpretation, Pedagogy*, edited by
Greta Gaard and Patrick D. Murphy, 49–73. Chicago: University of Illinois Press,
1998.

Southerland, Ellease. "The Influence of Voodoo on the Fiction of Zora Neale
Hurston." In *Sturdy Black Bridges: Visions of Black Women in Literature*, edited
by Roseann P. Bell, Bettye J. Parker, and Beverly Guy-Sheftall, 172–83. Garden
City, N.Y.: Doubleday, 1979.

St. Clair, Janet. "The Courageous Undertow of Zora Neale Hurston's *Seraph on the
Suwanee*." *Modern Language Quarterly* 50 (March 1989): 38–57.

Stein, Rachel. *Shifting the Ground: American Women Writers' Revisions of Nature,
Gender, and Race*. Charlottesville: University Press of Virginia, 1997.

Sutter, Paul. *Driven Wild: How the Fight against Automobiles Launched the Modern
Wilderness Movement*. Seattle: University Press of Washington, 2002.

Tarr, Carol Anita. "In 'Mystic Company': The Master Storyteller in Marjorie Kinnan Rawlings's *The Yearling*." *Journal of Florida Literature* 2 (1989–90): 23–34.

Tarr, Rodger L., ed. *Max and Marjorie: The Correspondence between Maxwell E.
Perkins and Marjorie Kinnan Rawlings*. Gainesville: University Press of Florida,
1999.

———, ed. *The Poems of Marjorie Kinnan Rawlings: Songs of a Housewife*. Gainesville: University of Florida Press, 1997.

Tate, Claudia. "Hitting 'A Straight Lick with a Crooked Stick': *Seraph on the Suwanee*, Zora Neale Hurston's Whiteface Novel." In *The Psychoanalysis of Race*,
edited by Christopher Lane, 380–94. New York: Columbia University Press, 1998.

Tindall, George B. *The Emergence of the New South, 1913–1945.* Baton Rouge: Louisiana State University Press, 1977.

Trefzer, Annette. "Floating Homes and Signifiers in Hurston's and Rawlings's Autobiographies." *Southern Quarterly* 36 (Spring 1998): 68–76.

———. "Possessing the Self: Caribbean Identities in Zora Neale Hurston's *Tell My Horse.*" *African American Review* 34 (Summer 2000): 299–312.

Twelve Southerners. *I'll Take My Stand: The South and the Agrarian Tradition.* 1930. Reprint, Baton Rouge, Louisiana State University Press, 1977.

Vallone, Lynne. "Gender and Mothering in *The Yearling.*" *Journal of Florida Literature* 2 (1989–90): 35–56.

Vance, Rupert B. *Human Factors in Cotton Culture.* Chapel Hill: University of North Carolina Press, 1929.

———. *Human Geography of the South.* Chapel Hill: University of North Carolina Press, 1932.

Walter, E. V. *Placeways: A Theory of the Human Environment.* Chapel Hill: University of North Carolina Press, 1988.

Ward, Cynthia. "From the Suwanee to Egypt, There's No Place Like Home." *PMLA* 115 (January 2000): 75–88.

Washington, Mary Helen. "A Woman Half in Shadow." In *I Love Myself When I Am Laughing . . .: A Zora Neale Hurston Reader,* edited by Alice Walker, 7–25. Old Westerbury, N.Y.: Feminist, 1979.

Watkins, T. H. *The Hungry Years: A Narrative History of the Great Depression in America.* New York: Henry Holt, 1999.

Watson, Jay. "The Rhetoric of Exhaustion and the Exhaustion of Rhetoric: Erskine Caldwell in the Thirties." *Mississippi Quarterly* 46 (Spring 1993): 215–29.

Westling, Louise. *The Green Breast of the New World: Landscape, Gender and American Fiction.* Athens: University of Georgia Press, 1996.

White, Richard. "'Are You an Environmentalist or Do You Work for a Living?' Work and Nature." In *Uncommon Ground: Toward Reinventing Nature,* edited by William Cronon, 171–85. New York: Norton, 1995.

———. *The Organic Machine: The Remaking of the Columbia River.* New York: Hill and Wang, 1995.

Whitehead, Alfred North. *Science and the Modern World: Lowell Lectures, 1925.* New York: New American Library, 1949.

Williams, Raymond. *The Country and the City.* New York: Oxford University Press, 1973.

Wittenberg, Judith Bryant. "*Go Down, Moses* and the Discourse of Environmentalism." In *New Essays on "Go Down, Moses,"* edited by Linda Wagner-Martin, 49–71. New York: Cambridge University Press, 1996.

Woodward, C. Vann. *Origins of the New South, 1877–1913.* Baton Rouge: Louisiana State University Press, 1951.

Worster, Donald. *Dust Bowl: The Southern Plains in the 1930s.* New York: Oxford University Press, 1979.

Index